View from the top of Dry Fork

# BEST DOG HIKES
# UTAH

## Nicole Tomlin

**FALCON**GUIDES

GUILFORD, CONNECTICUT

## FALCONGUIDES®

An imprint of The Rowman & Littlefield Publishing Group, Inc.
4501 Forbes Blvd., Ste. 200
Lanham, MD 20706
www.rowman.com

Falcon and FalconGuides are registered trademarks and Make Adventure Your Story is a trademark of The Rowman & Littlefield Publishing Group, Inc.

Distributed by NATIONAL BOOK NETWORK

Copyright © 2018 The Rowman & Littlefield Publishing Group, Inc.

Photos by Nicole Tomlin unless otherwise noted

British Library Cataloguing in Publication Information available

**Library of Congress Cataloging-in-Publication Data available**

ISBN 978-1-4930-3277-8 (paperback)
ISBN 978-1-4930-3278-5 (e-book)

∞™ The paper used in this publication meets the minimum requirements of American National Standard for Information Sciences—Permanence of Paper for Printed Library Materials, ANSI/NISO Z39.48-1992.

Printed in the United States of America

The author and The Rowman & Littlefield Publishing Group, Inc. assume no liability for accidents happening to, or injuries sustained by, readers who engage in the activities described in this book.

*This book is a tribute to dogs—all of our incredible dogs*
*who do their best for us over and over again.*

Thank you for the adventures my dear friend Tip, see you on the other side. RACHEL WARNER

# THE HIKES

## THE HIKES

### *Northern Utah*

### *Wasatch Front*

## High Country

## Canyon Country

## Southern Utah

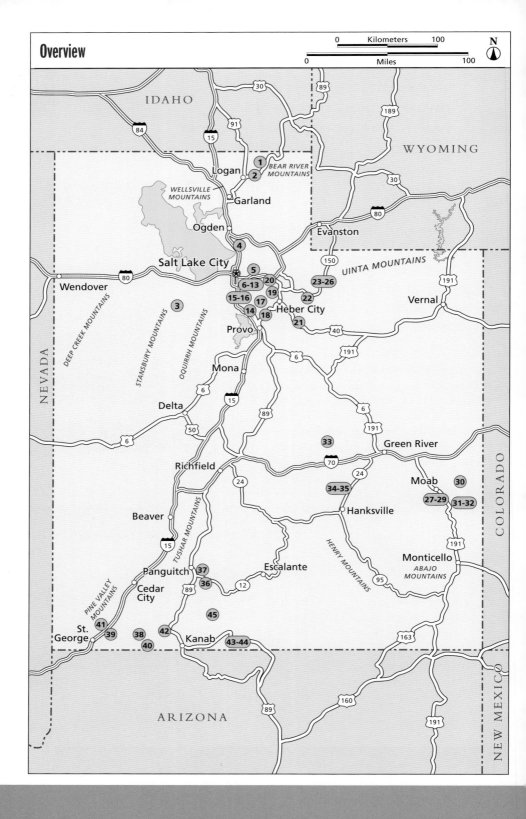

Kilometers

Miles

N

IDAHO

WYOMING

Logan

BEAR RIVER
MOUNTAINS

Garland

WELLSVILLE
MOUNTAINS

Ogden

Evanston

Salt Lake City

UINTA MOUNTAINS

Wendover

Vernal

DEEP CREEK MOUNTAINS

NEVADA

STANSBURY MOUNTAINS

OQUIRRH MOUNTAINS

Heber City

Provo

Mona

Delta

Green River

Richfield

Moab

Beaver

Hanksville

TUSHAR MOUNTAINS

Monticello

ABAJO
MOUNTAINS

Panguitch

Escalante

HENRY MOUNTAINS

Cedar
City

PINE VALLEY
MOUNTAINS

St.
George

Kanab

COLORADO

ARIZONA

NEW MEXICO

# MEET YOUR GUIDE

*"You may not agree, you may not care, but if you are holding this book you should know that of all the sights I love in this world—and there are plenty—very near the top of the list is this one: dogs without leashes."*

—Mary Oliver, *Dog Songs*

In woods and deserts of Utah, I have hiked many miles with a number of incredible dogs. For starters, Bandit, Tay, Tip, Martin, and Wren have traveled with me through back trails into the wilderness and canyon country of this state. Over time I have become less and less interested in our destination. Now I love spending time with my dogs—in Utah nature—hiking, listening, and observing. With each step, I grow more fond of my companions.

In writing this book, Wren and Martin (the border collies) and I worked together in hopes of sharing the trails we have found important to building our relationship. We have grown closer as our odometer's mileage has increased. Covering ground together and spending time in the outdoors has changed us, for the better. In these pages we share what we have learned while hiking Utah—about the environment, history, and one another. We share with you our discoveries, loves, and struggles in the hopes that you and your dog will also grow more connected and happy.

Nicole with her companions. RACHEL WARNER

Some of the things we have learned together while out on the trail are:

1. **Safety:** Write down where you are going and when you plan on being back. Give this information to someone you trust. In the event of injury or if you become lost, this person will be able to tell Search and Rescue where to begin looking.

2. **Preparedness:** Utah is a wild place and many of the trails in this book require a level of self-sufficiency that is unique to this area. It is important to bring "survival gear." This includes an extra wool outer layer and rain gear for you, and extra water and food for you and your dog. Utah weather can change minute to minute, and getting caught unprepared could be miserable at best, life-threatening at worst.

3. **Positive Impact:** Positive Impact is a Boulder Outdoor Survival School (BOSS) philosophy that I share. Simply stated: Leave a place better than how you found it.

4. **Curiosity:** The environment around you becomes infinitely more interesting if you understand the complexity of what is surrounding you. Take a birding class, read about plants, practice using a topo map and compass, go to survival school, sit quietly outside for 15 minutes a day—become immersed in and eager to learn about nature.

5. **Fun:** If you or your dog stop having fun, it is time to reconsider the hike or activity at hand.

Dogs without leashes.

# ACKNOWLEDGMENTS

I have learned many important lessons while working on this project, but none as great as the lesson of friendship and support that was shown to me by a select few brilliant, patient, loving, and creative beings. Rachel, Liz, Lya, Robin, Leslie, Kristi, Wren, Martin, and my mom, thank you. My life is better with you in it.

# TRAIL FINDER

## VOICE CONTROL (OFF-LEASH)

Adams Canyon
Battle Creek Loop
Bloods Lake
Bowman Fork to Alexander Basin
    Trailhead
Chute Canyon
Crimson Trail
Deseret Peak
Dog Lake
Eagle Crags
Grandeur Peak (Mill Creek Canyon)
Grandstaff Canyon to Morning Glory
    Natural Bridge
Horsetail Falls
Hunter Canyon
Lick Wash

Little Grand Canyon
Lone Peak Trail to the Second
    Hamongog
Miners Trail
Mountain View via Miners Basin Trail
Onion Creek Narrows
Paria River
Pipeline Trail (Burch Hollow to Elbow
    Fork)
Run-a-Muk
Silver Lake in American Fork Canyon
Stewart Falls
Water Canyon
Wild Horse Canyon
Willow Creek
Yant Flat

## BEST PHOTOS

Battle Creek Loop
Bay Bill and Merwin Canyons
Bowman Fork to Alexander Basin
    Trailhead
Chute Canyon
Corona Arch
Crimson Trail
Crystal Lake Loop
Deseret Peak
Eagle Crags
Grandeur Peak (Mill Creek Canyon)
Grandstaff Canyon to Morning Glory
    Natural Bridge
Horsetail Falls
Hunter Canyon
Lick Wash
Little Grand Canyon
Lofty Lake Loop

Lone Peak Trail to the Second
    Hamongog
Losee Canyon
Mountain View via Miners Basin
Neffs Canyon
Nobletts Spring
Onion Creek Narrows
Paria River
Ruth Lake
Silver Lake in American Fork Canyon
Thunder Mountain
Toadstools
Warner Lake to Dry Creek
Water Canyon
Wild Horse Canyon
Willow Creek
Yant Flat

## FAMILY FRIENDLY

Bloods Lake
Bonneville Shoreline Trail: Thousand Oaks Section
Chute Canyon
Crystal Lake Loop
Dog Lake
Eagle Crags
Grandstaff Canyon to Morning Glory Natural Bridge
Hunter Canyon
Lick Wash
Lofty Lake Loop
Miners Trail
Onion Creek Narrows
Pipeline Trail (Burch Hollow to Elbow Fork)
Red Reef at Red Cliffs Recreation Area
Run-a-Muk
Ruth Lake
Stewart Falls
Toadstools
Wild Horse Canyon
Yant Flat

## WATER FEATURES

Adams Canyon
Battle Creek Loop
Bay Bill and Merwin Canyons
Bloods Lake
Chute Canyon
Crimson Trail
Crystal Lake Loop
Dog Lake
Fehr Lake Trail
Ferguson Canyon
Grandstaff Canyon to Morning Glory Natural Bridge
Heughs Canyon
Horsetail Falls
Hunter Canyon
Little Grand Canyon
Lofty Lake Loop
Mountain View via Miners Basin Trail
Neffs Canyon
Nobletts Spring
Onion Creek Narrows
Paria River
Red Reef at Red Cliffs Recreation Area
Ruth Lake
Silver Lake in American Fork Canyon
Stewart Falls
Warner Lake to Dry Creek
Water Canyon
White Pine Lake–Logan Canyon
Wild Horse Canyon
Willow Creek

## FINDING SOLITUDE

Bay Bill and Merwin Canyons
Chute Canyon
Deseret Peak
Eagle Crags
Lick Wash
Little Grand Canyon
Lone Peak Trail to the Second Hamongog
Losee Canyon
Mountain View via Miners Basin Trail
Paria River
Wild Horse Canyon
Willow Creek
Yant Flat

# TOP FIVE HIKES

**Deseret Peak (Northern Utah):** Located west of Salt Lake City in the Stansbury Mountains, this difficult hike is both beautiful and remote, with views from the top of Deseret Peak that rival any in Utah.

Martin overlooking the valley below just before the summit of Deseret Peak.

Martin enjoying Silver Lake.

**Silver Lake in American Fork Canyon (Wasatch):** In the stunning American Fork Canyon, the hike to Silver Lake is a classic Utah hike. Aspen groves, challenging switchbacks, and a perfect payoff at trail's end make this a memorable hike.

**Crystal Lake Loop (High Country):** Deep in the Uinta Mountains, the Crystal Lake Loop trail passes other Utah beauties—Wall Lake, the Notch, Twin Lakes—and offers many other spectacular vantage points.

Wren at the Notch.

Heading out of Little Grand Canyon.

**Little Grand Canyon (Canyon Country):** Little Grand Canyon is an iconic example of what the Swell in Central Utah's canyon country boasts; it is a wild and mysterious place with endless opportunities for adventure, exploration, and moments of awe.

**Yant Flat (Southern Utah):** Yant Flat is a fun short hike on which to spot some of Utah's unique sandstone formations, streaked and spiraled in all combinations of colors and shapes. The opportunities for photographs and challenging terrain are plentiful.

Exploring the candy cliffs of Yant Flat. RACHEL WARNER

# BEFORE YOU HIT THE TRAIL

## STATE OVERVIEW

Hiking with my dogs in Utah, I have already lived a fulfilling life. A dog story is pinned to almost every corner of this state, from Wren and Martin learning how to be canyon dogs in the Grand Staircase National Monument or spending time with Tip at Ruth Lake in the Uintas, to running with Tay through the sage flat of the north country or exploring Logan Canyon with Nema. Dogs, who never seem to live long enough, are remembered and therefore honored with a visit to their favorite trails. It is a gift to have beautiful spaces to create memories and to remember beautiful dogs. Both have the ability to strengthen and break your heart.

During the miles I have spent locked into a pack, with the lead dog happily blazing trail, collecting orange feathers of the Flicker, I have often asked myself if things could be better than this. I am proud to be from Utah and to have had the reverie of its beauty modeled to me by my family. Many of us have wandered into some slickrock cathedrals and set up camp to recoup from a bad time or two and come out better for it. I have done the same. I have, not nearly enough, tramped through Utah's muddy rivers or

Utah is beautiful.

wondered about their headwaters a horizon or two away. I have hiked to a peak or two and overlooked meadows full of elk and stood amazed. I have been lucky to have seen some of the sand-covered hillsides in primrose on a fall day after being deep in the desert. I hope to share some of that luck with those who are seeking views, miles, and adventures in the company of their undoubtedly incredible dog.

We are all from somewhere, and that place makes up pieces of who we are. For me, I have been put together bit by bit, mile by mile on the trails of Utah. Growing up in the foothills of giant mountains and then moving to the red rock canyon country can drastically shift a person's perspective. This shift has the ability to take what you think you've seen of beautiful and gently redefine it for you in the most elegant way.

I am from Utah, have lived here most of my life. The life that I have shared with the geography of this state has also been shared with my dogs. They have had good dog lives, full of open miles with naps under aspen trees and munching kipper snack under trees on mesa tops. I think Utah can give dogs and people a chance at getting it right. Living together with open space to explore is lucky enough; and still, Utah has thousands upon thousands of acres to gain perspective. Hiking in Utah offers us a chance not only to log miles but also to ponder the importance of wilderness in our lives. I am grateful for the spaces with open gates that my dogs and I have hiked through into a better understanding of one another.

The landscapes of this state are drastic—one might even say violent at times. From the uplifts of the Waterpocket Fold to the hoodoos at Bryce Canyon National Park, they are always naturally beautiful. The vastness of the exposed geology is a wonderland for those interested in the fabric of the earth itself. Inland seas, fault lines, massive uplifts, canyon-carving glaciers, enormous sand dunes, massive floods, volcanoes, and swift extinctions are just a few pieces of Utah's geologic past. While anyone appreciative of the more delicate creatures, such as sego lilies or sacred datura, will find room to wonder, in Utah there is also a harshness that exists in a high-desert world, a stark beauty that holds many secrets.

I am also grateful to all the creatures that have walked these spaces before me. In the south we share this place with many who have disappeared from the Ancestral Puebloans, and before them the mighty dinosaurs whose traces are now in remote and quiet places. Their painted handprints line alcoves, and their footprints are locked in stone across the southern Utah canyon country. In the north rock climbers scale the faces of Lone Peak and the Cottonwood Canyons. Powder hounds chase winter on the slopes of Alta while cutthroat trout inhabit the rivers and bald eagles hunt the waterways. Utah is dogmatic in its profession of grandeur, and we are the lucky recipients. Our roads are not all paved and our stars still glow magnificently in small towns with what some may consider hard-to-pronounce names. Again, we are lucky for these inconveniences—it is what makes our place beautiful.

For many, the story of the state of Utah is connected to early pioneer settlers. The people of the Latter-Day Saints religion followed a temperamental trail to this promised land. Spurred on by conviction and hope, the Saints arrived in the valley of the Great Salt Lake and began shaping the land into their rendition of paradise. From this central hive, satellite towns were developed all across the area, and eventually after some negotiations, the State of Deseret became Utah.

In July of 1847 Utah as a state began taking shape into what it has become today. The walk to the promised land could be understood as a metaphor that has shaped its people even to modern day. As the pioneers hiked west looking for a place to begin again, something cemented into their hearts and that something gets played out time and time again as we take to trails looking out at a place that offers a life and a promise of greatness. Utahns have always walked—it is who we are. Our modern lives trace the ancestral hunting grounds and migration routes of generations of people and animals before us.

This region was very different before the pioneer wagons rolled in, the oxen unhitched, and the handcarts unloaded. Before this area was claimed as the land of Zion, indigenous peoples—the Utes, the Paiutes, the Shoshone, and many other tribes—inhabited this land. Long before the Pipeline Trail was laid with pipe to move water to the dry valley below, people walked

Exploring Eagle Crags near Zion. RACHEL WARNER

these areas hunting and gathering the essentials for their way of life. Without a doubt, they walked on trails that we do today. These trails are similar to those used by the elk and the mule deer who knew the streams and the forests by following ancestral memory to the meadows in the low country, and the migration routes as the snows filled the high country. These small cuts through the hills were used by skillful hunters, scouts and trappers, loggers, miners, and finally recreationalists. History repeats itself, and no doubt the view from Grandeur Peak held the gaze of humans for centuries. We walk through history each and every step forward. Our trails have not changed drastically, and perhaps the reasons for walking them has only slightly shifted. Hiking in Utah has a special place in its creation story.

Over the course of writing this book, I have only begun the unraveling of this great story and its millions of years in the making. Within each chapter of creation, I have learned about the smaller forces at work that are busy creating beauty in small and magnificent ways. My curiosity to understand this place has led me to study the magnificent formations that make up Utah, from the stone lace in the Swell to the China Wall along the Crimson Trail. I know now about the forces that put up the fins of sandstone in Moab and others that are tearing them down, inch by inch. I've also discovered the magic of cryptobiotic soil, a biological crust formed by microscopic algae, fungi, and other organisms that is formed over hundreds of years, similar to coral reef. This black, ridged soil is found throughout southern canyons of Utah and is a vital part of the ecosystem and incredibly fragile. Some of the most important geology in this state is the smallest. Nature's creation and destruction is at times what is most beautiful about it. It is in this cycle that things can begin again, over and over. Utah has reinvented itself over and over. There is nothing to me as beautiful, peaceful, or fulfilling as walking with my dog through the red rock canyons and high mountains of this state.

By writing this book, I invite you to be curious and hope to share some of my favorite places with you and your dog. My hope is that we will together enjoy, share, and protect the wilderness that is vital to the psyche of a Utahn. From the immense geology to the trail as our cultural identity, this place is as unique for those visiting as it is for those who

One of Utah's many archaeological sites.

call it home. I have written this book in hopes of sharing with those who want to know a bit of what is special about this little place in a big world.

## WHY I HIKE WITH MY PUPS

I hike with Wren, my dog, because I believe covering ground together is foundational to our relationship. By participating in an activity that we both enjoy, our bond has formed and grows. Wren and I have spent years as partners in the backcountry, and at this point, I have found no better hiking buddy. Because of her superior senses, I have been able to see and experience an array of things that without her keen nose and sharp eyes I would have missed—a doe nibbling on a willow branch or a chipmunk high in a blue spruce.

**My best friend, Wren.**

Because I am interested in being more connected to and aware in the wilderness, I let Wren be my teacher. She has proven herself over and over by finding the best way down a slickrock face, discovering water, detecting rising temperatures, and spotting wildlife. Her senses have capabilities I revere.

Hiking with my dog gives purpose and joy to an activity. Caretaking an animal pushes me to do things for them and myself that I may not think to do. Dogs are my teachers, companions, and guides in the backcountry. Our rewards are great when we allow dogs to fold into our lives in ways that meet the needs of both.

## TRAINING AND TRAIL ACCLIMATION

If you own a dog, and if you are honest, you will be able to recall the up and downs that are inherent in this relationship. It is not easy, it is not straightforward, and it isn't free of heartaches. This partnership is fraught with hardships and frustration and—most of all—joy. Some dogs come into our lives seemingly pretrained, ready to learn, happy to obey, and others defy logic in their obstinance. Each and every one of them presents his own take on the world around him and gives what he can. To own a dog is both rewarding and challenging as are all things that require a commitment. Your life and its structure will change or has changed with your companion, and many of us are happy to do so. And it is not always easy, straightforward, or simple.

Wren demonstrating proper leash etiquette. RACHEL WARNER

The dogs we love challenge us to become patient, open, and thoughtful people who are vigilant to their needs and advocates for their well-being. We are responsible for their behavior, their health, their well-being, and—quite possibly—their happiness. Their needs become braided into ours or ours into theirs as our lives shift into a partnership that is without a doubt rewarding, and occasionally trying. The journey of dog ownership is not all that different from Joseph Campbell's well-known *Hero's Journey,* filled with the same tests and trials as our favorite characters in myths and stories.

## The Dog Journey

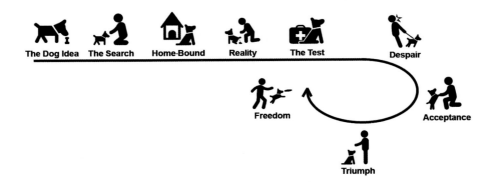

**The dog idea:** This is the moment that it becomes possible to consider owning a dog. Life circumstances change, and there is an opening for another being to share your world.

**The search:** This is a vital part of your happiness and compatibility with your dog. Researching different dog breeds, spending time observing different dog personalities at dog parks, talking with people who own dogs, volunteering at shelters to help walk dogs, even fostering different dogs will help you gain clarity on what type of dog will best fold into your life. Ask yourself questions like: How much activity am I comfortable with? What personality am I looking for in a dog? How much time am I willing to put into training? These will help you narrow down what type of dog fits best with your life.

**Home-bound:** This is a wonderful and exciting time. There is a thrill and a novelty to this new addition to your family and life! There is optimism and a thrilling sense of adventure. Idyllic thoughts surround the relationship that you are going to have with this perfect dog.

**Reality:** Maybe it is harder than you thought, and balancing needs is becoming difficult. You are tired and your dog needs to be walked. You have to clean up after your not-yet-trained puppy for the fifth time today. At three in the morning, she isn't quite as cute howling at ghosts in the corner as she was when you first brought her home.

**The test:** Your new dog is sick and has to go to the vet after getting into the trash . . . again. It is expensive. It is emotionally taxing. It is exhausting. You are worried and feel inadequate. If you were a better dog owner, these things wouldn't happen. Maybe you are a cat person after all. You and your relationship with your dog are being tested in a big way. You decide to persevere.

**Despair:** It isn't working. The training, the time, the advice your dog-owner friends and family members are giving you. You have tried everything to make your dog into what you think she should be, and it still isn't easy. You start to wonder if you are capable of the task at hand, the training, the shifting, the embracing of your dog's needs, and her limitations.

**Acceptance:** This is a powerful moment when after spending significant and meaningful time with your dog, you begin to understand who she is and what she needs. The relationship is getting stronger and trust is being built, and day by day things are actually improving. The fondness and even love of her quirks and idiosyncrasies is taking hold. A bond is forming.

**Triumph:** Your dog comes when he is called for the first time at the dog park. You see your dog as the amazing creature he is and you are proud of the work and understanding you have gone through. You accept your relationship with your dog and recommit to the life you are building together, with the understanding that hardship and readjusting expectations are just part of your life together. It is a glowing time, filled with possibility and joy.

**Freedom:** You and your dog are a team. You help each other and feel connected and hopeful. Your world expands with a trust and understanding of commands. Off-leash is becoming a reality. You have molded into each other's lives with a clear understanding of needs and expectations.

**Repeat 4–9:** Your relationship with your dog will cycle through the stages of reality, test, despair, acceptance, triumph, and freedom over and over as your bond deepens, time passes, and adventures are had. Your relationship is tested, and if you are up for the journey to be had, your companionship will grow stronger.

Much of what you will do to prepare your dog for hiking with you will depend on the personality and needs of your dog. The dog's journey teaches us that creating balance is a vital part of connecting with your dog, shaping different elements with your dog's personality to help her become more well adjusted and capable of accompanying you on adventures.

Without shaping, without boundaries, most dogs will continue to test your relationship. They will, in their ways, continue to ask you what is okay to do or not do. It is up to you, as their guardian, to learn how to request behaviors that will positively affect both you and your dog. It is vital for the happiness of both that you are willing to set the boundaries that will bring a sense of freedom to the relationship. Without clear expectations, your dog will behave in ways that may make taking them to the trail uncomfortable

Calliope, a wonder dog, adopted from Best Friends Animal Sanctuary. RYAN MCDERMOTT

for you and others, which ultimately confines your lives to a narrow scope of activity. Narrowing the scope of a dog's activity ultimately leads to a dog suffering from our limitations around requests. It is important to understand our responsibility in creating well-adjusted dogs.

It is vital that you understand that "good" hiking dogs are dogs that are emotionally plastic, have an understanding of basic commands, and are capable of behaving appropriately in a variety of situations. Good hiking dogs have been taught, spent time with, and held accountable for their actions. Dog owners that are willing to work toward bettering the relationships with their dogs and are willing to accept what their dog lacks or needs will have a better chance of gaining the relationship that will allow them to enjoy all that hiking has to offer.

To prepare your dog to hike, time spent socializing and training your dog is vital to her development.

## SOCIALIZING

Socializing is allowing your puppy the opportunity to spend time in a variety of different scenarios that will help her develop curiosity instead of fear. This is very important with puppies due to the time frame of their brain development. After three months the brain in your dog has formed important associations that may be difficult to alter in the future. It is regarded as "best practice" in dog ownership to help your dog become as well adjusted as possible by socializing her as much as possible when she is young. Socializing is also going on adventures with your already-grown dogs, expanding their world and exercising their bodies and minds in a positive way that will help build trust and help them internalize a sense of safety, confidence, and relaxation in new situations.

If you adopt a dog, this will be part of the acceptance stage in your relationship. You will learn over time what your dog needs to feel safe and what scenarios will bring out different elements of your and your dog's relationship. Through time spent socializing your dog, you may learn that behaviors that you thought needed shaping are—in certain contexts—her most endearing qualities.

## TRAINING

Training is the word we use to help shape behaviors in a way that will allow you to have the relationship you would like with your dog. Training is best achieved through positive reinforcement about how you will be together. You can teach your dog to walk on a leash without pulling, making it enjoyable to hike on-leash together. It is possible to teach your dog not to jump up on strangers, again keeping your dog's world open to all the places that strangers are.

Consistently practicing voice recall off the trail can be useful when you need your dog to come to you while on the trail. Seeking mode is a useful dog-training strategy. Take the time to learn about seeking mode and how to use it to help your dog overcome discomfort, and integrate it into your daily training.

While socializing and training your dog, it is important to notice how it feels to be with your dog. If there is anxiety in your body, your dog will likely sense that and react to that fear. It is important to consider how you may perhaps unknowingly be adding to your dog's stress. Remaining calm or neutral in scenarios not only helps your dog, it is often important for your safety as well. Dogs are living beings with their own patterns of behaviors. This is especially the situation when adopting an older rescue dog. Take time to understand your dog's unknown triggers.

There are always moments of struggle in relationships, and getting the support you need to help you with your dog is an important part of owning a dog. For example, if you have a high-energy dog and are not able to give him the outlets he needs to express that energy, consider doggy day care. Puppy classes are places where your dog can learn to navigate social situations and agility obstacles. These obstacle may not only be fun to experiment with but also can be good training for obstacles you will experience out on the trail. It again depends on your individual dog and the commitment you have to creating a loving bond. In the journey of learning how to train, connect, and care for a dog with specific needs, you will have the opportunity to grow as a dog person.

Ultimately, time spent training your dog can be very enjoyable. Yes, there might be limitations intrinsic to your relationship depending on the circumstances surrounding your dog—perhaps their past, their breed, their body type, their disposition—but most dogs are willing to change and grow right alongside us. It is helpful if you are having small issues to seek help early before patterns of behavior become more difficult to alter. Continue to be curious

**Nema and Stephanie.**

about dogs and how relationships form with dogs. Read, listen, and research. You will find more to discover. As Alexandra Horowitz describes in her books and lectures on the umwelt of dogs, if we spend time observing dogs being dogs, questions [and answers] will unfold. Researching those moments will allow for stronger relationships between you and your pet.

Here are the most important things to do when creating a trail dog:

**Millie showing off her harness and collar.**
RACHEL WARNER

- Trail dogs need you to clean up after them so the trail they love so much will continue to be available to them.

- Provide identification on a collar or harness, and also a microchip. Be sure to put a phone number in addition to yours on their tag in case something happens to you on the trail and you are not able to take care of your dog.

- Trail dogs need you to take care of them and keep them healthy in the way that you and a veterinarian or holistic health-care provider decide is best for your particular dog.

- Spend time socializing and training your dog. Practice walking on leash and voice recall.

## SAFETY AND PREPARATION

Following are general safety and preparation guidelines that you should attend to when hiking with your dog. Throughout the book you will find trail-specific cautions and preparation advice to help you and support your dog in having an optimal hike.

### KNOW YOUR DOG'S BREED

Different breeds of dogs have different thresholds with "trail dog" elements. Know your breed, its strengths, and what is possible. Dogs with short nasal passages, such as bulldogs and pugs, are physically unable to be as athletic as a Labrador or poodle. Large breeds, such as Presa Canarios and Great Danes, have high risks of joint problems and should not be asked to pound out the miles with you as you endlessly explore the Wasatch Range. Small dogs such as dachshunds can be feisty mile eaters but also are susceptible to back problems as they age. Again, it is important to remember to think about your preferences as a hiker as you decide what dog will fit your lifestyle. Also remember, just because your dog will do what you ask of her, that does not mean that it is good for her to do so.

## PREVENTING HEALTH PROBLEMS

Preventing health problems is paramount to dog ownership. Work with your veterinarian to determine when you should spay or neuter your dog, which vaccines will keep your dog healthy, and to learn best practices for creating a trail dog.

## DOG FITNESS

Your dog's fitness is also crucial to a healthy life. Feeding habits and getting your dog to an appropriate weight are important for her overall health. Keeping your dog trim will allow her to enjoy the activities you are asking of her.

Awareness of potential physical and emotional issues, which are common among all dog breeds, could be reduced with thoughtful exercise options for your particular dog. With working breeds, chasing a ball may be tempting and seem fun, but be thoughtful of your dog's joints and mental health in regard to stimulating her "work/chase" drive. High-energy dogs need stimulation, and it is important to consider how this mental-physical stimulation happens. Perhaps your dog needs to spend more time playing with other dogs to feel calm and relaxed. Maybe your dog needs to spend more time with you so your dog feels more grounded with you. Maybe your dog is a brainiac and needs food puzzles, agility training, or a different kind of "job" to feel happy and secure. This will be part of your relationship adventure that will unfold individually over time.

Many breeds are susceptible to joint issues such as hip dysplasia (a deterioration of the joint socket or a genetic issue with the ball size of the ball-and-socket hip joint). It is vital to do research around these genetic or predisposition issues, talk with your veterinarian, and tailor your regimens around the information you have about your dog.

## DOG ENDURANCE

Just like it is important for you to be conditioned for the trail, your dog's endurance abilities and needs are vital. Start and build slowly. Puppy bodies and large breeds take time to develop properly, and taxing joints too early can result in damage long-term.

One way to build your dog's endurance is to start by walking your dog for 20 minutes a day, then increasing in length and difficulty over time. Another option is to be observant of your dog and his behavior and cater to his needs with thoughtful choices surrounding the signs of fatigue. Remember dog behaviors are very dog-specific. It can take time to know and understand what signs mean. The rule of thumb is to allow your dog time to adjust to a more active lifestyle over time.

## TRAIL PREPARATION

General trail-specific preparations can make sure you and your dog have a safe hike. If you are planning on hiking with your dog in the areas of Utah that are off-leash, it is imperative your dog has a high-function recall that can be depended on regardless of circumstances: deer prancing down the trail, other dogs running around, hikers enjoying their lunch—all of these scenarios will test your dog's capability to listen to your command.

When hiking in Utah, you and your dog may face many obstacles, especially on more technical trails. You will want to work with your dog to learn how to wait patiently as you find a safe way. For example, your dog may need to be lifted off a ledge, led down a steep section of slickrock, or carried across obstacles including water crossings. Plan to practice these skills before hiking the trail to get your pup acclimated to the process.

Other elements that are part of your trail dog's life:

There are different behaviors that are appropriate in the front country and the backcountry. It is your responsibility to know what is appropriate in each area and the risks involved with the behaviors you are asking of your dog. It is vital to monitor your dog intensely while spending time far away from definitive health care. Most dogs with loyal dispositions will not hesitate to participate in the activity asked of them, whether that is crossing a log over a very swiftly flowing river, climbing a steep rock face, or being out in the heat with you despite the repercussions to themselves. It is our responsibility to edit or censor our requests according to our dogs' overall well-being and preservation. Drowning, falling, heat stress, and becoming injured due to overexertion are very real dangers while hiking.

Be cognizant of the caretaking aspect of dog ownership as you explore the backcountry. It is often impossible to get out of the backcountry quickly, and this could, depending on the injury or situation you find yourself in with your dog, prove catastrophic for you or your animal.

It is important that you choose hiking buddies that line up with your own values around behavior, fitness, ethics, and other priorities in your life. By doing this you will provide your dog the space to be safe and comfortable and have fun. Some dogs are very impressionable, and pack behavior will very quickly override their individual behaviors. If you have this type of dog, it is important to spend time with other dogs that will help teach your dog behaviors that you value. If you become stressed in the presence of someone who feels it is appropriate to disobey watershed laws, does not clean up after their dog, or is overwhelmed by their dog's behavior and is unable or unwilling to seek guidance around shaping, these scenarios should be avoided. It is important to protect the relationship you have with your dog, and if your dog cannot hear your commands while chasing another dog that is not offering a good example, it is time to reconsider trail time with that particular pair.

Self-care while on the trail is also incredibly important to your dog, especially in the backcountry. Their lives depend on you in many circumstances, from simply being without restraint in the car you're driving to your choice of trail, how much water you bring for them, how well you train them, if you decide to check the weather, if you are prepared navigationally for the area you want to hike in, or what you do during an animal encounter. These will all very drastically affect your dog. Your happiness, comfort level, and footwear choice will all also affect your hiking buddy, and it is therefore vital that you learn how to

Wren navigating a water crossing.

**Wren is a great trail dog.** JASON HACKNEY

take care of yourself while hiking. It will be impossible for you to care for your dog appropriately if you are incapacitated.

The possibilities are almost endless after you and your dog develop a relationship based on trust and attentiveness, from teaching your dog to wear a dog pack by slowly introducing her to it, to wearing booties, to all the nuances that you and your dog will navigate together. Dog gear can be both useful and detrimental for your dog and it's important that it fits well. Consult with your veterinarian for more information about how to select and fit your pup's gear.

"Go slow to go fast" is a phrase from Boulder Outdoor Survival School lore, and this motto applies to just about everything including dog training and relationship building. By taking the time to prepare your dog for the rigors ahead by conditioning her slowly, by working with her at home on recall, patience, and emotional plasticity, you will be able to conquer the limitations that have perhaps held you and your dog back from accomplishing the goals you have set. Spending time with your dog and having fun exploring the world around you will help you build the confidence to overcome the obstacles that present themselves. As the relationship grows, you will be able to turn moments of potential frustration into teaching moments for your dog. As you gain experience on the trails, you will find what works for you and your particular dog. With your dog's well-being at the forefront of your consciousness while hiking, you will learn how to best meet the needs of you and your dog, which is a beautiful thing. And your dog will teach you, if you listen.

## WHAT TO EXPECT ON THE TRAIL

Throughout Utah, what you will need to expect on the trails drastically shifts as you move from the high alpine woods to the deep desert slots. Trail etiquette is important to

Martin on the boardwalk.

Navigating trail obstacles.
RACHEL WARNER

understand as you move through these distinctive and beautiful areas. Regardless of where you are hiking, it is vital for you to clean up after your dog. This means picking up their poop. While unpleasant, it is rapidly becoming a concern to local governing agencies, which will mean more regulations, less freedom, and ultimately less access to the beautiful areas we are currently enjoying. Using an airtight designated plastic storage container to transport the bags to trailhead trash cans helps remove some of the obstacles of being responsible with cleaning up. This is also part of positive impact and part and parcel to dog ownership.

It is important to know and obey laws enforced by the various governing agencies. For example, Mill Creek Canyon's leash laws in parking areas and trailheads need to be respected for the sake of all of our trail usage in the future. As hikers with dogs, we are all lumped together as one problem when bad behavior is being regulated. It is up to all of us to provide positive examples of community tolerance and cooperation in order to keep the regulations about our dogs to a minimum.

Voice control and on leash are distinctions that you will find in the hikes throughout this book. Knowing when and how to employ these guidelines is important. Some trails that are voice control may be better suited as an on-leash trail with your dog due to terrain, water crossings, and other hazards that present themselves to you and your dog. Keep in mind your dog's current ability and athleticism, knowing and embracing that that reality will continue to shift and grow as time marches on.

It is impossible to predict and prepare for everything that could affect you and your dog while on Utah trails. But what you can control are your behaviors and actions while hiking, such as having a well-trained and well-behaved dog, a clear sense of what your dog needs to feel safe while out hiking, a strong understanding of you and your dog's strengths and limitations, knowledge about where you are going, and what items you will need to bring to continue to have fun.

Part of what makes Utah wonderful for those seeking recreational opportunities has to do with multiuse. Horses, mountain bikers, runners, and other hikers all follow the same routes through the canyons throughout the state, and it is important to offer other users the courtesy they deserve by being aware of the guidelines created to keep everyone safe.

## HORSES

Horses have the right of way, period. Most dogs have not spent time with horses and may not understand what to do or how to behave. It is best practice to step off the trail with your dog to give the horse and rider plenty of room to pass by. It is helpful if you can remain standing, talking to the rider or your dog, so the horse is aware that you are a human and not a threat. If you are walking with your dog off-leash and your friendly dog decides to ignore your frantic calling her back to you, walk calmly to your pup. Running toward the horses hoping to remedy your dog's faux pas will only create more issues. Horses can be jumpy, especially on windy days, and the more you can remain calm and nonchalant, the better everyone's experience will be.

## MOUNTAIN BIKERS

Mountain bikers also share a good portion of Utah's trails. In order to keep you and your dog safe, it is wise to keep your dog leashed in high-density bike areas, as in sections in the La Sals and the Wasatch. Technically, bikers must yield to hikers and their dogs, but some do not. Training your dog to "yield" to the side of the trail as you communicate with the cyclist can help avoid an unfortunate situation.

## RUNNERS AND OTHER HIKERS

Becoming a student of people's and dogs' body language is an important study as a dog owner. Some people are uncomfortable with dogs in their space and request respectful distances between themselves and your dog. Be able to provide that for them, by training your dog or keeping her on a leash. Children who have fear around dogs need to be respected, and their requests for space dictated either verbally or nonverbally need to be heard for the longevity of multiuse spaces.

Keep in mind that nature can get pretty big out in the backcountry, and you and your knowledge are the best prevention strategy.

The illustration exaggerates how on Utah trails you and your dog may experience a number of hindrances and potentially dangerous obstacles. Be prepared for everything from uncleared trails, quicksand, high-water crossings, exposure, harsh and sudden weather, wild animals, insects, high elevations, long mileage, and flash floods. Being self-sufficient and capable of both navigation and an ability to make wise and informed decisions will keep you and your dog safe. Be alert and prepare to face

**JASON HACKNEY**

obstacles great and small as you negotiate the wild terrain. Having invested time and energy into your dog's training and trail acclimation will minimize the struggles you will face together.

There are so many things that are out of your control while out in the wilderness. Taking care of things you can—such as training, gear, navigation, conditioning both you and your dog, knowing first aid, and being aware of potential hazards in the area and signs of distress your dog displays—will be an important component to being a happy trail team.

## SEASONAL NUISANCES

Seasonal nuisances in Utah can be as big as dynamic weather and as small as a Russian thistle prickle. Other elements can include trail conditions and complicated terrain, which also make Utah's wilderness special and daunting. There are as many different combinations of potential issues as there are suggestions on how to avoid them. In general, weather is one the most difficult and potentially uncomfortable scenarios that will present itself to you while hiking in Utah. The very real dangers that you could put yourself and your dog in by not knowing, not understanding, or ignoring the weather of Utah cannot be understated. Human error can make uncomfortable weather potentially dangerous, particularly in hot cars. Bring proper clothing and know about how to keep your dog and yourself warm and dry in the high country. Learn about flash flood potentials and heat stress in canyon country to avoid putting yourself and your dog in a very precarious position.

Educate yourself and stay curious about important survival strategies. Reading books or taking a class can help you learn how to read the signs Mother Nature is providing for weather that may be brewing hours in the future. One really important but simple

Wren inspecting the remnants of a flash flood.

thing is to be flexible to changing your plan as new circumstances present themselves. Prevention is the best advice when it comes to being in situations that are difficult and perhaps life-threatening. Being willing to call a hike when the weather turns or considering hiking another day or a different trail are all ways to keep you and your dog safe while enjoying Utah's wild places.

Following are some of the most common seasonal nuisances to know before hiking on Utah trails.

## DRIVING DIFFICULTIES

While many of the hikes in Utah can be technical and challenging, sometimes the drive in or the approach is just as difficult. The roads wind way up mountain passes, in and out of desert rivers, and across washboards to deliver you to your trailhead. Many of these roads can become impassable during the rainstorms that frequent southern Utah areas during the monsoons of late summer. The soil around the Paria River, up near Moab, turns to a slick clay when wet, making it almost instantly impassable. Be cautious when driving through these areas, and do not attempt when and if rain is eminent.

## FLASH FLOODING

Flash flooding is one of the more serious hazards that tend again to be more common during the rainy time in the desert. It is imperative that you take precautions in slot or narrow canyons, avoiding these hikes when rain is forecasted, predicted, or even hinted at. Flash floods are powerful forces that have not only carved the landscape we know, they have taken lives. These massive floods can turn a dry wash into a raging river in a matter of moments. The tar-black mass of floodwater can uproot and drag cottonwood trees, enormous boulders, cars, and anything else that stands in its way. Trees get stuck high up in some of the canyons, wedged tightly between the walls. The height of the water levels is frightening.

## WINTER WEATHER

In winter your dog will love playing in the snow. Options to cross-country ski or snowshoe offer you and your dog more territory to cover during the winter months. It is a beautiful and wonderful thing to frolic through the snow with your dog. The downside of this activity is the snowballs that form on the coats of dogs and grow larger as your dog moves through the snow. They can get grapefruit size and are incredibly painful to your dog. It is important to stop when your dog begins showing signs of discomfort and help him remove the snowballs. There are products such as Mushers-Secret that are supposed to help, but personally I have had little success with them. Providing booties and snowsuits for your dog is just about the only thing you can do to prevent these nuisances from occurring.

## PESKY CRITTERS

Utah is generally pretty bland when it comes to pesky critters such as fleas and ticks, but in heavily populated mule-deer country and high mountain areas, ticks and burrs are present and more bothersome. It is important to become habituated to checking yourself and your dog for these hitchhikers on a daily basis. Running your hands over your dog's body is an important tool in maintaining the health of your dog. Starting at your dog's head, rub your fingers over your dog's face and neck, look inside her ears, then move your hands across her back, chest, stomach, and back legs. The feel of a tick is noticeable and needs immediate attention. See your veterinarian for best practice with regard to removing ticks. There are many different thoughts and theories on how to best remove the tick without it causing more harm and possible infection to your dog. It is also important to check yourself as well. Ticks in Utah are not so much carriers of dreaded Lyme disease, but the ticks in this area do carry Rocky Mountain spotted fever. If bitten by a tick, try to save it to be tested by a doctor.

Specific hikes and areas in Utah have nuisances and elements unique to themselves. It is important to be cognizant of these specifics and reference the individual hikes for more specific information. In this wonderful state of Utah, be prepared, stay safe, and always check the weather when hiking.

# HOW TO USE THIS GUIDE

Use the overview map to decide on a hike in the part of the state you would like to visit, then read the appropriate entry to begin more detailed planning of your trip. Each entry contains the following information:

**County:** This is the county where the trail is located.

**Start:** This is where the hikes begins; the trailhead.

**Distance:** The total distance in miles that the hike travels is listed here.

**Approximate Hiking time:** This is an estimate of how long it will take to hike the trail. Note, this is just an estimate and can vary widely according to hiking pace and stops along the way.

**Difficulty:** A subjective opinion made by the author of the difficulty of the hike. Hikes are classified as easy, moderate, or difficult.

**Trailhead Elevation:** The height above sea level of the trailhead.

**Highest Point:** The highest point above sea level along the trail.

**Best season:** A suggested best time of year in which to hike the trail.

**Trail surface:** This indicates what type of surface you will be hiking on, such as dirt trail, boardwalk, paved path, etc.

**Other trail users:** This section lists other trail users you might expect to see during your hike, such as hunters, mountain bikers, horseback riders, etc.

**Canine compatibility:** This tells you if it is legal to bring your dog on the trail.

**Land status:** This indicates who owns or manages the land on which the trail passes; for example, national forest or private resort.

**Fees and permits:** This self-explanatory entry will ensure that you have enough cash or that you have obtained proper paperwork if required.

**Trail contact:** The address and phone number for acquiring up-to-date local information is included here.

**Nearest town:** The closest city or town with basic amenities is listed here.

**Trail Tips:** Practical advice for enhancing your hiking experience.

**Nat Geo TOPO! (USGS):** The National Geographic TOPO!/United States Geological Survey map that is applicable to the hike.

**Nat Geo Trails Illustrated Map:** The National Geographic Trails Illustrated Map that is applicable to the hike (if available).

**Finding the trailhead:** Directions to the trailhead are provided. Often, two or more sets of directions are listed to get you to different trailheads or to guide you from different starting points. This information should be used in conjunction with the maps in this guide, USGS maps, and state road maps.

**Trailhead GPS:** The global positioning coordinates to the trailhead.

**What to See:** Generally, the hike described is the most interesting or most scenic hike in the park or area. Alternate routes or suggestions for other nearby hikes may also be included here.

# Map Legend

## Municipal

≡🛡70🛡≡ Interstate Highway

≡🛡191🛡≡ US Highway

≡(24)≡ State Road

≡[103]≡ Local/County Road

= = = = Unpaved Road

┝━┿━┥ Railroad

─ ─ · ─ ─ State Border

## Trails

- - - - - - Featured Trail

- - - - - - Trail

↗ Trail Direction Arrows

## Water Features

⬭ Body of Water

∿ River/Creek

∿ Intermittent Stream

≋ Waterfall

∥ Cascade

ᕼ Spring

## Symbols

⑳ Trailhead

🅿 Parking

🚻 Restroom

▪ Building/Point of Interest

🖼 Scenic View/Lookout

▬ Bench

≍ Bridge

🚰 Water

▲ Campground

🅰 Picnic Area

⬦ Gate

≍ Pass

▲ Peak/Mountain

× Elevation

○ Town

## Land Management

▭ National Park/Forest

▭ Wilderness Area

▭ State/County Park

# NORTHERN UTAH

*"Each fresh peak ascended teaches something."*
—Sir Martin Convay

The hikes of northern Utah—through Logan Canyon, the Stansbury range, and the Northern Wasatch—share a unique relationship formed by the ancient inland seas that over the millennia have done their part to form parts of this beautiful state. Throughout this area, historical evidence is present of the sculpting and layering by tons of ancient water that once lapped against shores. Years of sedimentary layering now forms our mountains.

Today, what is left of these aquatic times can be measured in the salinity of the Great Salt Lake, the namesake of the capital of Utah. The hydrographic Great Basin, which encompasses 20,000 square miles, is one of three physiographic provinces in Utah, and the home to the majority of Utahns. Phantom lake shorelines along the Wasatch Range, now used as hiking trails, indicate the various water levels that once filled parts of the Great Basin.

Wren looking around at White Pine Lake.

The waterways are part of the defining characteristics of this area. Although water is present, there are not any outlets to the ocean. Because of its now dry climate, the water that makes its way into this basin will evaporate, become groundwater, or flow into one of the lakes in this area.

In the glacial- and Lake Bonneville–shaped canyons and mountains up Logan Canyon, you and your dog will hike past wildflowers and wild edibles. Chokecherries, poppies, yellow dyer's woad, Indian paintbrush, sticky geraniums, cinquefoils, and scarlet gilas are just a few of the species that paint the hillsides in summertime. Adams Canyon to the south, near Ogden, Utah, offers views of the Great Salt Lake and beautiful flora and fauna that grow streamside in this otherwise dry area. This is an area where giant pine trees shade much of the lower-mountain floor. Deseret Peak, the most western of the hikes explored in this book, is both rough and rugged and absolutely beautiful. Along the hike you will witness the vast emptiness of the Bonneville Salt Flats and Utah's West Desert. The hikes in this area give a hiker and their dog the opportunity to witness the eons of the past firsthand, with beautiful views the whole time.

# 1 WHITE PINE LAKE– LOGAN CANYON

## WHY GO?

From Tony Grove, the Logan Canyon White Pine Lake Trail winds up through the willows and aspen trees to open hillsides. From there the trail drops deep into the timbered streamside vegetation, which is both inspiring and daunting. White Pine Lake, shimmering and gorgeous, is tucked back in the shadows with Mount Magog and Mount Gog casting a watchful eye from above. There is water available throughout the hike to keep your pup happy.

### THE RUNDOWN

**County:** Cache
**Start:** From Tony Grove Day-Use Area
**Distance:** 7.2 miles out and back
**Hiking time:** 3.5–4.5 hours
**Difficulty:** Moderate due to a difficult climb and longer mileage
**Trailhead elevation:** 8,423 feet
**Highest point:** 8,832 feet
**Best seasons:** Late spring, summer, fall
**Trail surface:** Dirt, some rocky switchbacks, boarded bridges, can be muddy in the fall
**Other trail users:** Horses, hunters, backpackers

**Canine compatibility:** On leash
**Land status:** Uinta-Wasatch-Cache National Forest
**Fees and permits:** None
**Trail contact:** Logan Ranger District, 1500 E. US 89, Logan, UT 84321; (435) 755-3620; www.fs.usda.gov/ uwcnf
**Nearest town:** Logan
**Trail tips:** No cell service. This hike can easily be made into a backpacking trip.
**Nat Geo TOPO! Map (USGS):** 7.5-Minute *Naomi Peak*
**Nat Geo Trails Illustrated Map:** *713: Logan Bear River Range*

### FINDING THE TRAILHEAD

From the mouth of Logan Canyon on US 89, drive 19 miles up the canyon and turn left (west) at the sign for Tony Grove Campground onto Tony Grove Road 003. Follow the road up the winding grades, gaining elevation until you reach a large parking lot at the end of the road overlooking Tony Grove Lake. From the parking lot, you'll find the White Pine Lake Trail at the northern edge of the parking area, opposite the restrooms.
**Trailhead GPS:** N41 53.714' / W111 38.553'

## THE HIKE

If views from the parking trailheads were rated, the view of Tony Grove Lake would be vying for the top position. In the 1880s this area was frequented by the hardworking loggers and stockman who cast a judging eye toward the elite socialites, called "Tonies," who enjoyed the recreational opportunities that this area afforded. So the nickname "Tony" attached to the area. It is worth taking a moment to look at Tony Grove Lake, and let your dog get a drink before heading up the trail.

To the north of the parking area, you'll find the start of the trail. Make your way up the trail, then sign in at the trail register, continuing north. At mile 0.2 you will pass by a

trail junction to the beautiful Naomi Peak Trail, a trail to be hiked another day. Meadows that can be seen from the trail are a favorite hangout for deer and elk. In the fall you will most likely share this trail with hunters.

The trail crosses Bunchgrass Creek—step carefully to avoid getting your shoes wet. In between bunches of willows, your dog can find pools of water in which to lie down and cool off if needed. As you continue to climb out of the Tony Grove drainage area and ascend the small ridge to the north, make sure to turn around and give the stunning valley behind you a nod. The landscape changes after the ridge, with rolling hills and displays of stunted sages and grasses. Views down the smaller side canyons draw the eye south.

After climbing steadily in and out of small aspen stands, at mile 2.4 the trail will continue to climb to a very drastic ridgeline, with a steep descent plunging down to the canyon floor on the north side. The trail's mood shifts from the sunny hills to the steep, dark wooded hillside, where you will notice a temperature drop. Toward the end of the descent, water will again be available for your dog. For the remaining two trail junctions, continue left (west) toward White Pine Lake, which is located under the high quartzite cliffs in the distance.

At mile 3.2 you will cross a bridge. At the trail junction remember to veer left and continue west. At mile 3.6 you will arrive on the eastern shore of White Pine Lake. The lake is a beauty, snuggled between Mount Gog to the north and Mount Magog to the south. These oddly named peaks could reference biblical happenings in Ezekiel and Revelations or perhaps they are named after Gogmagog, a legendary British giant. The dog-loving locals will also call them "dog and my dog."

This area is popular for camping. There are campsites and a toilet at the northern end of the lake. After you are done soaking in the beauty of the cliffs, the sky, and the sight

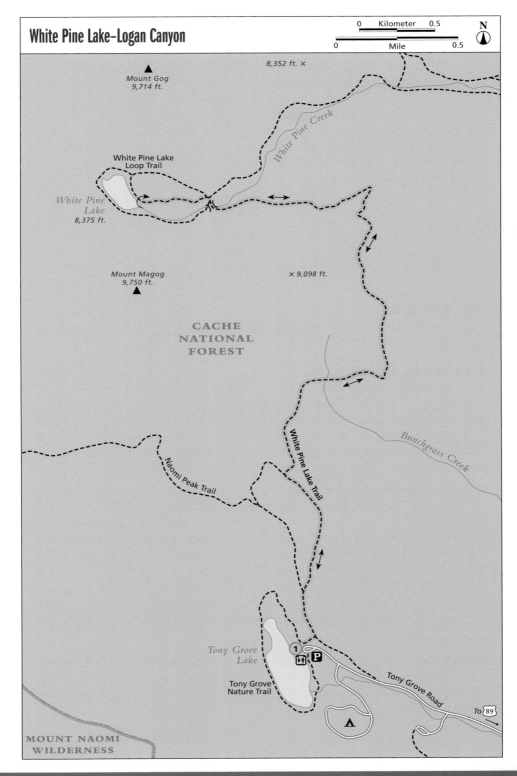

# White Pine Lake–Logan Canyon

0    Kilometer    0.5

0    Mile    0.5

N

▲ Mount Gog
9,714 ft.

8,352 ft. ×

*White Pine Creek*

White Pine Lake
Loop Trail

*White Pine
Lake*
8,375 ft.

Mount Magog
9,750 ft. ▲

× 9,098 ft.

CACHE
NATIONAL
FOREST

*Bunchgrass Creek*

Naomi Peak Trail

White Pine Lake Trail

*Tony Grove
Lake*

Tony Grove
Nature Trail

Tony Grove Road

To 89

MOUNT NAOMI
WILDERNESS

of the water ruffling the logs along its banks, return the way you came. Head up and out of the canyon on the switchback trail.

## MILES AND DIRECTIONS

**0.0**  Follow the signs north of the parking area at Tony Grove Lake.

**0.2**  Stay right (north), following the signs for White Pine Lake at the junction with Naomi Peak Trail.

**0.9**  Stay right, heading north, as you cross another junction.

**1.3**  Cross Bunchgrass Creek.

**2.4**  Descend steeply from the ridge to the canyon bottom.

**3.2**  Cross a small bridge.

**3.3**  Continue left (west) at the junction, following the signage for the lake.

**3.6**  Arrive at White Pine Lake. Return the way you came.

**7.2**  Arrive back at the Tony Grove Day-Use Area.

## NEARBY HIKES

Tony Grove Nature Trail, Mount Naomi, Jardine Juniper

## CREATURE COMFORTS

**Tony Grove Campground**, FR 140, Richmond, UT 84333; (801) 226-3564; www.recreation.gov. Tony Grove is a primitive campground in a beautiful setting at the center of a variety of recreational options near the White Pine Lake Trailhead. It is mostly shaded near Tony Grove Lake and is popular during wildflower season. Vault toilets are available, but there are no water, electrical, or sewer hookups. Plan to "pack out" your garbage. This campground is not recommended for long trailers or RVs.

**Holiday Inn Express Hotel & Suites Logan**, 2235 N. Main St., Logan; (435) 752-3444; www.ihg.com/holidayinnexpress/hotels/us/en/logan/ognes/hoteldetail?cm_mmc= GoogleMaps-_-EX-_-US-_-OGNES. The Holiday Inn in Logan is a nice, affordable hotel centrally located near Logan Canyon. Most rooms are standard, but there are suites and kitchenette rooms available. All stays include a hot breakfast and free parking. There is a pet fee per night and pets are limited to two per room.

**Caffe Ibis**, 52 Federal Ave., Logan; (435) 753-4777; www.caffeibis.com. Caffe Ibis is a staple in Logan serving delicious coffee and cafe fare, including vegan options. Their coffee is known as the "best in the state." Outside seating is available, or take your snacks to go as you head up Logan Canyon.

**Morty's Cafe**, 780 E. 700 North, Logan; (435) 535-3276; mortyscafe.com. Morty's is a burger joint near Utah State University that serves iconic burgers, sandwiches, shakes, and famous scone fries. There is a great patio with views of the mountains and Logan, but no pups, please.

# 2 CRIMSON TRAIL

## WHY GO?

On the Crimson Trail you will climb high through the alluring "crimson" sea of oak leaves in the fall, tiptoe above the "China Wall," and then descend to the banks of the Logan River, where trout can be seen flicking through the currents. This hike has some exposure at times, making it less appealing for families with small children. Leash laws apply in Logan Canyon.

---

### THE RUNDOWN

**County:** Cache
**Start:** Spring Hollow Campground, 4.3 miles from Logan
**Distance:** 4.3-mile loop: Spring Hollow Campground to Crimson Trail to Riverside Nature Walk
**Hiking time:** About 2 hours
**Difficulty:** Moderate. There are some steep ascents and descents and exposed narrow sections with drop-offs while hiking atop the famous China Wall.
**Trailhead elevation:** 5,120 feet
**Highest point:** 6,083 feet
**Best seasons:** Spring, fall
**Trail surface:** Dirt trail, tree root navigation, some rocky sections, limestone travel

**Other trail users:** Runners
**Canine compatibility:** On leash
**Land status:** Cache National Forest
**Fees and permits:** None
**Trail contact:** Logan Ranger District, 1500 E. US 89, Logan, UT 84321; (435) 755-3620
**Nearest town:** Logan
**Trail tips:** Enjoy the climb, the view is spectacular. Plan to eat lunch at one of the many trail "pull-offs" overlooking Logan Canyon for a wonderful way to spend an afternoon.
**Nat Geo TOPO! Map (USGS):** 7.5-Minute *Logan UT*
**Nat Geo Trail Illustrated Map:** *713: Logan/Bear River Range*

---

### FINDING THE TRAILHEAD

Parking for the Crimson Trail is located at the Spring Hollow Campground/day-use area, approximately 4 miles up Logan Canyon. From Main Street in Logan, Utah, turn right (east) on 400 North (US 89) through town, past the Utah State University Campus (Go Aggies!). As you approach Logan Canyon, you will pass the Logan Canyon Visitor Center on the right side (south) of the road. The visitor center is a recommended stop. You can gather lots of maps, advice, and interesting tidbits. Continue up Logan Canyon for approximately 4 miles, following the Logan River past First Dam Park, Second Dam, Bridger Campground, and Third Dam. Turn right (south) onto FR 038 toward the Spring Hollow Campground. If you pass Dewitt Picnic Area, you have gone too far. Drive into the Spring Hollow Campground. The day-use parking area is across a bridge and immediately to your right. After parking, walk south up the paved road, through the campground to the Spring Hollow Trail, a very obvious trail just past the group campsite. The trail will cross a bridge heading south for approximately 0.5 mile. The Crimson Trailhead will be indicated by a small wooden sign and will direct you to your left (north).
**Trailhead GPS:** N41 44.948' / W111 42.970'
**Parking GPS:** N41 45.196' / W111 43.022'

## THE HIKE

Logan Canyon is an all-American sweetheart with irrefutable beauty around every bend. From family-friendly trails to the upper echelons of athletic pursuits, the canyon offers every type of experience a person and pup could desire.

Seniors of the historical Brigham Young College in Logan, Utah, annually hiked the Crimson Trail and affectionately named it after their school colors. Crimson is certainly a metaphor of the students' journey, from the leg-burning switchbacks to the stride across the China Wall, a lodgepole limestone formation where encrusted fossils still sleep, to the quiet dare to the timid to have a look down to the canyon floor below, and, at last, the winding descent to the quiet shores of the Logan River. The path of a student: the trials, the triumphs, the moments of clarity, and the fearful steps into the unknown all are mirrored by this lesser-known trail.

Through the frilly limbs of Rocky Mountain juniper, the Crimson Trail offers amazing views down Logan Canyon along the hike. Approximately 1.6 miles into the hike, on the north side of the canyon, it is possible to see the famous Wind Caves of Logan Canyon, an eroded limestone cave that is known locally as the "witch's castle," the home of Hectate, Logan Canyon's very own witch. With your leashed dog nearby, pause high on the ledge and take in the amazing view.

After 2.4 miles the trail travels across the notable Lower Mississippian Lodgepole Limestone that characteristically creates the cliff-like feature of the China Wall. This layer of rock has many caverns, carved in it by wind and water. It is home to fossils of brachiopods, corals, and occasionally, trilobites. Be careful as you skirt the 200-plus-foot cliffs as it is a bit taxing on the nerves at a point or two.

After traversing the exposed clifftop of the China Wall, the descent through the forest is a welcome reprieve. The conifer forests are cooler than the cliffs above and are home to chattering squirrels and lovely breezes. At 3.6 miles the Crimson Trail "T's" with the Logan River and the Riverside Nature Trail. Turn left (west) downstream to head back to the parking area at Spring Hollow Campground. Be on the lookout for moose and enjoy the signage with information about the riparian zone, the Wind Caves, and other interesting pieces of the information about the area provided along this river walk.

## MILES AND DIRECTIONS

**0.0** Head south uphill through Spring Hollow Campground from Spring Hollow Day-Use parking area.

**0.3** Arrive at the Spring Hollow Trailhead.

**0.5** Veer left onto the Crimson Trail, climbing steeply.

**1.6** Look north toward the Wind Caves for a beautiful view.

**2.4** Cross the China Wall/Lodgepole Limestone geologic feature.

**3.3** At the T at the Logan River, head west to Spring Hollow Campground.

**4.3** Arrive back at the parking lot.

## NEARBY HIKES

Spring Hollow Trail, Riverside Nature Trail

Looking down Logan Canyon.

# Crimson Trail

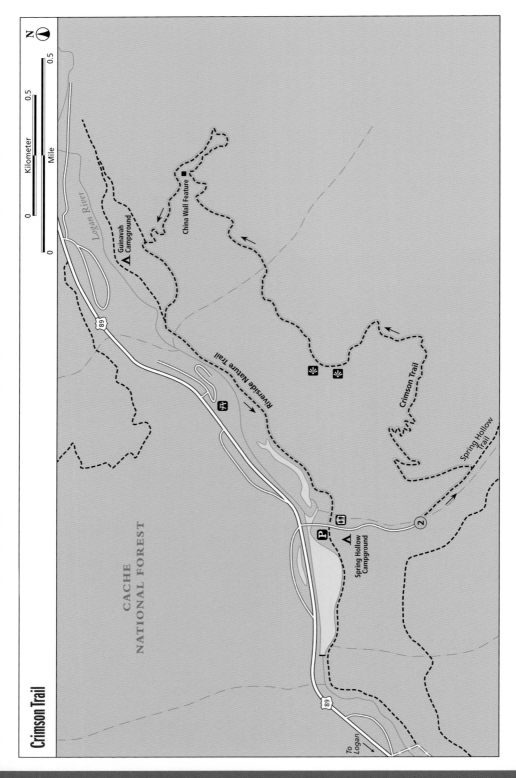

## CREATURE COMFORTS

**Spring Hollow Campground**, FR 038, Logan, UT 84321; (877) 444-6777; www .recreation.gov. Spring Hollow is a pleasant campground located 4 miles up Logan Canyon and is open May through September. It is shaded and has vault toilets, water, fire pits, paved parking, and group sites. You must reserve five days in advance on www .recreation.gov. This is a great campground for access to the Logan-area trails.

**Guinavah–Malibu Campground**, FR 034, Logan, UT 84321; (877) 444-6777; www .recreation.gov. Nestled in a 75-year-old black willow forest along the banks of the Logan River, this location offers beauty, access to trails, canoeing, and tubing. Open May– Sept with group sites and an amphitheater available. Must reserve five days in advance on www.recreation.gov. There are no hookups or water at this location.

**Airbnb Logan**, Airbnb.com. There are a number of pet-friendly vacation rentals around Logan if hotels and camping aren't your preference.

**Crumb Brothers**, 291 S. 300 West, Logan; (435) 753-0875; www.crumbbrothers.com. Crumb Brothers is an amazing bakery for a treat fest after a hike. They bake everything in-house and their sandwiches are delicious. Try the Cuban. They are closed Mon–Tues but are a great post-hike snack place on the weekends. Plan for a picnic.

# 3 DESERET PEAK

## WHY GO?

From the well-earned summit of Deseret Peak, the highest peak in the Stansbury range, you can smell the distinct aroma of the Great Salt Lake and see views of the west desert salt flats, Tooele, and the Oquirrh Mountains. This trail is a wild one, wandering through layers of geology, meadows, and valleys of glacier graveyards, along false summits littered with scree fields, and past windy canyons. It can be done as a loop or an out-and-back. The trail is an adventure well worth the commute.

### THE RUNDOWN

**County:** Tooele
**Start:** Deseret Peak Trailhead
**Distance:** 8.9-mile loop
**Hiking time:** 4–5 hours
**Difficulty:** Strenuous due to steep climbs, technical sections, and exposure
**Trailhead elevation:** 7,475 feet
**Highest point:** 11,031 feet
**Best seasons:** Spring through fall. The road is closed in winter.
**Trail surface:** Dirt, scree, rocks
**Other trail users:** Horses, runners
**Canine compatibility:** Voice control
**Land status:** National Forest

**Fees and permits:** None
**Trail contact:** Salt Lake Ranger District, 6944 S. 3000 East, Cottonwood Heights, UT 84121; (801) 733-2660
**Nearest town:** Grantsville
**Trail tips:** Bring lots of water, and prepare for very steep climbs. It can get chilly at the summits so bring layers.
**Nat Geo TOPO! Map (USGS):** *Deseret Peak East, Deseret Peak West*
**Nat Geo Trails Illustrated Map:** N/A

### FINDING THE TRAILHEAD

From Salt Lake City, head west on I-80 toward Reno/Salt Lake International Airport. After 21 miles take exit 99 onto UT 36 toward Stansbury/Tooele. Continue south for 3.5 miles on UT 36, then turn right (west) on UT 138, and continue for 11 miles through Grantsville. UT 138 will become Main Street, and as you pass the cemetery, turn left (south) onto West Street/Mormon Trail Road, following the signage for South Willow Canyon Road. Continue for 4.3 miles, then take a right (west) onto the dirt South Willow Canyon Road. Follow this winding road for 7.2 miles until it terminates at Loop Campground. Do not attempt the South Willow Canyon Road if heavy precipitation is expected as this road is very susceptible to flooding. Once at Loop Campground, follow the road around to the right to a small parking area with vault toilets. The trailhead is to the south from the parking area.
**Trailhead GPS:** N40 28.974' / W112 36.413'

## THE HIKE

The drive on South Willow Canyon Road is stunning and winds through a narrow gorge that sets the adventure bar pretty high. To begin, head south of the parking area to Mill Fork Trail, which is easy to spot, just to the right (west) of the toilets. You will enter the Deseret Peak Wilderness Area shortly after you begin your hike. You will follow Mill Fork as it winds along the trail adjacent a creek bed, dodging aspens, to a crossing at 0.9

Martin and Wren making it look easy on the technical section.

mile. If it is running, this is a good place to let your dog cool off before the trail begins in earnest. The drainage is wide and has steep sides. Make your way across the rocky bottom, popping up on the east side, and veer to the left on a narrow trail that continues east. You will see a small sign to Deseret Peak. The trail will slowly climb through the conifer trees, eventually crossing into a long, narrow meadow that the trail crisscrosses toward the cliffs to the south.

There are dozens of deer that call this area home, and they will often be just a blur as they hightail it away from you. The views to the north are beautiful and provide opportunity for a small break as the steepness increases.

After approximately 2 miles you will traverse the meadow in and out of the dark timber, and for the next mile the challenge will become great as you scale the glacial cirque to the ridge above. This section is difficult and rocky, be careful as you ascend toward the locally endeared spot called Lunch Ridge. From the saddle, there are a couple trail options that are viable substitutions for added adventures, but to Deseret Peak the trail is to the right and climbs up the rocky slope. The wind can be fierce up here—layer up to avoid getting chilled, especially if you've been sweating (you will be sweating) after your climb. As the trail makes its way up to what you hope will be Deseret Peak but isn't, be sure to look south down the elegant canyons and into the Tooele Valley. From the top of the second ridge, the trail swings west, and suddenly the starkness of the salt flats and the smell and humidity of the Great Salt Lake are evident. This sulfury smell, like rotten eggs, is caused by bacteria, decaying algae, and decomposing brine shrimp along the shallow waters of the Great Salt Lake. Depending on the direction of the wind, you may get lucky on your hike and avoid the stench, but don't be surprised if you can smell it when you get back to town. Occasionally, Salt Lake Valley residents find themselves downwind.

Beyond the false summit, continue your rocky ascent, with views to the north visible between gaps in the rocky cliffs. Be careful as there is some exposure on this section. The actual summit at 4.3 miles, atop a rocky outcropping, is a spot from which to enjoy the 360-degree views. Hold on to your hat here as the winds are fierce, but the views are pretty much jaw-dropping. After your fill from this scenic outpost, make your decision to return to the parking area the way you came or finishing the loop. The loop trail continues to the north along a very rocky trail on the ridge. It descends almost as quickly as it ascended a mile or so back.

This trail is referred to as the Pocket Fork Trail. Pocket Fork is narrow as it winds back and forth along the hill, descending quickly into the charred remains of a forest. The trees are an eerie and haunting sight, but they're beautiful in their odd shapes and burned-out interiors. Continue descending with views of pristine canyons that fall away to the west. At mile 5.4 there is a brief technical section that may require some scrambling. Choose your footing carefully and continue along a small traverse. Next you will see a small sign after a brief climb directing you up a small ridge. Follow this trail as you ascend the ridge past a stunning old limber pine bracing against the wind. This tree points the way down off the windy rocky ridge down into the wind break of the valley below. This trail also knows the switchback routine as it drops you quickly through the rocky steep sections to a signed trail junction. At mile 6.6 turn right on the Loop Campground Trail. This trail will take you south and drop you quickly over another ridge. There are multiple springs on this side of the cliffs, and your dog will enjoy a long drink. The view of the peaks above are an incredible sight. Continue along the trail until at mile 8 you will have

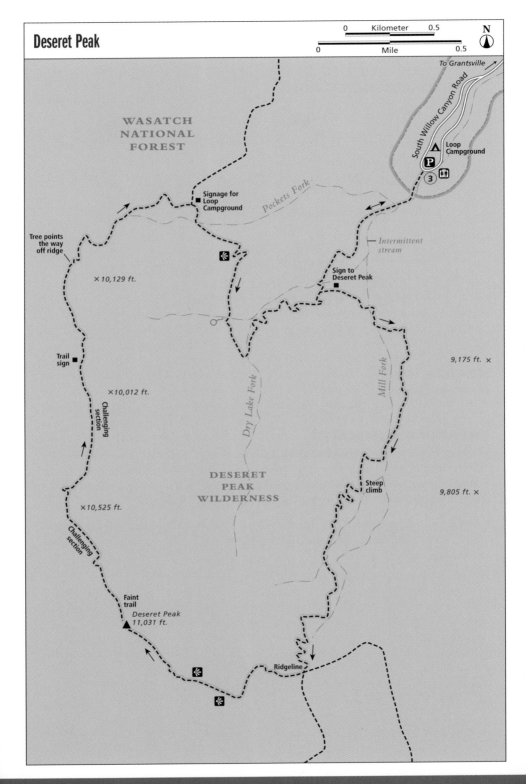

**Deseret Peak**

completed your loop. You will meet up with the trail you hiked in on. Descend through the aspens back to your vehicle.

## MILES AND DIRECTIONS

**0.0**  The trail begins to the south of the Loop Campground parking area.

**0.9**  Cross South Willow Creek, then stay left toward the signed junction. Follow the trail right (south) for Deseret Peak.

**2.2**  Climb the switchbacks toward the Cirque.

**3.0**  Climb a very steep rocky ascent to Lunch Ridge. Continue west, uphill toward Deseret Peak.

**4.3**  Arrive at the summit of Deseret Peak. Continue north for the Pocket Fork Trail.

**5.4**  Descend the short technical section.

**5.5**  Follow the trail up the ridge, as indicated on the trail sign.

**6.6**  Follow signage to Loop Campground toward the south.

**7.5**  Allow the pups to access the spring for a drink.

**8.0**  Arrive at the junction with the trail you started on, and follow it left (north).

**8.9**  Arrive back at the parking area.

## NEARBY HIKE
Butterfield Canyon

## CREATURE COMFORTS
**Holiday Inn Express Hotel & Suites Tooele**, 1531 N. Main St., Tooele; (435) 833-0500; www.ihg.com/holidayinnexpress/hotels/us/en/tooele/tvyut/hoteldetail. Not far from the Stansbury Mountains, the Holiday Inn in Tooele is a great pet-friendly hotel with a heated pool, hot breakfast, and fitness center. There is a pet fee.

**Kravers**, 500 Village Blvd. #202, Tooele; (435) 843-1688. Kravers is a well-known spot in Tooele that offers quick-bite American food. Perfect for grabbing burgers, sandwiches, and fries to-go.

# 4 ADAMS CANYON

## WHY GO?

Adams Canyon is a rugged adventure beginning with a challenging, sandy climb up nearly a dozen switchbacks. The start is challenging, but you'll soon be rewarded with views of Adams Canyon and the North Fork of Holmes Creek. Once inside this rough and rocky canyon, the hike is exciting!

### THE RUNDOWN

**County:** Davis
**Start:** Adams Canyon Trailhead
**Distance:** 3.6 miles out and back
**Hiking time:** 2–3 hours
**Difficulty:** Moderate due to challenging sections with some exposure
**Trailhead elevation:** 4,806 feet
**Highest point:** 6,002 feet
**Best seasons:** Spring or fall. Can be hiked year-round.
**Trail surface:** Rocks, gravel, stream crossings
**Other trail users:** Hikers and equestrians until the Shoreline Trail junction

**Canine compatibility:** Voice control
**Land status:** Uinta-Wasatch-Cache National Forest
**Fees and permits:** None
**Trail contact:** Salt Lake Ranger District, 6944 S. 3000 East, Salt Lake City, UT 84121; (801) 236-3400; www.fs.usda.gov/uwcnf
**Nearest town:** Layton
**Trail tips:** Adams Canyon is a rugged trail with steep sections and uneven surfaces. Use caution.
**Nat Geo TOPO! Map (USGS):** *Kaysville*
**Nat Geo Trails Illustrated Map:** *700: Ogden, Monte Cristo Range*

### FINDING THE TRAILHEAD

The trailhead for Adams Canyon is directly east of US 89 in Layton, Utah, near Holmes Reservoir. From the intersection of Oak Hills Drive and US 89, head north on US 89 for approximately 100 feet, then turn right (east) onto a road spur connecting to Eastside Drive. Turn right (south) onto Eastside Drive and continue for 0.2 mile until you reach the dirt parking area. This is the Adams Canyon Trailhead. The trail begins just north of the chain-link fence.
**Trailhead GPS:** N41 03.982' / W111 54.574'

## THE HIKE

From the parking area, the trail begins heading east just north of the fence surrounding the small reservoir. A short distance up the trail, there is a sign detailing the history of the canyon and its namesake, Elias Adams, a pioneer who made the trek to Utah in the mid-1850s and established a whipsaw mill near the canyon.

The trail begins very sandy as it follows the ancient Lake Bonneville shoreline switchbacking up the hillside. This can be a challenging start and is exposed, but the climb is worth it. There is a convenient bench waiting for you at the top. Once the switchbacks have been conquered, the canyon ahead will beckon you forward. At mile 0.7 there is a junction with Lake Bonneville Shoreline Trail. This is good place for the dogs to get water. Continue east up the canyon. From this point forward, water will be accessible for your pup and the surroundings are truly breathtaking.

Heading into the canyon after the switchbacks.

The trail continues on the north side of the canyon along Holmes Creek, where there are a few rocky sections that require thoughtful navigation. As you climb up into the deeper recesses of this canyon, you'll notice the trees and their expansive root systems. At mile 1.4 there is a particularly impressive arboreal specimen on the south side of the trail, and you will pass underneath the sprawling branches.

The climb continues up through the trees and around the rocky faces of outcroppings. There are a couple sections that have well-worn trees or tree-root handholds—use caution if putting weight on objects with unknown integrity. Go slow and climb with caution.

At mile 1.6 there is a challenging section with a few different routes to choose from. Take a moment and look at your options. With dogs, do not attempt the route across the face. It would be very easy for them to slip and fall into the creek bed below. The other two options are safer: one being to climb down and around the problem, the other is to go over it. After navigating this section you will cross the creek at mile 1.8 and get a good look at the falls. The water rushing back down the canyon is a beautiful sight, with the iron-rich rocks almost glowing underwater. This is a fun place to hang out, but use caution around the water since sometimes the creek may be too swift for little doggies and humans. Return the way you came when you desire.

## MILES AND DIRECTIONS

**0.0** Follow the trail located east of the parking area, just north of the chain-link fence. Prepare to climb.

**0.5** You'll reach the top of the sandy switchbacks.

**0.7** Stay right (east) past the trail junction with the Bonneville Shoreline. Do not cross the bridge.

**1.6** Approach a technical section.

**1.8** Cross the stream to the falls. Return the way you came.

**3.6** Arrive back at the trailhead.

## NEARBY HIKES

Hobbs Canyon, Bonneville Shoreline, Kays Creek

## CREATURE COMFORTS

**Home2Suites**, 803 Heritage Park Blvd., Layton; (801) 820-9222; home2suites3.hilton .com. The Home2Suites hotel is conveniently located in Layton with easy access to the highway and hikes in the area. It is a modern hotel with friendly staff and a full breakfast. Pets are allowed with a deposit.

**Bomb Dilla Food Truck**, www.facebook.com/Bomb-Dilla-1311291045635821/. Bomb Dilla is an LA-inspired food truck specializing in quesadillas. They rotate between Salt Lake and Weber County locations, but if in Layton near Hill Air Force Base, they are worth a visit. Try their Cali-Killer and tater tots, a great way to replenish calories after a big hike.

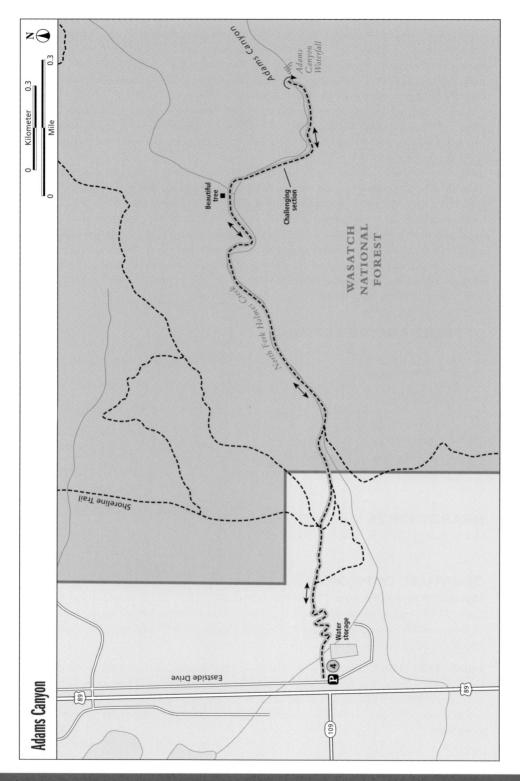

Adams Canyon

**Two Bit Cafe**, 126 25th St., Ogden; (801) 393–1225. Located north of Layton in downtown Ogden on historic 25th Street, Two Bit Cafe is a nice spot to unwind after a long day of hiking. They serve farm-to-table options and have an outdoor patio for pups. If you time your visit right, you'll get great food plus live music or a magic show.

# WASATCH FRONT

*"The idea of wilderness needs no defense, it only needs defenders."*

—Edward Abbey

The canyons of the Wasatch Range offer you and your dog chances to walk through timeless geological displays, views of spectacular waterfalls, and the opportunity to push yourself athletically. Some of the hikes are steep, perhaps even downright brutal, while others are tranquil and easygoing. From the granite cliffs of Lone Peak to the pioneer history of Neffs Canyon and Battle Creek to the grandeur of American Fork Canyon, the trails in this area of Utah are inspiring, beautiful, and challenging.

There are important regulations to remember while exploring the Wasatch trails, most importantly the watershed regulations. Most of the water used by Salt Lake City households comes from the watershed area of the canyons above Salt Lake City. The drainage basin and snow runoff of these areas create Salt Lake City's water supply, making it imperative to practice the ethics prescribed to maintain a healthy water system. Dog waste can transmit disease that can cause illness to humans and is difficult to remove through water-purification practices. More information about the watershed can be found at www.slcgov .com/sites/default/files/documents/ offleash/2012/dog%20brochure.pdf.

Dogs are, therefore, not allowed in these areas around Salt Lake City:

Enjoying the views of the Wasatch Front.

- Bell Canyon Creek and tributaries
- Big Cottonwood Canyon
- Big Willow Creek and tributaries
- City Creek Canyon (northeast of the treatment plant)
- Deaf Smith Canyon Creek and tributaries
- Emigration Canyon (above Burrs Fork)
- Lambs Canyon
- Little Cottonwood Canyon (including the town of Alta)
- Little Willow Creek and tributaries
- Mountain Dell Canyon
- Parleys Canyon
- South Fork of Dry Creek

You will incur hefty fines if you are caught with your dog in these areas. The major areas include signage that will warn you that your dog is not allowed. Still, not knowing these regulations will not get you out of a ticket.

This section of Utah hikes includes trails from northern Mill Creek Canyon to southern American Fork Canyon and many places in between. This area of Utah offers you and your dog lots of opportunities to explore canyons, cool off at flowing waterfalls, and rest at many sit-spots with views of the mountains beyond. In the lesser-known Heughs and Ferguson Canyons, you will be able to enjoy streamside ecology and plant life including box elders and cottonwoods. In other areas of the Wasatch, you will also see white pines, scrub oaks, glacial lilies, great western sage, lupines, yarrow, and hundreds of other varieties. This balanced ecosystem has great diversity and distinctive ecology.

Recreationally, from fishing to world-famous rock climbing, Utahns are lucky to get to spend time in these hills. Remember, because 85 percent of the population of Utah is located along the Wasatch Front, these trails are impacted significantly when humans are negligent. Clean up after your dog and obey the watershed regulations. Follow the odd-even leash-law days prescribed by Mill Creek Canyon to help ensure our dog-friendly areas remain so.

# 5 MINERS TRAIL

## WHY GO?

One of the few dog-friendly areas in Emigration Canyon, Miners Trail starts off as a level stroll, passes a dependable stream, and after a steep climb ends at a beautiful view of the vast topography of the Wasatch Range. From open expanses to the cloistered feel of the dark woods, this hike has variety, challenge, and beauty that hikers and dogs will love. Bring plenty of water for you and your dog.

### THE RUNDOWN

**County:** Salt Lake
**Start:** From Miners Trailhead in Emigration Canyon
**Distance:** 5.0 miles out and back
**Hiking time:** 2–3 hours
**Difficulty:** Moderate due to elevation gain toward the end
**Trailhead elevation:** 6,411 feet
**Highest point:** 7,569 feet
**Best seasons:** Spring, fall
**Trail surface:** Dirt, shale
**Other trail users:** Horses, hikers
**Canine compatibility:** Voice control
**Land status:** National Forest
**Fees and permits:** None
**Trail contact:** Salt Lake Ranger District, 6944 S. 3000 East,

Cottonwood Heights, UT 84121; (801) 733-2660
**Nearest town:** Salt Lake City
**Trail tips:** Parking is very limited at the Miners Trail. Try to hike during non-prime times such as early afternoons on weekdays, or have an alternate plan if the parking lot is full. Bring plenty of water—the first water for dogs is 1.8 miles from the trailhead.
**Nat Geo TOPO! Map (USGS):** 7.5-minute *Mountain Dell, UT*
**Nat Geo Illustrated Map:** *709: Wasatch North*

## FINDING THE TRAILHEAD

 From the Hogle Zoo on 2600 E. Sunnyside Ave. in Salt Lake City, continue east into Emigration Canyon past the legendary Ruth's Diner. Follow Emigration Canyon Road approximately 6 miles up the canyon, then turn left into Pinecrest Canyon just before the sharp right-hand dog-leg turn heading south. Continue up Pinecrest Canyon Road for approximately 0.5 mile, then veer left continuing on Pinecrest Canyon Road as it intersects with Killyon Lane. Continue for 1.4 miles, watching for a small parking area to your left with a large sign that reads "Attention Big-Game Hunters." Park in this pullout. Do not park along the road as there is private property on either side of Pinecrest Canyon Road. The trailhead begins to the south of the parking area.
**Trailhead GPS:** N40 48.445' / W111 43.365'

## THE HIKE

From the parking area, the trail begins to your left (south) past a gate that prevents motorized vehicles from entering the trail. The conifer woods are thick for the first handful of steps, but they quickly peter out into scrub oak hillsides scattered with arrowleaf balsamroot and great western sage. The wide trail is comfortable and relatively level, making it a nice place to catch up with a friend. Looking back down into Pinecrest and the steep walls of the canyons, this canyon feels more remote than it is. The trail continues south,

Enjoying a pretty summer day.

**Almost to the saddle.**

arching around the mountain, until a view gives way down Emigration Canyon and over to the grander peaks toward Parleys Canyon. It is quite something. The trail loses its dirt-packed footing from time to time for more geometric shale coverings, which are fun to look at and have an interesting sound when you walk over them.

As the trail turns north, it is now possible to look down into the Brigham Fork drainage. Physical evidence of mining culture is very prevalent in this area. Like the timber industry that was vastly responsible for the trails in Mill Creek and the Cottonwood Canyons, the mining industry provided many modern routes in this area. Emigration Canyon is famous for being the very last leg of the long Mormon trek west. "This Is the Place" Park and Monument, celebrating the legendary statement uttered as the Mormon pioneers entered the Salt Lake Valley, is just west of the steep walls of this canyon.

Stay to the main trail as it gets rockier. Above you and to the north, the canyon walls begin to look a little bit like the red rock sandstone of southern Utah. The trees start getting bigger and the sound of water becomes audible for hot pups. At mile 1.8 the trail crosses a reliable stream. If hiking in the summer, this is not a bad place to relax with your dog for bit. When you are ready to continue, the trail picks up and takes you over a steep incline to the west, then turns right (north) under the limbs of a rather impressive fir tree.

Keep your eyes peeled for remnants of the past. There are old mines in this area with barred-off entrances. The trail stays in the big trees, and it is easy to forget the wide-open sections of the trail that were downright hot not half a mile earlier. The trail winds through the forest and follows a draw up and up. At mile 2.3 the trail gets steeper, and you may need to use caution around fallen trees. Continue your travels up to the top of the ridge.

After catching your breath enjoy a look around. From the ridge, you are on the boundary of the Red Butte Canyon, which has watershed regulations and is out-of-bounds for pups, so keep to the trail. Find a good place to sit and enjoy the view all the way to Salt Lake City. From this vantage point, there are ridges and peaks in almost every direction. Head back the way you came.

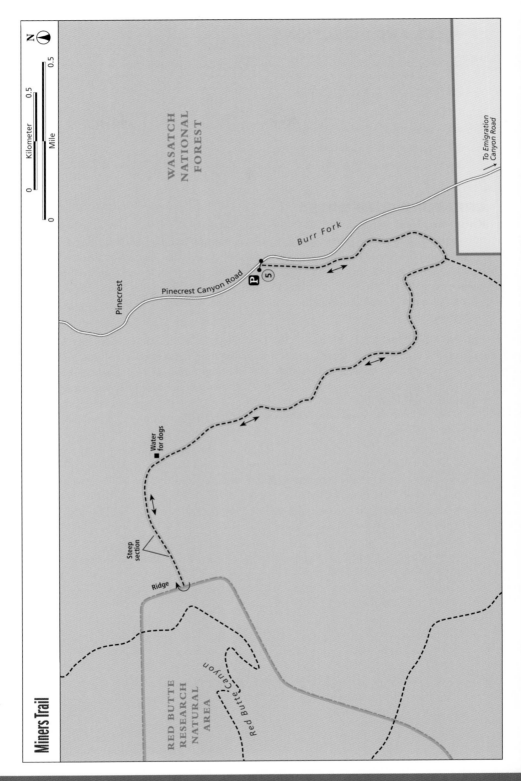

Miners Trail

N

0 Kilometer 0.5

0 Mile 0.5

Pinecrest

Pinecrest Canyon Road

WASATCH
NATIONAL
FOREST

Burr Fork

To Emigration
Canyon Road

P ⑤

Water
for dogs

Steep
section

Ridge

RED BUTTE
RESEARCH NATURAL
AREA

Red Butte Canyon

## MILES AND DIRECTIONS

**0.0**  The trail begins to the south of the parking area past a barricade for motorized vehicles.

**0.7**  Stay right (north) on the main trail.

**1.8**  Pass a stream with water available for dogs. The trail continues up the hill.

**2.3**  Ascend a short, steep section.

**2.5**  Arrive at the ridge. Head back the way you came.

**5.0**  Arrive back at the trailhead.

## CREATURE COMFORTS

**Kimpton Hotel Monaco**, 15 W. 200 South, Salt Lake City; (800) 805-1801; www.monaco-saltlakecity.com. This hotel is simply extraordinary! The Monaco is a beautiful hotel that is centrally located in downtown Salt Lake City near many great restaurants, shopping, entertainment, and sights. The rooms are appealing and comfortable and include yoga mats, coffee, and the suites include whirlpool tubs. They don't charge a pet fee, but mention your dog during the reservation process and they'll give your pup a toy and treat at check-in.

**Pig and a Jelly Jar**, 401 E. 900 South, Salt Lake City; (385) 202-7366; www.pigandajelly jar.com. Pig and a Jelly Jar serves southern comfort food for breakfast and lunch. They are known for their chicken and waffles and morning mimosas, but also have healthy options that are appropriate for food allergies and diet preferences. Their outdoor patio is permitted for dogs.

# 6 GRANDEUR PEAK (MILL CREEK CANYON)

## WHY GO?

Grandeur Peak brings you the best of the Wasatch: views, cardio, plenty of dog company, and challenge. It's a classic hike for the peak-bagger, the view seeker, and the mile logger. The hike starts creekside, ending about 2,500 feet higher in elevation, with a rather exposed middle section. Once you reach the summit of Grandeur, which affords spectacular views of the Salt Lake Valley and beyond, you will quickly forget the heat of the middle section. This hike has a little bit of everything, even stairs.

### THE RUNDOWN

**County:** Salt Lake
**Start:** Church Fork Picnic Area. Parking for Grandeur Peak is along the Mill Creek Canyon Road on the north side.
**Distance:** 6.4 miles out and back
**Hiking time:** 4–5 hours
**Difficulty:** Moderate due to exposed hot south-facing sections and elevation gain
**Trailhead elevation:** 5,735 feet
**Highest point:** 8,299 feet
**Best seasons:** Early summer, fall
**Trail surface:** Dirt, rocks, stairs, boulders, steep sections
**Other trail users:** Runners, possibly cyclists
**Canine compatibility:** Voice control odd-numbered days, on leash even-numbered days
**Land status:** National Forest
**Fees and permits:** Small cash-only day-use fee; annual pass available

**Trail contact:** Salt Lake Ranger District, 6944 S. 3000 East, Salt Lake City, UT 84121; (801) 733-2660
**Nearest town:** Salt Lake City
**Trail tips:** Bring a camera, snacks to be enjoyed at the summit for both you and your pup, and adequate water for the hike. You can hike this trail year-round, but use caution in the summer and winter. In the summer there are long exposed sections that get very hot, and in the winter it is absolutely vital to take and use removable traction devices for your boots as it can be very icy.

This hike accesses Grandeur Peak from Mill Creek Canyon. The same peak can also be accessed from another trailhead at the base of Parleys Canyon.
**Nat Geo TOPO! Map (USGS):** 7.5-minute *Sugar House, UT/Mt. Aire, UT*
**Nat Geo Trails Illustrated Map:** *709: Wasatch Front North*

## FINDING THE TRAILHEAD

The Church Fork Picnic Area and parking for the Grandeur Peak Trailhead is 3.8 miles up Mill Creek Canyon past the fee station. From southbound I-215, take exit 4 at 3900 South and turn left (east), going under the overpass. At the light turn left (north) onto Wasatch Boulevard. The Olympus Cove park-and-ride will be on your left (park here to carpool). From Wasatch Boulevard heading north from the park-and-ride, take your next right (east) onto 3800 South, which soon becomes Mill Creek Canyon Road. As you proceed up the canyon, you'll pass Camp Tracy Boy Scout Camp on the south side of the road, and Church Fork will come up quickly on the north side of the road, just before you reach the Millcreek Inn. There are many places to park along the road. *Do not* enter the picnic area to park: Hiker parking is along Mill Creek Canyon Road.

From Mill Creek Canyon Road, walk through the Church Fork–area gates, down briefly into a ravine, before you climb up the Church Fork picnic area road. Follow this road until it terminates at a picnic parking area. There will be signs indicating the trailhead for Grandeur Peak to the north side of the road. Begin up the trail heading north.

**Trailhead GPS:** N40 42.038' / W111 44.549'

## THE HIKE

Grandeur Peak is one of the many beautiful faces of the Wasatch Front. For the avid hiker, it is also one of the most accessible peaks to climb. The trailhead for Grandeur Peak is at the northern end of the Church Fork picnic area. After parking on Mill Creek Canyon Road, proceed to the Church Fork Picnic area, entering the area on foot. It is mandatory that you keep your dog(s) on leash, regardless of odd- or even-day restrictions, while in parking areas and trailheads. The winding Church Fork Picnic Road has toilet facilities. During the winter months only the toilet area closest to Mill Creek Canyon Road is open. Continue to follow the road up as it winds toward the picnic area.

The trail begins in the northeast corner of the parking area, where Grandeur Peak signage will welcome you onto the trail. From this point, pups are welcome to roam as they wish on odd-numbered days. Just before 0.5 mile you will cross over a quaint bridge. During the winter months the ice formations are worth pausing to enjoy. The trail continues and will intersect with the Pipeline Trail just a bit farther. The Pipeline Trail traverses Mill Creek Canyon east to west following a long-gone water pipeline. (See the Pipeline Trail hike for more details.)

To continue to Grandeur Peak, follow the signs heading north uphill, crossing over some downed trees to where you will begin your climb in earnest to the peak. Through the firs and dark timber, the trail gains elevation as it follows the Church Fork drainage eventually up some stairs at mile 0.8.

There are plenty of opportunities for dogs to get a drink, and the temperatures are cool and refreshing with the breeze coming off the rushing water. The trail will leave the wooded oasis and stream at mile 1.2, so encourage your pup to get a last drink and dip in the water before making the trek across the south-facing exposed hillside, switchback-ing up to the saddle. You will notice the temperature immediately getting warmer after one switchback. As you leave behind the pines, you will begin seeing Oregon grape and scrub oak along the ground.

It is a steady incline, and the views of yonder hills get better and better as the elevation gain goes from the 6,000s to the 7,000s. At mile 2.1 the trail gets a bit rougher and rocky. Continue through the rubble and orange-colored rocks as you proceed to the saddle. About a half mile farther, there will be a small trail offshoot to a viewpoint with a glimpse into Parleys Canyon and the Pharaohs Glen Quarry, which is excavating Twin Creek limestone. Mount Olympus looms large to the south.

As you continue from the saddle to the summit, you'll be traversing the most difficult part of the hike. It will be both steep and rocky. After your climb there is a good place to catch your breath before rounding the bend and making your summit bid.

Once around the corner the view to the west of the Oquirrh Mountains becomes visible. It will be easy to call it quits as you turn onto the west flank of the mountain, but

continue east, climbing a few more feet, which will afford you incredible views of the Salt Lake Valley from the point of the mountain to the south and Antelope Island to the northwest and beyond. There are many great places to sit and relax with your pooch. A favorite view is east, over the peaks and ridges toward Park City. The wilderness seems vast. Be sure to stay hydrated and enjoy the 8,000+-foot vantage point. Return the way you came.

## MILES AND DIRECTIONS

**0.0**  Vehicle parking is located along Mill Creek Canyon Road near the entrance to the Church Fork Picnic Area.

**0.1**  Depending on where you park, this number will change, but enter the picnic area on foot and on leash and walk north up along the road to the trailhead.

**0.4**  Follow the trail at the northeast corner of the parking area, following the signs. You'll cross a bridge.

**0.5**  Continue north past the junction for the Pipeline Trail.

**0.8**  Cross another bridge, then continue up some stairs.

**1.2**  Begin the steeper climb up the switchbacks. Let your dog get a drink before climbing west.

**1.9**  Pause here for incredible views.

**2.1**  The trail becomes rocky at this point—travel cautiously.

**2.5**  Pass a small side trail to the north that offers views to Parleys Canyon. Continue on the main trail.

**3.0**  Enjoy a view of Mount Olympus to the south.

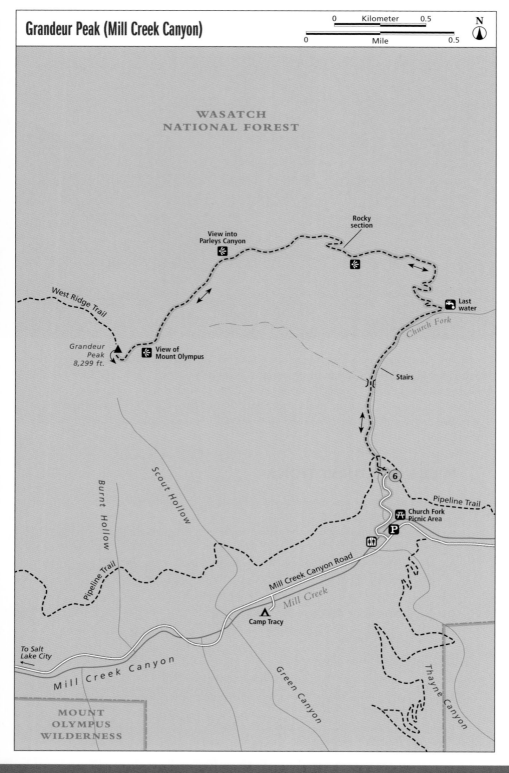

# Grandeur Peak (Mill Creek Canyon)

WASATCH
NATIONAL FOREST

View into
Parleys Canyon

Rocky
section

West Ridge Trail

Last
water

Grandeur
Peak
8,299 ft.

View of
Mount Olympus

Church Fork

Stairs

Pipeline Trail

6

Church Fork
Picnic Area

Scout Hollow

Burnt Hollow

P

Pipeline Trail

Mill Creek Canyon Road

Mill Creek

Camp Tracy

To Salt
Lake City

Mill Creek Canyon

Green Canyon

Thayne Canyon

MOUNT
OLYMPUS
WILDERNESS

**3.2** Arrive at the summit of Grandeur Peak, then return the way you came.

**6.4** Arrive back at your car.

## NEARBY HIKES
Mill Creek Canyon hikes, Neffs Canyon, Mount Olympus

## CREATURE COMFORTS
**Airbnb**, www.airbnb.com/a/Salt-Lake-City. Various options in Millcreek City and Salt Lake City. There are many great vacation rental options in the Salt Lake Valley that are pet-friendly and comfortable. Sugarhouse and the Avenues are great neighborhoods to stay in.

**Wasatch Brew Pub Sugarhouse**, 2110 S. Highland Dr., Salt Lake City; (801) 783-1127; www.wasatchbeers.com. Wasatch is a local favorite with delicious brews, a good selection of salads, burgers, and much more. They serve award-winning brews on rotating taps as well as cocktails, mocktails, and options for kids. Their tuna tartare is a favorite, and the tater tots with whiskey bacon dip are delicious. They are permitted for dogs on their patio.

**BOWMAN FORK TO ALEXANDER BASIN TRAILHEAD**

## WHY GO?

With incredible views of the backcountry and ample miles to get an active dog tired, this trail is one of the best in Mill Creek Canyon. This hike is done as a shuttle starting at Bowman Fork and ending at Alexander Basin, but can also be done as an out-and-back. The trail offers shady stretches and tough climbs and there is water available for pups at the beginning of the hike. Hikers have the opportunity to push themselves while being rewarded with beautiful scenery.

### THE RUNDOWN

**County:** Salt Lake
**Start:** Burch Hollow parking area. This hike is also possible to start from the Terraces Picnic Area, if parking is available.
**Distance:** 5.6-mile shuttle
**Hiking time:** 2.5–3.5 hours
**Difficulty:** Strenuous
**Trailhead elevation:** 6,562 feet
**Highest point:** 8,604 feet
**Best seasons:** Year-round (great trail to snowshoe)
**Trail surface:** Rocky, streamside walking, bridge crossing, steep descents
**Other trail users:** Hikers, possibly horses
**Canine compatibility:** Voice control odd-numbered days, on leash even-numbered days

**Land status:** National Forest—Mount Olympus Wilderness
**Fees and permits:** Small cash-only day-use fee; annual pass available
**Trail contact:** Salt Lake Ranger District, 6944 S. 3000 East, Salt Lake City, UT 84121; (801) 733-2600; www.fs.usda.gov/uwcnf
**Nearest town:** Salt Lake City
**Trail tips:** Bring a camera!
**Nat Geo TOPO! Map (USGS):** 7.5-minute *Mt. Aire*
**Nat Geo Trails Illustrated Map:** *709: Wasatch Front North*
**Other maps:** Map of watershed areas and trails of Mill Creek available at: www.fs.usda.gov/Internet/FSE_DOCUMENTS/stelprdb5090538.pdf

## FINDING THE TRAILHEAD

From southbound I-215, take exit 4 at 3900 South and turn left (east), going under the overpass. At the light turn left (north) onto Wasatch Boulevard. The Olympus Cove park-and-ride will be on your left (park here to carpool). From Wasatch Boulevard heading north from the park-and-ride, take your next right (east) onto 3800 South, which soon becomes Mill Creek Canyon Road. As you proceed up the canyon, you'll pass the fee station. Continue up the canyon until the signs for the Terraces Picnic Area. If you are shuttling cars, continue past the picnic area as you'll want to park the shuttle vehicle at the Alexander Basin Trailhead. To get to the Alexander Basin Trailhead, drive 8 miles up the Mill Creek Canyon Road past Elbow Fork. The small parking area will be on your right (south). If you make it to the Big Water parking area, you have gone too far. Once the shuttle vehicle is parked, drive back down the canyon past the winter gate to the Burch Hollow parking area on the north side of Mill Creek Canyon Road, approximately 4 miles below where you parked the shuttle.

To the southeast you'll see the Terraces Picnic Area Road across a bridge. Walk with your dog on leash east up toward the Terraces Picnic Area, about 0.4 mile. Be

So pretty!

aware of traffic on this road. The trail begins on the north side of the picnic parking lot across from the pit toilets. If shuttling isn't an option, an out-and-back up Bowman Fork to White Fir Pass is a popular option. To do this, park at Burch Hollow parking area and begin the hike.

**Trailhead GPS:** N40 41.819' / W111 42.972'
**Shuttle car parking GPS:** N40 41.541' / W111 40.214'

## THE HIKE

Mill Creek Canyon has a significant place in the settlement of the Great Salt Lake Valley. After the Mormon pioneers' wagon wheels stopped, the surviving livestock were put out to pasture, the fields were plowed to grow food for the upcoming spring, and homes had to be built before the snows of winter. The Salt Lake Valley was lacking in timber. Many of the trails we enjoy today in Mill Creek Canyon are historically old logging roads, or routes between mills, and logging areas. The milled trees of Mill Creek Canyon became the walls and floors of the first homes of Salt Lake City.

From the parking area at Terraces Picnic Area, follow the trail northeast of the pit toilets. The trail forks almost immediately. Turn right (east) to stay on the Bowman Fork Trail. As you hike up the trail, you'll cross a short retaining wall along a cliff before dropping down toward the Bowman Fork Stream. Follow the stream up the trail through the woods, which—if not interrupted by happy, barking pups—will be quiet and lovely.

The first section has little elevation gain, as the trail parallels the stream heading up the draw. As you continue up the trail, you will frequently cross the stream over small bridges or logs. At mile 1.7 the trail will turn right (south) out of the Bowman Fork drainage, heading steeply uphill. Let your pups get a drink before switchbacking toward White Fir Pass.

At mile 2.1 there is an incredible lookout toward Mount Raymond to the southwest and Gobblers Knob to the southeast. There are places to sit and enjoy the view, and this is a popular place to turn around if doing a Bowman Fork out-and-back hike.

If shuttling via Alexander Basin, continue on the obvious trail hiking up the hill to the east. At mile 3.1 there will be signage for a steep smaller trail toward Alexander Basin to the left (north). Follow this until you reach the summit.

From here, you'll be descending toward the glacially eroded Alexander Basin. Evidence of moose and deer is common in this area, so be aware and respectful of this wild place. At mile 4.7 you will hike down into the basin until you reach another sign for Alexander Basin. Turn left (north) at the three-way trail junction to head back toward Mill Creek Canyon Road. It is possible to add mileage and some extra adventuring by turning right (south) and hiking uphill on the Alexander Basin Trail.

The remaining section of this hike is beautiful but also difficult. It is a very steep descent. Take your time and switchback when you can to reduce stress on your knees. At 5.6 miles you will arrive at your shuttle vehicle after a winding adventure through the backcountry. If the gates are closed for winter, it is possible to connect back to your car at the Burch Hollow parking lot by taking the road and then connecting to the Pipeline Trail at Elbow Fork. This makes for a long and spectacular day.

# Bowman Fork to Alexander Basin Trailhead

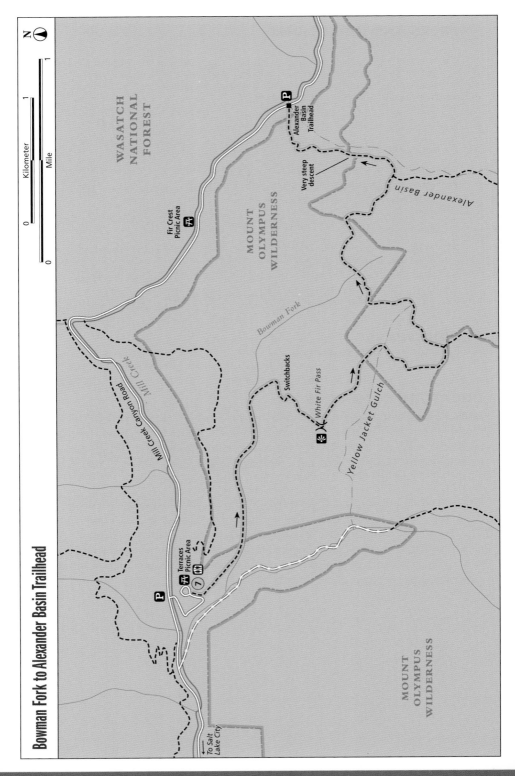

## MILES AND DIRECTIONS

**0.0** If you are doing this hike as a shuttle, park one vehicle at the Alexander Basin Trailhead approximately 8 miles up Mill Creek Canyon Road. Park your other car at the Burch Hollow Trailhead, approximately 4 miles down the canyon from the shuttle vehicle (3.7 miles up the canyon from the fee station).

**0.1** Cross Mill Creek Canyon Road heading south and walk up through the Terraces Picnic Area for 0.4 mile. The trailhead can be found on the left (north) side of the road, across from the restrooms.

**0.5** Veer right at the junction with Elbow Fork heading east up Bowman Fork.

**1.7** Let your dog get a final drink at the stream before beginning the climb out of the drainage toward White Fir Pass.

**2.1** White Fir Pass is a popular turnaround spot and offers incredible views of the backcountry.

**3.1** There will be signage for Alexander Basin. Take the trail to the left (north), and continue climbing uphill.

**4.7** You will arrive at another trail sign. Go left (north), heading steeply downhill.

**5.6** Arrive back at your shuttle vehicle at the Alexander Basin Trailhead.

## NEARBY HIKES

Pipeline Trail, Dog Lake, Neffs Canyon

## CREATURE COMFORTS

**Backcountry camping and backpacking** are allowed in certain areas of Mill Creek Canyon. Please leave no trace, and all camping must be at least 200 feet away from developed areas, trails, and water and 0.5 mile away from the road. Call the ranger station for more information and fire restrictions. Salt Lake Ranger District, 6944 S. 3000 East, Salt Lake City, UT 84121; (801) 733-2600; www.fs.usda.gov/uwcnf.

**Log Haven**, 6451 Mill Creek Canyon Rd., Mill Creek; (801) 272-8255; www.log-haven.com. Log Haven is a romantic restaurant located in a lodge in Mill Creek Canyon. They serve "mountain fare" including trout, steaks, salads, and campfire-inspired desserts. As of May 2017, Log Haven is permitted for dogs to be legally allowed on their patio. It is a gorgeous setting with upscale dining and award-winning cuisine. Reservations recommended.

# 8 PIPELINE TRAIL (BURCH HOLLOW TO ELBOW FORK)

## WHY GO?

This hike starts with a climb that will likely get your heart pumping a little bit, with a rewarding level coast to Pipeline's end and inspiring views of the city behind and the forests beyond. This hike is great during the early season to get the legs back in hiking shape after winter. It is a simple hike with miles to be had if sought.

### THE RUNDOWN

**County:** Salt Lake
**Start:** Burch Hollow Trailhead
**Distance:** 6.2 miles out and back
**Hiking time:** 3–4 hours
**Difficulty:** Moderate with some steeper climbs and the extended mileage
**Trailhead elevation:** 6,307 feet
**Highest point:** 6,702 feet
**Best season:** Year-round
**Trail surface:** Packed dirt and rock
**Other trail users:** Bikers, hikers, runners
**Canine compatibility:** Voice control odd-numbered days, on leash even-numbered days

**Land status:** National Forest
**Fees and permits:** Small cash-only day-use fee; annual pass available
**Trail contact:** Salt Lake Ranger District, 6944 S. 3000 East, Salt Lake City, UT 84121; (801) 733-2600; www.fs.usda.gov/uwcnf
**Nearest town:** Salt Lake City
**Trail tips:** Bring plenty of water for you and your dog, and watch out for rattlesnakes.
**Nat Geo TOPO! Map (USGS):** 7.5-minute *Mt. Aire*
**Nat Geo Trails Illustrated Map:** *709: Wasatch Front North*

## FINDING THE TRAILHEAD

From southbound I-215, take exit 4 at 3900 South and turn left (east) to go under the overpass. At the light turn left (north) onto Wasatch Boulevard—the Olympus Cove park-and-ride will be on your left. If you intend to carpool, then take your next right (east) onto 3800 South, soon to become Mill Creek Canyon Road. Continue past the fee station for 4.3 miles. Once you pass the Log Haven Restaurant, the Burch Hollow Trailhead will be to your left across from Porter Fork. There is a space to park on the north side of the road and additional parking a few hundred feet up the road.
**Trailhead GPS:** N40 41.964' / W111 43.269'

## THE HIKE

This trail was originally cut on the hillside to hold two water pipelines that supplied water-generated power to both the upper Mill Creek Power Plant and a second plant at the mouth of the canyon. Remnants of the original pipeline can be seen, but the pipeline for the most part has been removed, and this is now used as a trail.

The Pipeline Trail is predictable, fun, and simple. It is possible to hike this trail over and over and not see everything there is to see. This hike is a wonderful way to begin getting in shape, getting your trail dog ready for longer excursions into the wilderness, or just to go exploring without having to worry about navigating.

Gorgeous, typical Mill Creek.

From nose to tail, this trail is 14 miles one-way, with numerous options from four different trailheads along the canyon: Rattlesnake Gulch, Church Fork/Grandeur Peak, Burch Hollow, and Elbow Fork. There is also a highly regarded lookout option west of Rattlesnake Gulch overlooking the Salt Lake Valley. Depending on your time and energy levels, there are lots of creative options to get the mileage you'd like, doing anything from out-and-backs to shuttle hikes to loops.

From the Burch Hollow Trailhead, one of the prettiest sections of the trail, you will begin climbing almost immediately through the trees. It is a little on the steep side, but nothing too taxing. At mile 0.3 there is the east–west option for the Pipeline Trail: left (west) toward Grandeur Peak Trail or right (east) toward Elbow Fork. This trail description is given as you hike toward Elbow Fork.

Hiking up the canyon (east) on the Pipeline Trail, you will pass through three distinct sedimentary formations: Park City Formation, Woodside Shale Formation, and finally Thaynes Formation. These three formations were each created during different periods in geologic history. The Park City Formation is a Precambrian formation of limestone and fossils that formed 286 million to 248 million years ago (the time of the massive extinctions), during the time this rock was being created by the waters and upwelling of ocean currents. After the Park City Formation, you will cross over the red shales that are characteristic of the Woodside Shale, then finally into the Thaynes Formation, which is a mix of shale, fine-grained sandstone, and limestone, which was formed in the deeper waters of ancient times.

The Pipeline Trail is usually a packed-dirt trail, wide enough to easily allow others to pass. Keep an eye out for bikes. Unlike the upper Mill Creek trails, bikes are allowed on the Pipeline Trail every day, but on odd days dogs may be off-leash. Continue climbing the switchbacks looking over your shoulder toward the Salt Lake Valley—the views get more and more beautiful as you gain elevation.

At mile 1.7 the trail levels out and is fairly easygoing from here. There is a trail junction with the Burch Hollow Trail coming in from the north, an option to add some mileage and elevation. Continue hiking east on the wider Pipeline Trail, looking below at the Terraces Picnic Area and the conifer-forest canyon floor. Along the trail you will see occasional trail spurs to lookouts. Be sure to check these out, as the views are worth it. At mile 3.1 you will arrive at Elbow Fork. There are restrooms at this trailhead. Return the way you came.

## MILES AND DIRECTIONS

**0.0** Park your car at the Burch Hollow Trailhead just off Mill Creek Canyon Road to the north. The Pipeline Trail begins directly north of the parking area.

**0.3** The Pipeline Trail goes west toward Grandeur Peak Trail (Church Fork) or east toward Elbow Fork. Keep right to hike toward Elbow Fork.

**1.7** Continue east as the trail levels. You'll pass the Burch Hollow Trail coming in from the north.

**3.1** The Elbow Fork Trailhead is adjacent to the Mill Creek Canyon Road. Return the way you came.

**6.2** Arrive back at the trailhead.

# Pipeline Trail (Burch Hollow to Elbow Fork)

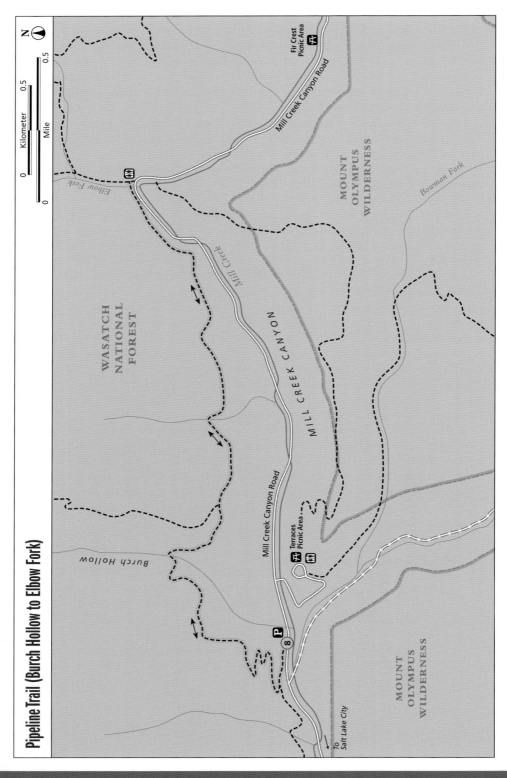

## NEARBY HIKES

Other sections of Pipeline Trail, Bowman Fork, Burch Hollow, Elbow Fork

## CREATURE COMFORTS

**Extended Stay America Sugarhouse**, 1220 E. 2100 South, Salt Lake City; (801) 474-0771; www.extendedstayamerica.com. This hotel is centrally located in Sugarhouse not far from the Salt Lake City–area hikes. It is within walking distance of grocery stores, numerous restaurants, bookstores, bars, and coffee shops and include kitchenettes in the rooms. It is also 1 block from Sugarhouse Park, a beautiful spot for a walk or picnic, and a 10-minute walk from the Fairmont Dog Park. There is a per-day pet fee, and height and length restrictions apply.

**Taqueria 27**, 4670 S. Holladay Blvd., Holladay; (801) 676-9706; www.taqueria27.com. T27 is an upscale taco joint with delicious food, an impressive tequila selection, and homemade guacamole. While they do not take reservations, they are permitted for dogs on their patio and have three locations throughout the Salt Lake Valley. Their duck confit tacos are delicious!

# 9 DOG LAKE

## WHY GO?

A Wasatch Front classic, this hike is a steady climb to a lake on the boundary of the Salt Lake City watershed in Mill Creek Canyon. Dog Lake provides plenty of opportunities to get exercise and enjoy the wildflowers with other dogs and hikers in a stunning forest setting. Water is available for your dog for a good portion of the hike, making it a summer-friendly excursion.

### THE RUNDOWN

**County:** Salt Lake
**Start:** Little Water Trailhead at the end of Mill Creek Canyon Road
**Distance:** 4.7-mile loop
**Hiking time:** About 2 hours
**Difficulty:** Moderate due to 1,000-foot elevation gain
**Trailhead elevation:** 7,650 feet
**Highest point:** 8,723 feet
**Best seasons:** Summer–fall. The upper Mill Creek Canyon Road closes Nov 1 at the gate just above Terrace Picnic Area.
**Trail surface:** Dirt trail, bridges, slightly rocky sections
**Other trail users:** Other hikers and trail runners, mountain bikers on even days, and possibly equestrians
**Canine compatibility:** Voice control odd-numbered days, on leash even-numbered days

**Land status:** National Forest
**Fees and permits:** Small cash-only day-use fee; annual pass available
**Trail contact:** Salt Lake Ranger District, 6944 S. 3000 East, Salt Lake City, UT 84121; (801) 733-2600; www.fs.usda.gov/uwcnf. Open Mon–Fri 8 a.m.–4:30 p.m.
**Nearest town:** Salt Lake City
**Trail tips:** This is a popular hike so avoid weekends if possible. Carpooling is recommended.
**Nat Geo TOPO! Map (USGS):** 7.5-minute Mount Aire
**Nat Geo Trails Illustrated Map:** 709: Wasatch Front North
**Other maps:** Map of watershed areas and trails of Mill Creek available at: https://www.fs.usda.gov/Internet/FSE_DOCUMENTS/stelprdb5090538.pdf

## FINDING THE TRAILHEAD

From southbound I-215, take exit 4 at 3900 South and turn left (east), going under the overpass. At the light turn left (north) onto Wasatch Boulevard—the Olympus Cove park-and-ride will be on your left (park here to carpool). From Wasatch Boulevard, head north from the park-and-ride, then take your next right (east) onto 3800 South, soon to become Mill Creek Canyon Road. Continue up the canyon for approximately 9 miles until it terminates at the Little Water and Big Water parking area. The Little Water Trail begins on the east side of the parking area, opposite the restrooms. There is signage for the trail.
**Trailhead GPS:** N40 41.077' / W111 38.796'

## THE HIKE

From the Little Water Trailhead, the trail begins to the east opposite the restrooms. As you begin, be sure to follow signs for Little Water at the junction just past 0.3 mile, staying to the east and avoiding the large bridge.

On odd-numbered days the pups are free to run, walk, or whatever gait most suits them off-leash. For the first mile or so, the trail follows Little Water Gulch, which is partly

Martin and Wren out for a swim.

what makes this hike so wonderful. The gentle rush of the creek, the green, water-loving fauna, the spruce and fir and aspen trees overhead, all make this hike a shady respite from summer temperatures at lower elevations.

As you continue you'll wander through the woods, ascend a short rocky section of trail, and then cross a small bridge. Stay to the right, heading south on the main trail as you climb steeply along the creek. The meadows, when the woods part, are beautiful, and the bee balm (also called horsemint) found along the trail edges is a cheerful sight to dog and hiker alike. As the trail ascends you may find yourself short of breath, especially if you are busy talking to your companion about all the amazing sights and sounds.

The trail will climb south, sometimes steeply, for approximately 1 mile, getting steeper as it winds up the gulch. Almost abruptly you'll follow a dog-leg turn to the south, then cross another bridge out of Little Water Gulch. This is a good place to catch your breath and let the pups get a drink. Use caution during the summer as this section is prone to stinging nettle, which can irritate your skin if touched directly.

Continue on the trail, heading west through dense pines. Soon you'll intersect the Great Western Trail (GWT), but continue south, following the signs for Dog Lake. At mile 1.5 there is a fantastic view toward the canyon bottom, which, if you are hiking in fall, will offer a vast expanse of a variety of colored autumn leaves. It is incredible and well worth making a return trip during the fall.

As you continue through the woods, you'll approach a trail intersection. Follow the signs heading south toward Dog Lake. You will climb to a definite berm, followed by a quick descent to the water's edge. For the pups who have been here before, this is their cue to tear down the hill like a bobsledder, crashing into the water to cool off and play. Your pup's antics will make you smile as it is hilarious to watch and makes it well worth the hike up.

Dog Lake, although not spectacularly beautiful on its own, will be a favorite for you and your dog friend. This hike is sure to be one to repeat. From your pup's perspective, there is nothing better than a hike in the woods with their human, dog friends to play with, and water. What the destination lacks in sheer beauty, it gains in the atmosphere around its edges. Chances are there will be lots of dogs at the lake, and watching them negotiate the sticks and balls while frolicking in the water is quite endearing. It is important to stay on the north side of the lake as the south side borders the Salt Lake watershed and dogs are prohibited.

After spending time in the quaking-aspen groves and in the company of multiple canines and their outdoorsy humans, head back up the hill. You can return to the parking area the same way you came in for an out-and-back, or alternatively, follow the signs to Big Water to make a loop.

The trails are similar, but the Big Water Trail descends more gently to the trailhead than the Little Water Trail. The return description, here, is by way of the Big Water Trail. There are at least two water sources available for your pup, as you descend through large spruce and fir trees.

The trail is very straightforward and signed well, so relax and enjoy the descent! Notice any birds as you walk. Mill Creek is the home to finches, spotted towhees, and warblers. Around mile 4.5, if following the Big Water Trail, you will find a junction. One trail heads west-northwest and the other stays north. Both trails lead to the Mill Creek Canyon Road, but it is advised to stay north for a direct route to the parking lot where

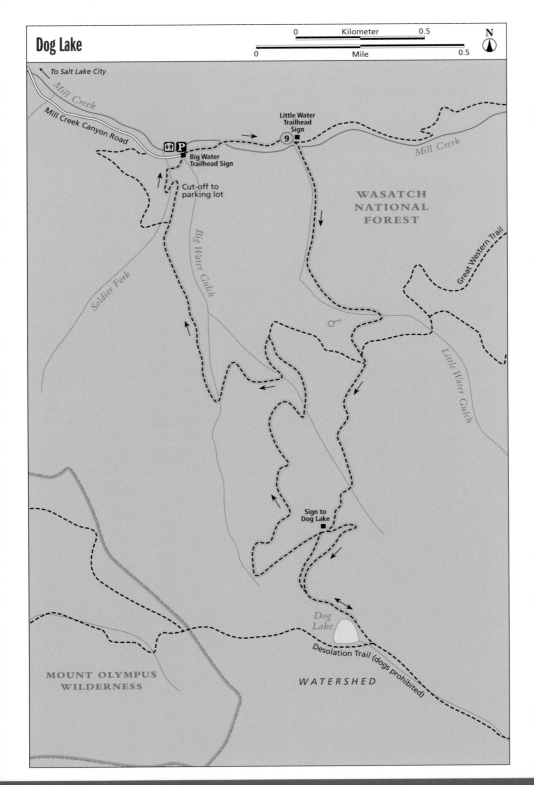

Dog Lake

To Salt Lake City

Mill Creek

Mill Creek Canyon Road

Big Water Trailhead Sign

Cut-off to parking lot

Little Water Trailhead Sign

9

Mill Creek

WASATCH NATIONAL FOREST

Great Western Trail

Soldier Fork

Big Water Gulch

Little Water Gulch

Sign to Dog Lake

Dog Lake

MOUNT OLYMPUS WILDERNESS

WATERSHED

Desolation Trail (dogs prohibited)

Kilometer

0    0.5

Mile

0    0.5

N

you began. Remember to leash up in parking lots and drive carefully back as the road is narrow.

## MILES AND DIRECTIONS

**0.0**  The trailhead for Little Water starts at the south end of the parking area for Big Water.

**0.4**  Follow signs for Little Water and climb along the stream to the south.

**1.0**  You will intersect the Great Western Trail. Continue south.

**1.6**  You'll approach a four-way trail junction. Follow the signs to Dog Lake.

**1.9**  Descend toward Dog Lake. Remember to stay on the north side.

**2.2**  Follow signs for Big Water to complete the loop, or take Little Water for an out-and-back.

**4.5**  Follow the north split in the trail to return to the parking area.

**4.7**  Arrive back at the parking area.

## NEARBY HIKES

Great Western Trail, Alexander Basin

## CREATURE COMFORTS

**Extended Stay America Sugarhouse**, 1220 E. 2100 South, Salt Lake City; (801) 474-0771; www.extendedstayamerica.com. This hotel is centrally located in Sugarhouse not far from the Salt Lake City–area hikes. It is within walking distance of grocery stores, numerous restaurants, bookstores, bars, and coffee shops and include kitchenettes in the rooms. It is also 1 block from Sugarhouse Park, a beautiful spot for a walk or picnic, and a 10-minute walk from the Fairmont Dog Park. There is a per-day pet fee, and height and length restrictions apply.

**Fisher Brewing Company**, 320 W. 800 South, Salt Lake City; (801) 487-2337; www.fisherbeer.com. Fisher is one of Salt Lake City's best breweries, and while new, it has a long history dating back to pre-Prohibition. The brewers have reformulated many of the recipes from the original Fisher and have a great collection of vintage collectibles. They have rotating beers on tap and a laid-back atmosphere. They don't serve food, but there are daily food trucks including pizza, tacos, and sandwiches. Check their calendar for the food trucks and be sure to watch for these favorites: Umani Pizza, Facil Taqueria, and Raclette Machine. They allow dogs on their patio on weekdays and before 6 p.m. on weekends.

# 10 BONNEVILLE SHORELINE TRAIL: THOUSAND OAKS SECTION

## WHY GO?

This quaint section of trail, on the bench near Salt Lake City, is just a taste of what the much longer Shoreline has to offer. The expansive Shoreline Trail spans the eastern bench of the Wasatch Mountains from Idaho to Nephi, Utah. It's an ambitious trail system that provides easy-to-moderate terrain for you and your dog. It is important to bring water for all hikers.

---

### THE RUNDOWN

**County:** Salt Lake
**Start:** From Mount Olympus Trailhead
**Distance:** 5.2 miles out and back
**Hiking time:** 2–3 hours
**Difficulty:** Moderate
**Trailhead elevation:** 4,825 feet
**Highest point:** 5,732 feet
**Best season:** Fall
**Trail surface:** Packed-dirt trail, rocky sections
**Other trail users:** Runners
**Canine compatibility:** On leash
**Land status:** National Forest
**Fees and permits:** None

**Trail contact:** Salt Lake Ranger District, 6944 S. 3000 East, Salt Lake City, UT 84121; (801) 733-2600; www.fs.usda.gov/uwcnf
**Nearest town:** Salt Lake City
**Trail tips:** This is just a small section of the Shoreline Trail. There are many other wonderful sections in and around Salt Lake City. The trail is steep at times and can be very hot in the summer.
**Nat Geo TOPO! Map (USGS):** 7.5-minute *Sugarhouse, UT*
**Nat Geo Trails Illustrated Map**: *709: Wasatch Front North*

---

### FINDING THE TRAILHEAD

 From 4500 South and Wasatch Boulevard, head south on Wasatch Boulevard for approximately 1.7 miles toward Mount Olympus. At the signed parking area for Mount Olympus Trailhead, turn left, following the short, steep spur up to the parking area. The trail begins to the south.
**Trailhead GPS:** N40 39.120' / W111 48.379'

## THE HIKE

From the parking area, walk south past the concrete barriers then head sharply left (east) up the earthen steps that create the trail. There is a lot of elevation gain on this first, short section—you will get warmed up in a hurry, but it isn't an extended climb. As you continue up the rocky slopes, the view of Salt Lake Valley and the Wasatch Peaks of the Wasatch Range gets clearer and better with each step. If you do this hike early, the view of the sun streaking across the Oquirrh Mountains to the west is worth the early alarm.

This trail follows the shoreline of an ancient inland lake called Lake Bonneville, a Pleistocene lake that existed around 15,500 years ago and covered most of the state of Utah. This giant lake cradled the Wasatch Range and was fed by many of the West's rivers, eventually filling it beyond capacity. The northern lake wall ultimately collapsed, receding into what we now know as the Great Salt Lake.

In 1990 the Bonneville Shoreline Trail became part of a 200-plus-mile dream to connect the Idaho border of northern Utah to Nephi, Utah, along the ancient shoreline. The Thousand Oaks trail section that you are hiking was completed in 2013 by a hardworking team of volunteers, which means in trail years it is still brand-new.

At mile 0.2 the views of the high-granite peaks of the upper terraces of the Wasatch Range are spectacular. At mile 0.4 there is a Y junction with the Mount Olympus Trail—turn left (north), to continue. You will still be climbing pretty significantly. At mile 0.7 there is another junction with the Mount Olympus Trail, which ascends 4,100 feet to the peak over 3.5 miles. Saving that for another day, and continue on the Shoreline Trail, switchbacking and winding through the oaks, which in the fall are brilliant red, and the juniper trees perched on seemingly impenetrable rocks.

At mile 0.9 there is a popular lookout point of the Salt Lake Valley that rivals that of the higher vistas. From this point, the trail levels out. It contours the hillside and keeps its northerly march. It can get hot while traversing the open hillside, but as you get closer to Olympus Cove, the residential subdivision, you will get more help with shade from the trees that line the trail on either side. At mile 2.3 the trail will switchback sharply to the west, an indication that you have completed the "out" in your out-and-back hike. If you continue down the stairs, you will be in the Olympus Cove neighborhood, which can also serve as an alternate trailhead for this section of the Shoreline Trail. Turn around and return the way you came.

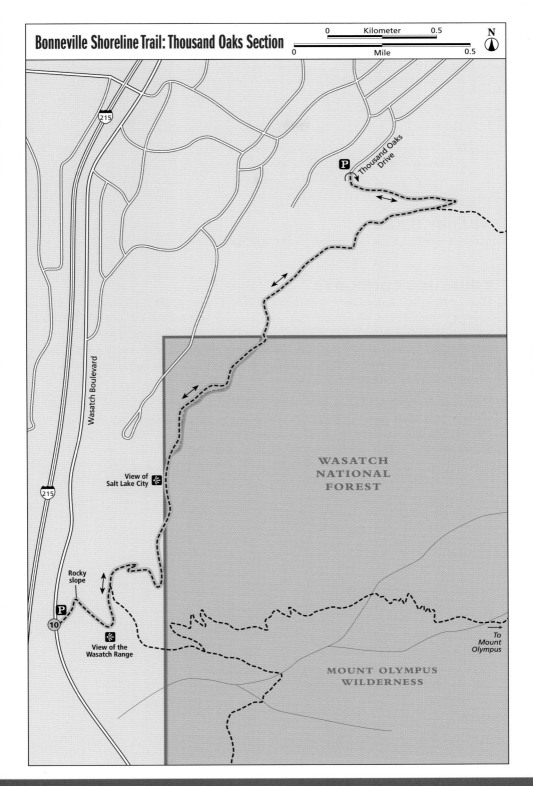

Bonneville Shoreline Trail: Thousand Oaks Section

Kilometer

Mile

N

215

Thousand Oaks Drive

P

Wasatch Boulevard

215

View of
Salt Lake City

WASATCH
NATIONAL
FOREST

Rocky
slope

P

10

View of the
Wasatch Range

MOUNT OLYMPUS
WILDERNESS

To
Mount
Olympus

## MILES AND DIRECTIONS

**0.0** Follow the trail to the south of the parking area through the barriers, then immediately east up the steps.

**0.7** Veer south at the junction with the Mount Olympus Trail. There is a sign for the Shoreline Trail.

**0.9** Enjoy a break, and the views, at the rock perch overlooking the valley.

**2.3** The trail will switchback sharply west, descending.

**2.7** Arrive at the Olympus Cove neighborhood and return the way you came.

**5.2** Arrive back at Mount Olympus Trailhead.

## NEARBY HIKES

Mount Olympus, Heughs Canyon, Neffs Canyon

## CREATURE COMFORTS

**Hyatt Place Salt Lake City/Cottonwood**, 3090 E. 6200 South, Holladay; (801) 890-1280; www.hyatt.com. The Hyatt Place in Cottonwood Heights is a centrally located hotel with easy access to I-215 and the Salt Lake–area hikes. It was recently built, with modern, comfortable rooms and standard amenities including a heated pool and hot tub. There are suites with kitchenettes available for extended stays, and all guests receive complimentary breakfast. Pet fee applies.

**Flatbread Neapolitan Pizza**, 2121 S. McClelland St., Salt Lake City; (801) 467-2180; www.flatbreadpizza.com. Flatbread Pizza has a large patio that is permitted for dogs and offers a delicious selection of gourmet pizzas, pastas, salads, and beverages. Located in Sugarhouse, it is a great spot for unwinding after a long day of hiking.

# 11 NEFFS CANYON

## WHY GO?

Neffs Canyon is perhaps best described by this quote from Georgia O'Keeffe: "Nobody sees a flower really; it is so small. We haven't time, and to see takes time—like to have a friend takes time." Every time you venture into this canyon, it offers something new and beautiful, and it takes time. Uphill from the beginning, this trail follows Neffs Creek, a spring- and runoff-fed waterway, to a vantage point worthy of its reputation. This trail is a welcome respite from the concrete and noise of the city, giving canines and humans ample time to reconnect to nature, water, and one another.

### THE RUNDOWN

**County:** Salt Lake
**Start:** Neffs Canyon Trailhead
**Distance:** 5.0 miles out and back
**Hiking time:** 2–4 hours
**Difficulty:** Strenuous due to steep climbs and some technical sections
**Trailhead elevation:** 5,573 feet
**Highest point:** 7,991 feet
**Best seasons:** Late spring (snow patches likely) to late fall
**Trail surface:** Varied. Loose limestone, creek bottom, water crossings, and some obstacles.
**Other trail users:** Hikers
**Canine compatibility:** On leash. (If your dog needs other dogs to be on leash, this is not a good choice of hikes. Many users do not follow the rule.)

**Land status:** National Forest
**Fees and permits:** None
**Trail contact:** Salt Lake Ranger District, 6944 S. 3000 East, Salt Lake City, UT 84121; (801) 733-2600; www.fs.usda.gov/uwcnf
**Nearest town:** Salt Lake City
**Trail tips:** Spring runoff can cause water-crossing hazards. During summer months rattlesnakes have been spotted from time to time along this trail. Parking lot closes at 10 p.m.
**Nat Geo TOPO! Map (USGS):** 7.5-minute *Mount Aire*
**Nat Geo Trails Illustrated Map:** *709: Wasatch Front North*

### FINDING THE TRAILHEAD

Located in the Olympus Cove Neighborhood, Neffs Canyon Trailhead is a little bit tricky to find. The address for the trailhead is 4326 White Way, Salt Lake City, UT 84124. From Wasatch Boulevard in Mill Creek City, turn east on 3800 South toward Mill Creek Canyon. At the first stop sign, turn right (south) on Parkview Drive and continue up the hill for 1.1 miles to Parkview Terrace. Turn left onto Parkview Terrace (4260 East), then turn right on White Way, continuing up the hill to the parking lot. Please don't park along the neighborhood road. From the trailhead parking lot, the trail begins just to the left (east) of the parking area past the sign.
**Trailhead GPS:** N40 40.636' / W111 46.580'

### THE HIKE

The old names that would have hung from the canyons and rivers before the dams and the mills have been mostly forgotten. The natural features of the Salt Lake area and beyond are, for now, labeled with names from the original wave of pioneers that claimed

this area as the promised land. Neffs Canyon is no different. John Neff was a prosperous Pennsylvania mill owner who converted to the Church of Jesus Christ of Latter-Day Saints in 1843. With his family, a fine team, and the best wagon money could buy, he set out west. As did many families, the Neffs suffered along the way, burying more than they ought to have, but nevertheless they arrived to "This Is the Place" on October 2, 1847. John Neff established himself as one of the most prominent Utah businessmen of his time. Interesting fact: Neffs Cave, debatably one of the deepest caves in the United States, was discovered in Neffs Canyon in 1949.

The hike up Neffs Canyon begins in homage to Mount Olympus. The view from the parking lot is spectacular. The trail's beginning is to the east of the parking lot and climbs quickly to an old jeep road. This wide path is great for viewing all the happy faces coming down from their hike as you start yours. As you head east and up, you'll soon see a water tank with a chain-link fence surrounding it to the north of the trail. This rocky two-track trail will take you to a grouping of boulders and a "no more motorized vehicles" guard at 0.5 mile. Beyond this landmark you'll find a number of trails. Yours is to the left, heading northeast along a drainage. You'll climb briefly, then drop across a dry riverbed as these trails connect with the main trail, continuing climbing east, sometimes steeply through the pines.

At mile 1.6 the trail gets challenging with very steep terrain and overexposed tree roots—use caution. You'll cross a stream near a small waterfall, which depending on the time of year, you may need to assist your dogs to cross safely. Not far from here, you will switchback up a very steep climb up exposed tree roots that is closer to a ladder than it is to a trail. Continue climbing until approximately mile 2, where the pines turn to aspens and the ambience changes with them. Aspens are stunning all year, but fall is their daring crescendo.

After winding through the aspen trees, the meadow arrives like a gasping breath after a consistently steep climb to the end. The views are spectacular and the cirque boasts the granite walls so adored by rock climbers. Have lunch, catch your breath, then return the way you came.

## MILES AND DIRECTIONS

**0.0** Begin at the trailhead to the east of the parking area near the signs.

**0.3** Climb past the water tank.

**0.5** Take the leftmost trail along the drainage. This will follow the drainage before dropping through a creek bed and connecting with the main trail.

**1.5** Enter the Mount Olympus Wilderness.

**1.8** Cross the small waterfall—use caution.

**1.9** Climb a very steep, rooty section.

**2.0** Enter the aspen grove.

**2.5** Arrive at the meadow. Return the way you came.

**5.0** Arrive back at the parking area.

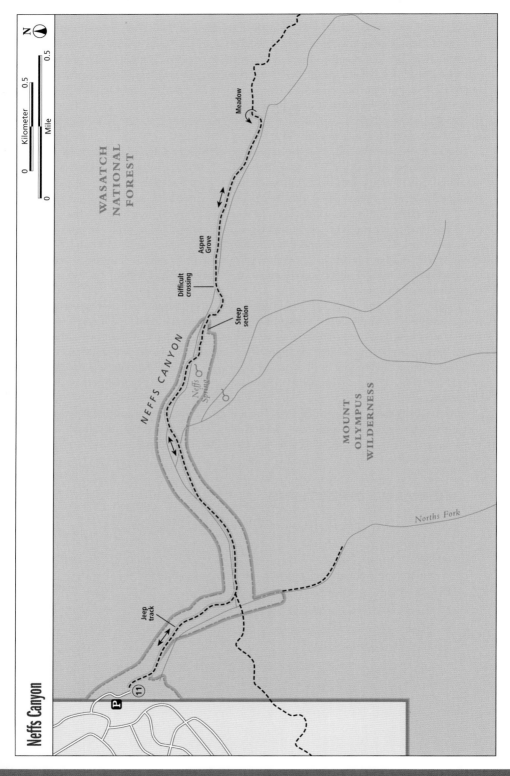

Neffs Canyon

## NEARBY HIKES

Bonneville Shoreline Trail, Mill Creek Canyon Hikes, Heughs Canyon

## CREATURE COMFORTS

**Hyatt Place Salt Lake City/Cottonwood**, 3090 E. 6200 South, Holladay; (801) 890-1280; www.hyatt.com. The Hyatt Place in Cottonwood Heights is a centrally located hotel with easy access to I-215 and the Salt Lake–area hikes. It was recently built, with modern, comfortable rooms and standard amenities including a heated pool and hot tub. There are suites with kitchenettes available for extended stays, and all guests receive complimentary breakfast. Pet fee applies.

**Lone Star Taqueria**, 2265 E. Fort Union Blvd., Cottonwood Heights; (801) 944-2300; www.lstaq.com. Lone Star is a local favorite serving incredible tacos, burritos, and other hearty options. They have an authentic salsa bar and soda selection. It is a great option for takeout, but the drive-through can get very busy.

# 12  HEUGHS CANYON

## WHY GO?

This short, rocky hike is a tough but rewarding adventure. From the beginning, the trail gains elevation while keeping the creek close almost the whole way. After crossing two bridges and a scree field, you will arrive at a beautiful waterfall. This is a well-earned and stunning achievement. There is plenty of water for your dog along the trail.

### THE RUNDOWN

**County:** Salt Lake
**Start:** Heughs Canyon Trailhead
**Distance:** 3.0 miles out and back
**Hiking time:** 1–2 hours
**Difficulty:** Moderate due to elevation gain, rocky footing, boulder field traverse
**Trailhead elevation:** 5,070 feet
**Highest point:** 6,150 feet
**Best season:** Fall
**Trail surface:** Gravel, rocks
**Other trail users:** Hikers only
**Canine compatibility:** On leash
**Land status:** National Forest
**Fees and permits:** None
**Trail contact:** Salt Lake Ranger District, 6944 S. 3000 East, Salt Lake City, UT 84121; (801) 733-2600; www.fs.usda.gov/uwcnf
**Nearest town:** Cottonwood Heights
**Trail tips:** There are a number of elements that make this hike challenging: patches of poison ivy, rattlesnake habitat, and a potentially difficult water crossing if it is a big runoff year. This is a very steep hike good for dogs and people who are in decent-to-good shape.
**Nat Geo TOPO! Map (USGS):** 7.5-minute *Sugar House, UT*
**Nat Geo Trails Illustrated Map:** *709: Wasatch Front North*

## FINDING THE TRAILHEAD

From Wasatch Boulevard and 4500 South, head south on Wasatch Boulevard, pass the trailhead for Mount Olympus, continue for 1 mile, then turn left (east) onto Canyon Cove Drive. Turn left (north) on the second street, Oak Canyon Drive. You will park on the east side of the road, immediately after Canyon Winds Lane (a private road). You will see signs informing the curious public about the parking regulations. Once parked, walk with your leashed-up pup toward a dirt trail, which opens through an oak tunnel at the end of the street. Stay north of a walled perimeter, which indicates private property.
**GPS for parking:** N40 38.400' / W111 47.789'
**Trailhead GPS:** N40 38.308' / W111 47.612'

## THE HIKE

Beyond the signed parking area, this trail is signless. Locals know this area as Heughs Canyon. The trail winds up the north side of Heughs Creek. On your steep climb to the falls, you will be a witness to the trail's history, geology, flora, and fauna.

A few hundred yards from the start, a debris pile from an old mine can be seen to the south of the trail. Along your hike in Heughs Canyon, you will be able to see a 4½-inch pipe used 150 years ago to bring water to long-forgotten apple orchards below.

Heughs Canyon Waterfall

**Martin navigating the scree field.**

In some years, California poppies grow near the trailhead. Their brilliant orange color is an eye-catching, lovely treat. At mile 0.6 there is a healthy patch of poison ivy on the south side of the trail. While you may be diligent in avoiding it, your pup may not. The culprit for the misery associated with poison ivy is the chemical urushiol. This oily substance can catch a ride on your dog's coat and then be transferred to your bare legs at the next doggie drive-by or lean-in. If you are allergic to this chemical, the itching will begin. Beware and keep your dog close at this point.

As you continue up the trail adjacent to the creek, you will walk by wild catnip, box elder trees, and glacial lilies hugging the canyon floor.

At mile 1 you will cross Heughs Creek on a primitive log bridge. When the water is low, this is a simple task. If the creek is full, be prepared to help your dog across. The logs in the creek are individually narrow and slippery, which makes it difficult for dogs to cross safely. A little farther along you will cross another, substantially more stable bridge. After the second bridge the trail continues steeply up the hill. At the top of the hill, the scree field will be visible on your right. About a third of the way across the scree field, there is a rather large cairn of stacked rocks on one of the bigger boulders. Head across the rocks toward the cairn and begin your slow traverse across the scree field veering south before the rock wall of the canyon. This is a difficult section for dogs not accustomed to route finding and problem-solving. Take it slow. If your dog has a propensity to become anxious when falling behind, be sure to stay with him. Pay attention while hiking this section. There are harsh angles on some of the rocks that would be very painful if landed on incorrectly. In canyon country, situations like these are common, and hiking trails like the Heughs Canyon Trail require some agility. Still, these experiences can be very beneficial for trust building between you and your dog.

# Heughs Canyon

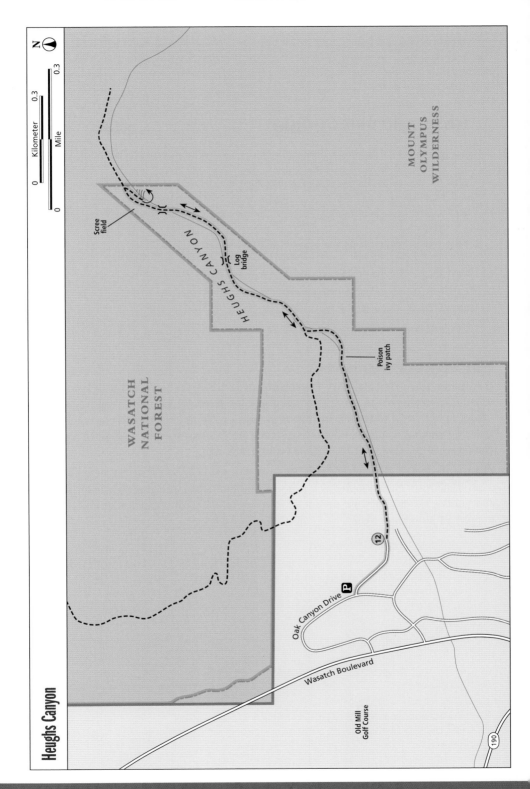

N

Kilometer
0          0.3

Mile
0          0.3

WASATCH
NATIONAL
FOREST

MOUNT
OLYMPUS
WILDERNESS

HEUGHS CANYON

Scree
field

Log
bridge

Poison
ivy patch

Oak Canyon Drive

P

12

Wasatch Boulevard

Old Mill
Golf Course

190

Once across the scree field, follow the eastern canyon wall and water south until the falls become visible. You will most likely get your feet wet if you decide to traverse all the way into the mist of the waterfall. Enjoy this hard-earned visual treat. When finished, return the way you came.

## MILES AND DIRECTIONS

**0.0** Park your car along the public street, then walk with your dog on leash to the trailhead.

**0.2** The trail begins at the end of the road and continues east under the branches of scrub oak.

**0.6** There is a large poison ivy patch to the right (south) side of the trail. Use caution.

**1.0** Use caution crossing the primitive log bridge over Heughs Creek. Use extra caution during high runoff times, helping your dog across if needed.

**1.2** You'll cross the final bridge and begin up the steepest part of the trail.

**1.3** Traverse southeast to the waterfall.

**1.5** Arrive at the waterfall. Return the way you came.

**3.0** Arrive back at the trailhead.

## CREATURE COMFORTS

**Residence Inn Salt Lake City Cottonwood**, 6425 S. 3000 East, Salt Lake City; (801) 453-0430; www.marriott.com. The Residence Inn hotel has kitchens in all rooms, an outdoor pool, and a reasonable pet deposit, making it enjoyable if you are staying in the area for a significant amount of time. It is located near a number of great restaurants, cafes, and pubs and minutes away from many of the area hikes.

**California Pizza Kitchen**, 6227 S. State St., #1, Murray; (801) 290-1124; www.cpk .com. California Pizza Kitchen is a national classic offering special pizza combinations and yummy salads. They are permitted for dogs on their patio and are located in the popular Fashion Place Mall.

# 13 FERGUSON CANYON

## WHY GO?

Ferguson Canyon is a challenging hike, both aerobically and technically, as you ascend from the canyon floor to a lookout high above the Salt Lake Valley. From the get-go, you will hike over obstacles. You will climb with the creek flowing beside the trail almost the whole way. It is a wonderful way to spend an afternoon and evening. This is a steep one, but plenty of water is available if your pup gets thirsty.

### THE RUNDOWN

**County:** Salt Lake
**Start:** Ferguson Canyon Trailhead
**Distance:** 4.0 miles out and back
**Hiking time:** 2–3 hours
**Difficulty:** Strenuous due to steep sections, exposure, and some technical sections
**Trailhead elevation:** 5,275 feet
**Highest point:** 6,618 feet
**Best season:** Spring
**Trail surface:** Rocky stairs, log crossings, gravelly hills, singletracks, river crossings with rocks
**Other trail users:** Rock climbers
**Canine compatibility:** On leash. Please clean up after your pup—there are garbage cans at the trailhead!

**Land status:** National Forest
**Fees and permits:** None
**Trail contact:** Salt Lake Ranger District, 6944 S. 3000 East, Salt Lake City, UT 84121; (801) 733-2600; www.fs.usda.gov/uwcnf
**Nearest town:** Cottonwood Heights
**Trail tips:** If you are comfortable using trekking poles, they would be helpful here as there are some very steep sections and numerous water crossings over logs and rocks. The trail is closed 10 p.m.–6 a.m.
**Nat Geo TOPO! Map (USGS):** 7.5-minute *Sugarhouse, Dromedary Peak*
**Nat Geo Trails Illustrated Map:** *709: Wasatch Front North*

### FINDING THE TRAILHEAD

The address for the trailhead is 7743 S. Timberline Dr. in Cottonwood Heights, Utah. This makes the trail easy to find. From I-215, take the exit for 6200 South (exit 6) and turn east toward the mountains. Stay on 6200 South until it becomes Wasatch Boulevard and continue 0.3 mile beyond Big Cottonwood Canyon Road (home of Brighton and Solitude Ski Resorts). Turn left onto Prospector Drive and very quickly turn right at the T intersection to continue up the hill. On the right there is a sign for overflow trailhead parking on a small dirt lot. Take note. You may need to backtrack depending on parking availability at the main lot. Follow the road for 0.4 mile, turn left on Timberline Drive (7780 South). Park on the road; the trailhead begins just ahead.
**Trailhead GPS:** N40 36.654' / W111 47.284'

## THE HIKE

If Mark Twain is right in saying "a gold mine is just a hole with a liar sitting at the top," Ferguson Canyon is either the liar or the hole. Many rumors dating back to the pioneer days have mentioned this area and the gold that is hidden somewhere within.

From the parking area, walk up the doubletrack maintenance road to the northeast. Just past mile 0.2 there is a water tank surrounded by a chain-link fence. Shortly after that the trail funnels down into a rocky narrow path with a couple "stairs" used to help manage erosion. This leads you steeply downhill, past old signage—now used for creative self-expression—and past some large boulders. Here is where you begin your climb.

At 0.7 mile you will hike through a rocky section with the trail hugging the south wall above you, lined with many routes used by both trad and sport climbers. At this point the hike veers north. There is a tempting side canyon to the east of the climbing wall, but stay to your left along the visible trail following the creek uphill.

Just beyond the rock-climbing wall, you get to pass under a little tree arch, an indicator that you are on the right track. There are braiding trails on this section, most of which will get you to where you are going. A good rule of thumb in Ferguson, aka "Fergie," Canyon: Continue uphill.

Depending on your specific route, you will have crossed the creek by now or you will cross it shortly. Use caution on the slippery rocks! Just before mile 1 you will find yourself at the base of a very steep and rocky section with very powdery dirt. To your right there will be a beautiful small waterfall flowing through the rocks. This section is difficult both on the way up and coming down.

After this climb the trail will descend sharply to a substantial bridge of stacked logs. Cross over them and turn left with the trail and resume climbing. This section can be slippery on the way down, so go slowly to avoid a mishap. At mile 1.2 cross the creek at the top of the hill. Use the rocks to find a dry way across—trekking poles can come in handy to balance on the boulders, if you have them. Continue through the trees,

Heading back to the car. STEPHANIE TOMLIN

following the drainage, and you'll soon pass a triplet of aspen trees on the south side of the trail. From here, the trail will turn sharply out of the drainage, climbing along the north canyon wall. There is no water available past this point for your dogs, so give them a moment to get a final sip before heading north to the high country. The trail is in a hurry to get out of the drainage, it is steep, and by most, it is considered difficult. Once you reach level ground again, the views of the valley below are astounding.

At mile 1.8, from the bench looking west, you will see the eye-catching Oquirrh Mountains and the Bingham Copper Mine. To the north you'll see the University of Utah, downtown Salt Lake City, and Antelope Island surrounded by the Great Salt Lake. Continue north on this trail, traversing the mountainside. There is a great spot to peer down into Big Cottonwood Canyon, a view rare for pups due to the watershed regulations. After a break and a snack, return the way you came, using caution on the steep, slippery sections.

## MILES AND DIRECTIONS

**0.0**  The trail begins heading north from the parking area on Timberline Drive up the doubletrack maintenance road.

**0.3**  Head east past the water tank surrounded by a chain-link fence where the trail transitions to singletrack.

**0.7**  Stay left (north) following the creek past the popular rock-climbing wall.

**0.9**  Climb up a steep, rocky section. There are also beautiful water features at this point on the trail.

**1.0**  Cross the bridge of stacked logs.

**1.2**  Cross the stream on boulders. Use caution.

**1.4**  The trail turns north, switchbacking to a lookout point.

**1.8**  Stop here at a very pretty view of the Salt Lake Valley and beyond. Return the way you came.

**4.0**  Arrive back at the trailhead.

## NEARBY HIKES

Bonneville Shoreline, Mill Creek Canyon, Bloods Lake

## CREATURE COMFORTS

**Spitz**, 3158 E. 6200 South, Holladay; (801) 930-5114; www.spitzslc.com. Spitz serves diner-style Mediterranean food including gyros, kebabs, salads, and more. They have two locations, one in Cottonwood Heights and another in Sugarhouse near many of the area hikes. This is a great to-go option and both locations have patios. Not permitted for pups, but they will give you a bowl of water and they have nearby spots for a picnic.

**Extended Stay America Sugarhouse**, 1220 E. 2100 South, Salt Lake City; (801) 474-0771; www.extendedstayamerica.com. This hotel is centrally located in Sugarhouse not far from the Salt Lake City–area hikes. It is within walking distance of grocery stores, numerous restaurants, bookstores, bars, and coffee shops and include kitchenettes in the rooms. It is also 1 block from Sugarhouse Park, a beautiful spot for a walk or picnic, and

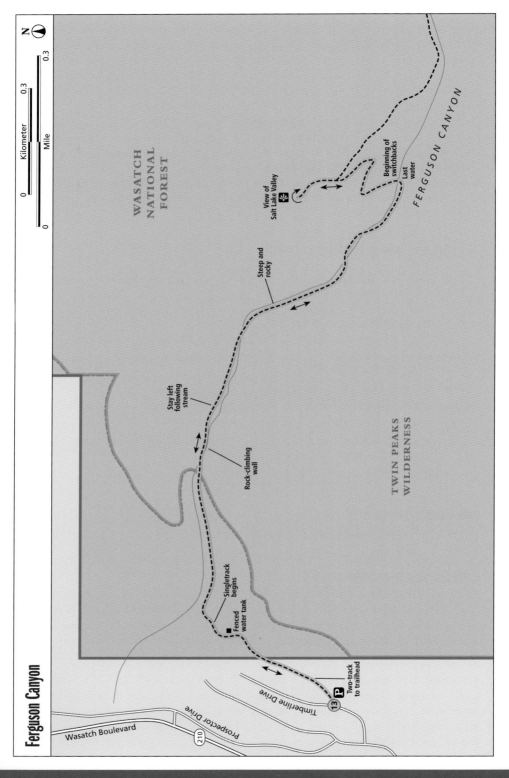

Ferguson Canyon

N

Kilometer
0          0.3

0          0.3
Mile

WASATCH
NATIONAL
FOREST

View of
Salt Lake Valley

Beginning of
switchbacks

Last
water

FERGUSON CANYON

Steep and
rocky

Stay left
following
stream

Rock-climbing
wall

TWIN PEAKS
WILDERNESS

Singletrack
begins

Fenced
water tank

Wasatch Boulevard

Prospector Drive

210

Timberline Drive

13  P

Two-track
to trailhead

**Nema and Martin ready to head out!**

a 10-minute walk from the Fairmont Dog Park. There is a per-day pet fee, and height and length restrictions apply.

# 14 BATTLE CREEK LOOP

## WHY GO?

Battle Creek Loop is a somewhat difficult and beautiful hike. From its crescendo high above the Utah Valley, the views offered are memorable. Along the way you will see numerous waterfalls, traverse cliffs, and pass by significant historical markers. This hike is multifaceted, with hot, exposed, steep, and slightly technical elements interwoven with high-profile views. You will want to bring water for your dog since water access is only periodically available on the trail.

### THE RUNDOWN

**County:** Utah County
**Start:** From Battle Creek Falls parking lot
**Distance:** 8.8-mile loop
**Hiking time:** 4–5 hours
**Difficulty:** Strenuous due to exposure, elevation, and technical sections
**Trailhead elevation:** 5,207 feet
**Highest point:** 7,745 feet
**Best season:** Fall
**Trail surface:** Talus, dirt, occasional primitive-bridge river crossings
**Other trail users:** Ambitious trail runners, horses, ATVs at the plateau between the two canyons, dirt bikes for the first mile

**Canine compatibility:** Voice control
**Land status:** National Forest
**Fees and permits:** None
**Trail contact:** Pleasant Grove Ranger District, 390 N. 100 East, Pleasant Grove, UT 84062; (801) 785-3563; www.fs.usda.gov
**Nearest town:** Pleasant Grove
**Trail tips:** This trail is best done in the cooler parts of the year or early in the day to avoid the exposed sections when the temperatures rise.
**Nat Geo TOPO! Map (USGS):** 7.5-minute *Bridal Veil Falls*
**Nat Geo Trails Illustrated Map:** *709: Wasatch Front North*

## FINDING THE TRAILHEAD

From I-15, take exit 275 toward Pleasant Grove. You will be able to see the giant *G* on the hillside and two parallel canyons to the north and south of the *G*. After exiting head 1.2 miles east on Pleasant Grove Boulevard toward the mountains, then turn right (south) onto State Street. Continue south for 0.4 mile, then turn left (east) on 200 South. Follow 200 South until it terminates at the parking area near Kiwanis Park. The trail will begin to the north.
**Trailhead GPS:** N40 21.779' / W111 42.034'

## THE HIKE

From the parking area south of Kiwanis Park, your hike will begin with a hot, sandy traverse to the north toward Grove Canyon. There are multiple ways to hike this section, so do your best to avoid needless elevation gain, and just continue north as your directional cue. This part of the trail is difficult in that it is wide open and a little chaotic-feeling. At mile 1.1 you will reach the mouth of the pretty Grove Canyon with Grove Creek flowing substantially. You will need to cross the creek and turn right onto a service road heading east. Allow your dog time to enjoy the water at Grove Creek. Not long after entering the canyon, you'll begin a steep climb up the road. At mile 1.4 there is a junction—take

Looking out toward Utah Lake.

the left (north) singletrack. The trail gets very steep for a few strides. Approximately 0.5 mile farther, let your dog get a final drink and a dunk as the next section is steep and exposed. Continue on the singletrack as the trail violently cuts back west and climbs out of the canyon bottom. As you continue to climb the trail, the views on all sides change drastically as the canyon walls drop away quickly.

Just past mile 2.4 there are two narrow parts to the trail that have some exposure. Be cautious as you walk through these sections. Once safely on the other side, continue hiking, enjoying the views down the canyon and up toward Grove Creek Falls. This pretty waterfall is not easily accessible, but the view from the Battle Creek Loop trail is beautiful and rewarding. After a seemingly long hot section of the trail, you'll come to a nice spot to sit on the famous "heart bench" and you'll have a chance to look out at the extreme topography. With the sound of the waterfall and the comfort of a seat, it doesn't get much better. This is a good place to have a snack before climbing again. There is a safe place for your dog to get a drink just a bit farther up the trail.

As you continue you'll cross a small wooden bridge, and the trail with enter the forest. Water will become abundant as you continue uphill. The trail winds in and out of the forest, entering the aspens as the trail brings the plateau closer. At mile 4.4 you will find the "Indian Camp" sign, which marks a somber reminder of the historical significance of this area. The nearby spring is beautiful, and the reflection of a sunset off of Utah Lake, if you get your timing right, is almost beautiful enough to honor the lives once lost here.

After a pause the hike continues up until you reach a T junction, which is a dirt road. Turn right (south) and continue on. Deer tracks are easy to see in the powdery dirt along the road, and their meandering is comical at times. At mile 5.7 there is a fork in the road with a twin dirt road heading west. Continue south toward Battle Creek Canyon and Big Baldy Peak. You will be surrounded by an expansive meadow. It is a moving scene, with the breeze rattling the seed heads of the grasses and the unison swaying. If you arrive near dusk, the sunset and the light are memorable.

At mile 5.8 there is an important wooden sign that will direct you off the road toward a small singletrack, dropping down and curving right (west) along drainages that roar with water in the springtime. At mile 6.5 there is another wooden sign in front of you confirming your location and providing correct direction of travel toward Battle Creek/ Curly Springs/Kiwanis Park. Before you reach the shores of Battle Creek, you will pass a lovely canyon scene with a gnarled tree in the middle. Then, the trail drops to the creek's edge. The trail will follow and cross the water a few times as you descend quickly. At mile 8.0 you will cross over a log bridge, which can be a little tricky on wobbly legs. Once across enjoy the hike down toward Battle Creek Falls and finally back to the car at mile 8.8. As this is a more heavily populated part of the trail, it is best to leash your dog on this lower section.

## MILES AND DIRECTIONS

**0.0**  Begin at the Battle Creek Falls parking lot.

**1.1**  Arrive at the entrance to Grove Creek Canyon, crossing over the creek after traversing the open sage flats between the two canyons.

**1.4**  Follow the steep upper singletrack trail leaving behind the doubletrack road.

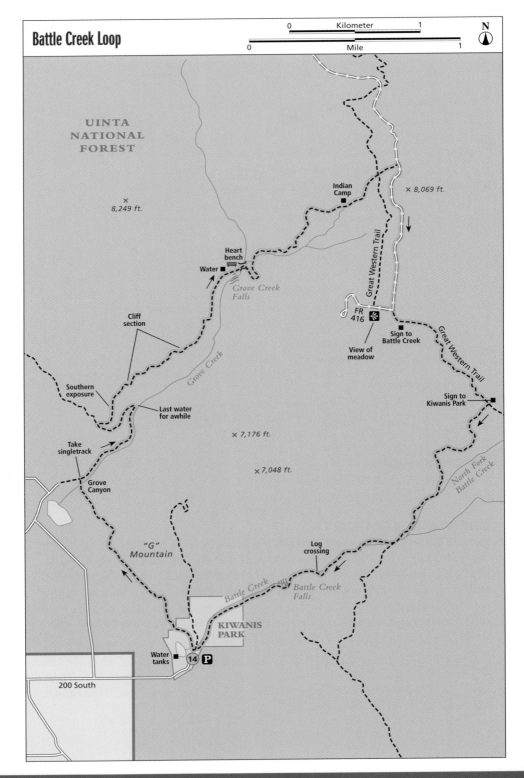

# Battle Creek Loop

0 Kilometer 1

0 Mile 1

N

UINTA
NATIONAL
FOREST

× 8,249 ft.

Indian
Camp

× 8,069 ft.

Heart
bench

Water

*Grove Creek
Falls*

Great Western Trail

FR
416

Sign to
Battle Creek

View of
meadow

Great Western Trail

Cliff
section

*Grove Creek*

Southern
exposure

Last water
for awhile

Sign to
Kiwanis Park

× 7,176 ft.

Take
singletrack

× 7,048 ft.

Grove
Canyon

*North Fork
Battle Creek*

"G"
Mountain

Log
crossing

*Battle Creek*

*Battle Creek
Falls*

KIWANIS
PARK

Water
tanks

14  P

200 South

| 1.8 | Let your dog get a last drink before heading up on the drastic switchback to the west, climbing out of Grove Creek drainage. |
| 2.4 | After climbing significantly you will have to cross two narrow sections. This is the first—use caution and stick to the inside of the hillside. Leash your dog if necessary. |
| 2.7 | Continue east. This is the last section with exposure. Take it slow and use caution. |
| 3.3 | Rest at the famous heart bench above Grove Creek Falls. |
| 3.4 | Cross the stream over a bridge with safe access for your dog to get a drink. |
| 3.5 | Continue climbing into the trees. |
| 4.4 | Arrive at the Indian Camp. |
| 4.7 | Turn right (south) on the dirt road and follow it across the plateau. There is also an optional singletrack trail. |
| 5.7 | Continue south past the dirt road. |
| 5.8 | At the Battle Creek sign, head south onto the trail. |
| 6.2 | Cross a small drainage. |
| 6.5 | Stay on the Battle Creek/Curly Springs/Kiwanis Park trail heading west. |
| 6.7 | Pass a beautiful tree standing alone in a meadow. The scene is idyllic. |
| 7.2 | Follow this creek the rest of the way down back to the car. |
| 8.0 | Cross over the water on a few logs. Use caution. |
| 8.2 | Battle Creek Falls will be falling to the pools below you. Use caution and do not allow your dog to get close to the slippery edge. It is polite to leash your dog at this point. |
| 8.3 | Cross over a bridge, and the trail continues west. |
| 8.8 | Arrive back at your car. |

## NEARBY HIKES

Scout Falls, Lone Peak, Horsetail Falls

## CREATURE COMFORTS

**Home2 Suites by Hilton at Thanksgiving Point**, 3051 Club House Dr., Lehi; (801) 753-5430. http://home2suites3.hilton.com/en/hotels/utah/home2-suites-by-hilton-lehi-thanksgiving-point-SLCTPHT/index.html. Home2Suites is a newer hotel located centrally to the Salt Lake and Utah County hikes. The rooms are large and comfortable with standard amenities as well as an included hot breakfast. The Thanksgiving Point area has shopping, restaurants, and some great museums and entertainment for the whole family.

**Cubby's**, 3700 North Thanksgiving Way, Lehi; (801) 766-8100; www.cubbys.co. Cubby's is a great fast-food spot that doesn't taste or feel like a fast-food restaurant. They serve organic burgers, sandwiches, and salads as well as a surprisingly tasty breakfast that will be sure to energize your adventure.

# 15 LONE PEAK TRAIL TO THE SECOND HAMONGOG

## WHY GO?

The Alpine approach to the Second Hamongog on Lone Peak, while a remote and challenging hike, is an opportunity to enter the rugged Lone Peak Wilderness with your pup. Beginning on a dirt road, the trail steeply climbs before becoming a singletrack at the first Hamongog then winding its way through meadows under spectacular views of Mount Timpanogos. Bring plenty of water and snacks for you and your pup, as this trail is steep and exposed to the sun.

## THE RUNDOWN

**County:** Utah County
**Start:** From the gate at Aspen Drive in Alpine
**Distance:** 6.6 miles out and back
**Hiking time:** 3.5–4.5 hours
**Difficulty:** Strenuous due to a long steep climb and extended mileage
**Trailhead elevation:** 5,702 feet
**Highest point:** 8,085 feet
**Best seasons:** Fall, spring
**Trail surface:** Dirt, rock, with some obstacles
**Other trail users:** Horses, hikers, rock climbers, and some ATV usage on lower section
**Canine compatibility:** Voice control. On leash if prone to chase wildlife.
**Land status:** National Forest
**Fees and permits:** None
**Trail contact:** Pleasant Grove Ranger District, 390 N. 100 East, Pleasant Grove, UT 84062; (801) 785-3563; www.fs.usda.gov
**Nearest town:** Alpine
**Trail tips:** It is important to have a topo map and recommended that you read the "Lone Peak Cirque" section of the FalconGuide *Rock Climbing the Wasatch Range*. The more you read about this area, the better prepared you'll be with trail navigation. This is a remote area that offers challenging circumstances. Bring plenty of water and snacks.
**Nat Geo TOPO! Map (USGS):** 7.5-minute *Dromedary Peak*
**Nat Geo Trails Illustrated Map:** *709: Wasatch Front North*
**Other maps:** Map in FalconGuide *Rock Climbing in the Wasatch Range:* "Alpine Approach to Lone Peak Cirque"

## FINDING THE TRAILHEAD

From I-15, take exit 284 toward Alpine/Timpanogos Highway. Head east on Timpanogos Highway (UT 92). Continue approximately 6 miles to the junction with 5300 West (SR 74/Alpine Highway) and turn left (north). Head north. This road becomes Main Street in Alpine, Utah. At the roundabout take the second exit, continuing north on Main Street until you reach the intersection of Main Street and 200 North. Turn right (east) on 200 North and continue for 2 blocks until you intersect 200 East (Grove Drive), then turn left (north). Continue on Grove Drive for approximately 1.5 miles and be on the lookout for Alpine Cove Drive (sometimes referenced as Aspen Grove Drive). Turn left (north) on Alpine Cove Drive and follow it up briefly before turning left on Aspen Drive. Continue on to the dirt road past the Schoolhouse Springs Trailhead and stay to the right until you reach a small parking area near two large water tanks. To the north of the water tanks, you will see a large gate. Park respectfully; the route begins at the gate. According to the Forest Service website, this road passes through private property so stay on the road as you begin your hike.

**Trailhead GPS:** N40 28.955' / W111 45.594'

## THE HIKE

The initial climb toward the First Hamongog is a tough one and begins on a rough dirt road. It is steep and unrelenting at times, but as you climb, look out toward American Fork Canyon and Mount Timpanogos—they will only get more beautiful. At mile 0.4 the grade of the road continues to get steeper until your first switchback. Just before mile 0.8 continue on the main road—do not take the smaller dirt road to the left (west) downhill. Continue climbing as the road becomes steep along tight switchbacks.

At mile 1.3 there is an important right (east) turn immediately before an old plank board fence, a tree, and some boulders that sends you up a small side trail to the northeast. Do not continue on the dirt road northwest. Follow the smaller trail heading northeast up a smaller draw that is rocky, narrower, and eroded by runoff—very different than the previous wide dirt road. Hike up the draw. It will make a T intersection with another dirt road not long after the turn. Turn right (east) to follow the road uphill. *Make note of this junction, as you will need to find it on the way down.*

After the T intersection the dirt road is less steep and views open up toward Alpine through the oaks, flaming red in the fall, and Utah Lake. At mile 1.7 you will pass a green gate. This is another important marker to pay attention to. On the return trip this gate will remind you to watch for your left turn. As you head up past the gate, there is a road-like trail to your right that will look tempting on the way down, but remember the turn to the parking area will be *after* the green gate.

Continue climbing until, at mile 1.9, you will cross over the culvert, some boulders preventing motorized traffic, and into the Lone Peak Wilderness Area. You will arrive shortly after to the First Hamongog, a beautiful mountain meadow.

This pretty meadow, with its odd name rooted in biblical texts, is stunning and worth a pause. At this point the dirt road becomes a singletrack. Continue on the main trail (north). There will be signage for the Second Hamongog Trail, which will direct you left (west) about halfway up the meadow. This junction is at approximately 2 miles and is another important intersection to note for your return.

Once headed left (west) on the Second Hamongog Trail, take time to enjoy this section of the trail. The oaks, dark timber, and small boulder obstacles all make for an exciting trip up toward the destination. Keep a lookout for snakes, for they can frequent the area. The Second Hamongog, or meadow, will be close when you see giant boulders mixed in with trees around mile 3.3. This will be very apparent when you arrive. Be sure to walk the trail through the meadow and take in the spectacular views of the mountains and glacially eroded features high up in the cliffs. At the end of meadow, there is a sign to Lake Hardy to the right (east). There is usually running water just past this sign as the trail dips through a drainage to the left (west), or there is another water source farther up the trail if necessary for your dog. When you are ready, return the way you came. *Remember to watch for your left turn after the green gate.*

## MILES AND DIRECTIONS

**0.0**  Park your car west of the water tanks. The hike begins at a metal gate, north of the water tanks, heading north on dirt road.

**0.4**  Begin climbing the switchbacks.

**0.8**  Continue on the main road. Do not take the side road to the left (west).

A beautiful morning.

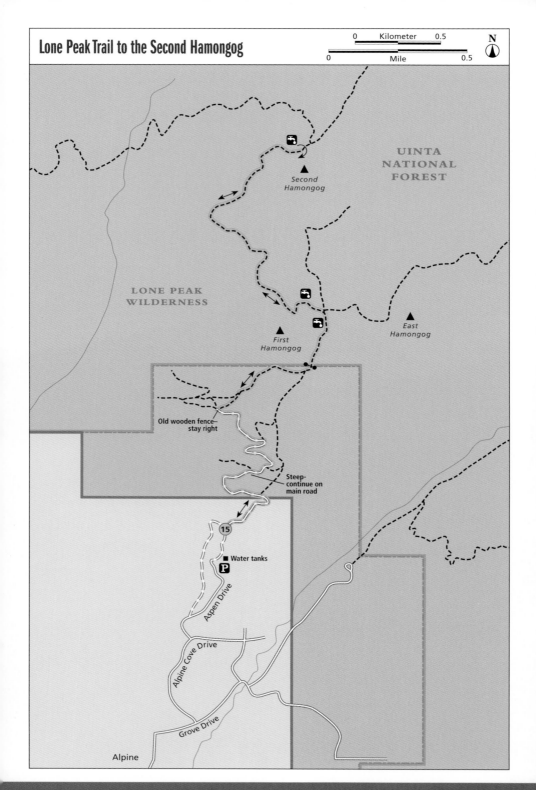

# Lone Peak Trail to the Second Hamongog

0    Kilometer    0.5

0    Mile    0.5

N

UINTA
NATIONAL
FOREST

Second
Hamongog

LONE PEAK
WILDERNESS

First
Hamongog

East
Hamongog

Old wooden fence—
stay right

Steep—
continue on
main road

15

■ Water tanks
P

Aspen Drive

Alpine Cove Drive

Grove Drive

Alpine

| 1.0 | The road becomes very steep, climbing sharp switchbacks. |
|---|---|
| 1.3 | Turn right off the main road at the old fence. The correct trail sends you uphill again, through a smaller rocky trail. GPS: N40 29.490' / W111 45.568' |
| 1.4 | Follow the wide dirt road, turning right (east). This is a very important turn. GPS: N40 29.557' / W111 45.470' |
| 1.7 | You will pass by a green gate. |
| 1.9 | You'll reach the First Hamongog, with water available for your pups. |
| 2.0 | Turn left to the Second Hamongog Trail. |
| 3.3 | Arrive at the Second Hamongog. Return the way you came. |
| 6.6 | Arrive back at the parking area. |

## NEARBY HIKES

Battle Creek, Stewart Falls, Horsetail Falls

## CREATURE COMFORTS

**WoodSpring Suites American Fork**, 57 N. 900 West, American Fork; (801) 492-1600. WoodSpring Suites is a pet-friendly hotel near Alpine and American Fork Canyon.

**Blues Street BBQ**, 648 E. State St., American Fork; (801) 692-7700; https://bluesstreet bbq.com. Blues Street is a standout BBQ spot with homemade sauces, Memphis-style ribs, and amazing mac and cheese. They have a dog-friendly patio and live music on the weekend.

# 16 HORSETAIL FALLS

## WHY GO?

Horsetail Falls is one of the prettiest waterfalls in Utah. The short, steep ascent to the falls has some boulder negotiation, pleasant shady sections, and water is available toward the halfway point. Timing is important, though, as it is very hot in the summer. You and your dog will enjoy this adventure, and the views are spectacular!

### THE RUNDOWN

**County:** Utah County
**Start:** Dry Creek trailhead in Alpine
**Distance:** 4.2 miles out and back
**Hiking time:** 2–3 hours
**Difficulty:** Moderate due to some exposure, technical sections, and danger near the falls
**Trailhead elevation:** 5,667 feet
**Highest point:** 7,178 feet
**Best seasons:** Spring, fall
**Trail surface:** Granite boulders, rocky, dirt
**Other trail users:** Horses, runners
**Canine compatibility:** Voice control
**Land status:** National Forest
**Fees and permits:** None
**Trail contact:** Pleasant Grove Ranger District, 390 N. 100 East, Pleasant Grove, UT 84062; (801) 785-3563

**Nearest town:** Alpine
**Trail tips:** The lower section of this hike can get quite hot, especially in the summer. Spring, fall, and winter will prove to be a much more enjoyable experience. Also use caution near the falls as the water is moving quickly at the base and is dangerous. Do not allow dogs to be in the water unleashed above a waterfall or near the base as the current is swift.
**Nat Geo TOPO! Map (USGS):** 7.5-minute *Dromedary Peak*
**Nat Geo Trails Illustrated Map:** *709: Wasatch Front North*

### FINDING THE TRAILHEAD

The Dry Creek Trailhead is tucked against the hills above east Alpine, Utah. From I-15, take the Highland/Alpine exit to the Timpanogos Highway (SR 92). Turn east and follow the Timpanogos Highway toward the mountains for approximately 7.5 miles. Turn left (north) on Main Street (5300 South) and continue straight (north), taking the second exit through the roundabout. At 200 North turn right (east), then take an almost immediate left (north) onto Grove Drive. Follow Grove Drive up past the cemetery as it winds up through neighborhoods eventually narrowing, passing the rodeo grounds. Grove Drive will "T" with Oakridge Drive. Turn right (east), then immediately left (north), staying on Grove Drive. The road will end at the large parking lot for Dry Creek. There are decommissioned large wooden signs that are not useful. The trail begins on the mountain side (east) of the lot and climbs immediately.
**Trailhead GPS:** N40 28.948' / W111 45.021'

## THE HIKE

Horsetail Falls is over 100 feet tall and is considered to be in the prestigious company of the other cascading Utah giants: Bridal Veil Falls, Battle Creek Falls, and Stewart Falls. The waterfall, like a horse's tail, begins from a narrow shoot and then fans out, cascading down the rock wall until it rejoins the currents below.

Nestled in the 30,078-acre Lone Peak Wilderness, the trail to Horsetail Falls shares proximity to some of Utah's finest peaks: Lone Peak and the Pfeifferhorn. This is a wild and beautiful area of Utah. From the very first step on the Dry Creek Trail, you will start ascending. The rough beginning sets the tone for a splendidly rocky trail that winds its way up to the base of Horsetail Falls. You will pass through dark timber and then into the light of the overlooks. Water is scarce for the first mile. It is best to not attempt this hike midday in summer. If you head out early, you can be safely under tree cover by the time the summer sun rises.

The start of the trail is two-track and has many smaller side trails tempting you up and calling you down. To get to Horsetail Falls, stay on the main trail, which heads east and climbs steadily. At 1 mile the trail narrows significantly. At 1.1 miles there is a drainage, lively with the spring runoff, that needs crossing. Looking up the drainage you will see erosion work on the tree roots along the gully. From here, the less pronounced trails frequently split off the main trail, reconnecting back to itself at various points along the way. Stick to the main trail as it forks around trail obstacles, always continuing east, and you'll get to your majestic destination: Horsetail Falls.

At mile 1.6 there is a creek crossing below the trail. You can hear the sound of a small waterfall, a relief at this point of your journey. Be sure to let your pup get a drink. Soon after the creek crossing, there are two trail options of equal merit, to the left and right. On the left trail you will have beautiful views of the valley and the waterfall. The right trail is less scenic but quicker with fewer rock obstacles. They both meet back up 50 or so yards down the trail.

Heading north on the left trail, just before mile 2, there is another creek crossing, a good place for pups to get a drink and cool off. Soon, the trail comes to a T junction. Take the trail headed north, following the scratched-in arrow on the wooden sign to Horsetail Falls.

At the falls please use caution: *Waterfalls are very dangerous to both dogs and humans.* Water has incredible force, and it can be deadly if a dog or person or both get swept over the falls. It is best to give dogs access to water at the creek along the trail before making your way to the falls. On the lower trail to the falls, there is a small clearing where you and your companion can take a break to enjoy a snack and nature's water show. Have fun and be careful as you explore around the falls. When you are finished, return the way you came.

## MILES AND DIRECTIONS

**0.0**  Follow the trail to the east side of the Dry Creek Trailhead parking area.

**0.5**  Stay on the main trail, ignoring the smaller trails splitting off. Continue climbing.

**1.1**  You will cross a drainage.

**1.6**  Arrive at a creek crossing that is a wonderful opportunity to water your pups.

**1.7**  Follow the trail to the left.

**1.9**  You'll cross a log bridge over a running stream and approach a T intersection with Dry Creek and North Mountain heading to the south. Take left fork (north) to Horsetail Falls.

# Horsetail Falls

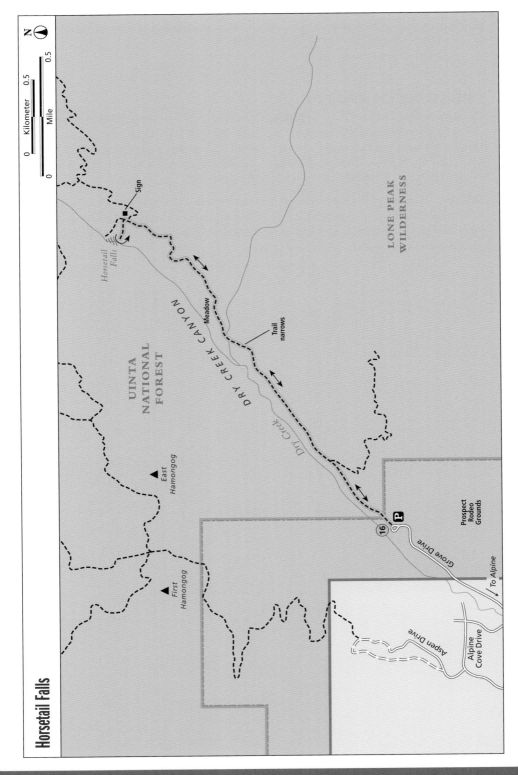

N

0        Kilometer        0.5

0        Mile        0.5

UINTA
NATIONAL
FOREST

LONE PEAK
WILDERNESS

Horsetail
Falls

Sign

Meadow

DRY CREEK CANYON

Trail
narrows

Dry Creek

East
Hamongog

First
Hamongog

Prospect
Rodeo
Grounds

Grove Drive

To Alpine

Aspen Drive

Alpine
Cove Drive

P

16

**2.1** Arrive at the falls. Plan to *leash your pups* and *use caution* as the water moves quickly. Head back the way you came.

**4.2** Arrive back at the trailhead.

## CREATURE COMFORTS

**Hampton Inn Provo**, 1511 S. 40 E St., Provo; (801) 377-6396; http://hamptoninn3 .hilton.com/en/hotels/utah/hampton-inn-provo-PVUHHHX/index.html. The Hampton Inn in Provo is easily accessible from I-15 and the hiking areas around Utah County. It is near both Utah Valley University and Brigham Young University and is surrounded by great restaurants and other attractions. Multiple pets allowed.

**Bombay House**, 463 N. University Ave., Provo; (801) 373-6677; www.bombayhouse .com. Bombay House is a popular Indian restaurant in Provo and Salt Lake City. They serve delicious curries, tandoori, and other traditional Indian fare. Their tikka masala is great and all their food can be ordered to-go.

# 17 SILVER LAKE IN AMERICAN FORK CANYON

## WHY GO?

The trail up to Silver Lake is easy to follow and has water available for pups. As it climbs, sometimes steeply, to a gorgeous mountain lake, it delivers almost unbelievable views of the valley below.

### THE RUNDOWN

**County:** Utah County
**Start:** Silver Lake Trailhead
**Distance:** 4.4 miles out and back
**Hiking time:** 2–3 hours
**Difficulty:** Moderate due to some steep ascents and exposure on southern-facing slope
**Trailhead elevation:** 7,586 feet
**Highest point:** 8,958 feet
**Best seasons:** Spring, fall
**Trail surface:** Dirt, boulders, primitive-bridge/stream crossings
**Other trail users:** Hikers, backpackers
**Canine compatibility:** Voice control
**Land status:** National Forest
**Fees and permits:** Small 3-day-pass fee

**Trail contact:** Pleasant Grove Ranger District, 390 N. 100 East, Pleasant Grove, UT 84062; (801) 785-3563; www.fs.usda.gov
**Nearest towns:** American Fork/ Alpine
**Trail tips:** The drive to the trailhead is partially unpaved. A high-clearance vehicle is recommended but not always necessary. It can get hot as you climb toward the lake, so be aware of rising temperatures and allow your dog some time at the water crossings.
**Nat Geo Topo! Map (USGS):** 7.5-minute *Timpanogos Cave, UT, Dromedary Peak, UT*
**Nat Geo Trails Illustrated Map:** *709: Wasatch Front North*

## FINDING THE TRAILHEAD

From I-15 in Lehi, Utah, take the Highland/Alpine exit toward Timpanogos (exit 284), Head east on the Timpanogos Highway (UT 92) for approximately 12 miles toward American Fork Canyon. You will see the canyon long before you enter it! From the fee station, continue east for 4.5 miles and turn north to Tibble Fork Reservoir on UT 144. At mile 2.4 the reservoir is on your right. From the parking area, it is possible to get some beautiful photos of Mount Timpanogos. Follow UT 144 north uphill around a sharp dog-leg turn onto FR 010. On your right (east), turn onto Silver Lake Road and follow the dirt road as it deteriorates and switchbacks up rather steeply and without guardrails. If you enter Granite Flat Campground, you have gone too far. This stretch of road may be a difficult drive—a high-clearance vehicle is recommended. Follow this road around switchbacks and over potholes for approximately 3 miles. You will pass Silver Lake Flat Reservoir on your right (east). Continue to the parking area for the Silver Lake Trail toward the northern end of the reservoir. There is a large parking lot with a vault toilet and information kiosk next to the trailhead.
**Trailhead GPS:** N40 30.421' / W111 39.384'

## THE HIKE

During the 1860s when the mining boom was in full swing in Utah's Cottonwood Canyon, it was only a matter of time before prospector's boots pushed the frontier south. The

**Wren shaking off the heat.**

routes into American Fork Canyon were difficult, and the promises fickle. Nevertheless Jacob and William Miller set out and found gold-filled ore. This induced the high-spirited frenzy that gold often does, and mining in the area flourished. However, by 1878 the seduction ended, the financial backing diminished, miners turned to ghosts, and the infrastructure of smelters and railroads evaporated with it.

The modern-day Silver Lake Trail, now used for recreation, travels north, meandering through the aspen trees and winding around rocky sections as you climb gently from the parking area. After approximately 0.5 mile on the right side of the trail just past an impressive upright boulder, your pup will enjoy a trail spur to Silver Creek. It is very peaceful at water's edge, and this little side trail is worth the pause to check out. The lushness of the lower section provides habitat to a variety of species. Look for deer and moose as you travel through this area.

The route is easy to follow, a confident trail that continues into the Lone Peak Wilderness Area without fanfare. Just before mile 1 there is a shallow but wide creek crossing. This is an ideal place to let your dog get a drink and cool off. Be careful on this crossing, though, as the rocks can be slippery.

After the crossing the trail no longer winds under the canopy of trees but instead switchbacks on the hot, south-facing hillside. This section is steep and exposed, but the views south will encourage you onward. At mile 2.2 you will crest a steep hill for your first peek of the shimmering beauty called Silver Lake. It will be a welcome sight to both you and your hot pup. Hike north until you find a spot to hike down to the water's edge.

Silver Lake is a man-made reservoir nestled in a glacial cirque. The green lake water surrounded by the rugged cliffs of Mount Timpanogos gives this place a pristine and inspiring distinction. The Timpanogos area of the Wasatch mountain range is primarily limestone created by compacted sediment from ancient oceans over 300 million years

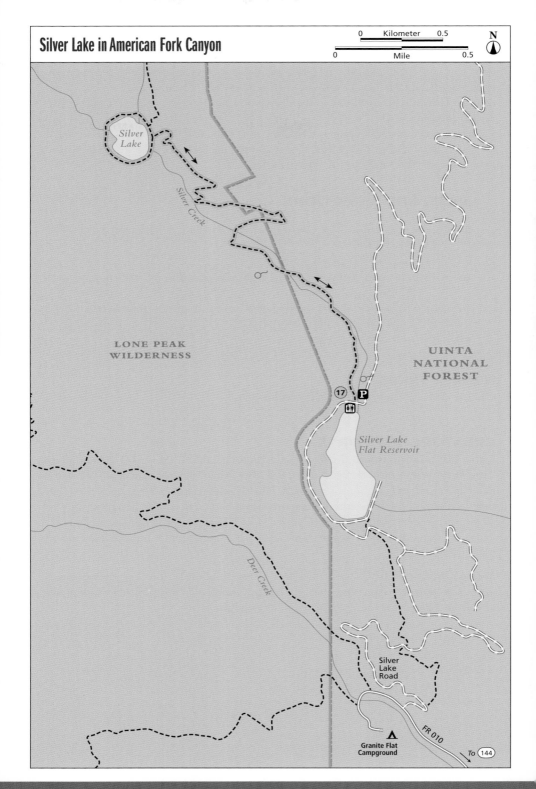

Silver Lake in American Fork Canyon

0    Kilometer    0.5

0    Mile    0.5

N

Silver Lake

Silver Creek

LONE PEAK
WILDERNESS

UINTA
NATIONAL
FOREST

17  P

Silver Lake
Flat Reservoir

Deer Creek

Silver
Lake
Road

Granite Flat
Campground

FR 010

To 144

ago. Glaciers and water erosion are, to this day, shaping the face of this mountain range, which can be seen in spades around this area.

As you hike the Silver Lake area, you will be kept company by White Baldy, a peak to the north, and the rising brook trout snatching treats from the lake's surface. If the hatch is right, the aquatic display is impressive, and maddening, especially for a fisherman caught without a pole.

There are a number of camping areas fairly close to the trail if an overnight is desired. If more mileage and adventure is needed, it is also possible to hike farther to Silver Glance Lake. Return to the trailhead the way you came.

## MILES AND DIRECTIONS

**0.0**   Park your car above Silver Flat Reservoir. The trail begins at the north end of the parking area, just past the restrooms.

**0.5**   Enter the Lone Peak Wilderness Area.

**1.0**   Ford Silver Creek. This water is important for your dog, as the next section is hot and steep.

**2.2**   Crest a small hill to Silver Lake. There is a trail around the perimeter worth exploring. Return the way you came.

**4.4**   Arrive back at the trailhead.

## NEARBY HIKES
Cascade Springs, Timpooneke Trail to Scout Falls

## CREATURE COMFORTS
**Little Mill Campground**, Little Mill Campground Road, Provo, UT 84604; (801) 226-3564; www.recreation.gov (search Little Mill). The campground is approximately 4 miles up American Fork Canyon and near Tibble Fork Reservoir. There are shaded sites near a creek with vault toilets but no water or hookup services. This is a great spot for accessing the American Fork Canyon hikes, Mount Timpanogos attractions, and incredible sights along the Alpine Loop Scenic Byway heading toward Sundance. Reserve on www.recreation.gov.

**Marco's Pizza**, 4723 W. Cedar Hills Dr., Cedar Hills; (801) 763-0000; www.marcos.com. This popular pizza chain offers great pizza, wings, and cheesy bread in Alpine and Highland. They deliver and offer takeout for a yummy picnic.

# HIGH COUNTRY

*"When you go to the mountains, you see them and you admire them. In a sense, they give you a challenge, and you try to express that challenge by climbing them."*

—Edmund Hillary

The miles of crisscrossing trails in Utah's high country meander through the sage flats of Park City, throughout the Uinta mountain range, and past the cascading waterfalls of Provo Canyon. These hikes lead the beginner-through-intrepid hiker into a memorable adventure at lofty elevations. From certain vantage points, the horizons are immense and foreboding, dappled with meadows and lakes, and occasionally ending in cascading water. It is a paradise for the seekers of the forests and all the inspiration that those spaces conjure. You and your dog will be able to negotiate winding trails leading to ledges overlooking valleys filled with potential adventure and unrelenting beauty.

**Enjoying the mountains!**

A majority of the hikes in this section are located in the high mountain country of the Uintas. The Uintas have roots leading back to the Precambrian era—some rocks date back 2.5 billion years. The evidence of immense geologic pressure, seen in the nearly vertical fault lines, gives this area a ruggedness that is not replicated anywhere else in the state. It is also one of the most significant mountain ranges that runs east to west in the country and the tallest mountain range in Utah. With its talus slopes, glacial moraines, immense basins dotted with lakes teeming with cutthroat, rainbow, tiger, brown, and other species of fish, this area is a hiker's paradise. The slopes of these mountains are home to quaking aspens and coniferous trees such as lodgepole pine, Douglas fir, and Engelmann spruce. If you are lucky, you will catch a glimpse of mountain creatures including elk, deer, moose, black bears, and mountain lions.

These areas in the Uinta Mountains have much to offer in terms of beauty, solitude, adventure, and miles, but there is also a seriousness to them that should not be taken for granted. Knowing where you are and having a good sense of the terrain around you will help keep you oriented and safe. Carrying a compass in the high wooded country is also vital—always know how to get back to your car. If you do become lost, stay where you are and create a shelter for yourself and your dog to keep warm and dry. Always tell someone where you are hiking—it is crucial in this area.

While hiking in the high country, it is important to remember the threat of after-noon thunderstorms, with their bone-quaking cracks of thunder that howl through the mountain valleys and passes. This can wreak havoc on you and your dog and can be very dangerous. Plan your hikes around the weather patterns of the time of year that you will be traveling. Also, be thoughtful of your dog and the stress these storms could create for her and plan accordingly. Some dogs will bolt during thunderstorms and may become lost. Also bring extra layers of clothing in case a rare but not unheard of blizzard in May or June occurs.

The High Country section includes hikes around Park City, the Uintas, and Provo Canyon, which are not far from Salt Lake City.

# 18 STEWART FALLS

## WHY GO?

Stewart Falls is a classic Utah dog hike north of Sundance Resort in Provo Canyon. Although popular, the sight of the 200-foot waterfall at the trail's end is worth every step. The trail has moderate climbs, can get hot, and is busy on weekends. If you can plan a midweek early start time, it will be a rich and rewarding experience for both you and your dog.

### THE RUNDOWN

**County:** Utah County
**Start:** From Aspen Grove parking area
**Distance:** 3.5 miles out and back
**Hiking time:** 2–3 hours
**Difficulty:** Moderate due to sun exposure, a rocky section, and a steep section near the falls
**Trailhead elevation:** 6,860 feet
**Highest point:** 7,159 feet
**Trail surface:** Rock, packed dirt
**Other trail users:** Hikers
**Canine compatibility:** On leash
**Land status:** Uinta-Wasatch-Cache National Forest/Mount Timpanogos Wilderness Area

**Fees and permits:** Small 3-day-pass fee
**Trail contact:** Pleasant Grove Ranger District, 390 N. 100 East, Pleasant Grove, UT 84062; (801) 785-3563; www.fs.usda.gov
**Nearest town:** Provo or Heber
**Trail tips:** This is a popular hike. It is best done early or at off-peak times.
**Nat Geo TOPO! Map (USGS):** 7.5-minute *Aspen Grove*
**Nat Geo Trails Illustrated Map:** *709: Wasatch Front North*

### FINDING THE TRAILHEAD

From the mouth of Provo Canyon, drive 7 miles north and turn left (west) on the Alpine Loop Scenic Byway (SR 92) to Sundance Resort. This turn is almost immediately after the tunnel. Drive 2 miles up the canyon, passing Sundance Resort on your left, and continue driving to the fee station. The large Aspen Grove parking lot is located on the left side of the road just past the fee station. The trailhead is on the west side of the parking lot, just to the north of the restrooms.
**Trailhead GPS:** N40 24.254' / W111 36.325'

### THE HIKE

From the Aspen Grove parking area, work your way to the trail's beginning just to the right (north) of the vault toilets. After a few strides there is a trail junction. Take the left (south) fork to Stewart Falls. The west fork would take you on a difficult trail to Mount Timpanogos. After the junction the trail will wind through the trees, climbing steeply up a small hill with rocks and roots exposed by years of wear by the paws and soles of happy hikers. After the hill the trail will continue to climb in and out of the dappled shade provided by conifers, then eventually aspens.

There are side trails that dive off east toward the BYU Alumni Center, but the main trail is obvious and well worn. At mile 0.5 you'll pass a large water tank on the left side of the trail. It stores water for the camps and buildings below.

Hiking up the hot section. Remember to bring water and a hat!

If visiting in the summer or fall months, the hiking will get hot at this point. The trail lacks a lot of shade as cover. Be sure to keep an eye on your dog and watch for signs of overheating (excessive panting, lying down repeatedly, and lagging behind). There are places along the way that afford some shade if you start getting hot. Look for small side trails and fallen aspen logs to sit on while enjoying a snack and some water and give your dog a chance to cool off some if the temperatures are rising.

This hike provides ample opportunity for your dog to socialize as you travel along. If you have an antisocial dog, do not attempt this hike on the weekends. The narrow sections make meet-and-greets frequent and unavoidable. As you continue along, there will be sections with exposed tree roots, so watch your step.

At mile 1.7 you will traverse a scree field that is somewhat rough. This is not a good place to stop for a break because of the danger of rocks falling. Once across this section of the trail, you will begin to descend toward the falls. There are a couple tricky spots to navigate, and mild teamwork might be necessary so your dog will not be challenged.

At mile 1.8 you will arrive at an obvious lookout point for the falls. From this vantage point, you will be able to witness the splendor of Stewart Falls and its two-tier cascade of glacial runoff. This waterfall is an impressive 200 feet tall, and you'll likely see kids and dogs running around at the base, cooling off. From your vantage point, there is the option to get closer to the waterfall to your left. Follow the side trail going east that will steeply descend toward the river below. As you get closer to the water, the mist coming off from the falls will coat you and your dog with little water droplets that shimmer in the sun. On a hot day nothing could be better. There will be a cacophony of happy dog voices and much splashing and carrying on. Your dog may want to join. When you are finished cooling off, turn around and hike back up the steep hill, turning right and making your way back to the parking area.

## MILES AND DIRECTIONS

- **0.0**  Follow the trail for Stewart Falls to the north of the restrooms at the parking area for Aspen Grove.
- **0.1**  Stay left, heading south and following the sign for Stewart Falls.
- **0.4**  Continue on the main trail south, avoiding the side trail to the Aspen Grove Amphitheater.
- **1.0**  There is an opening in the trees with views to the south, a great place to take pictures.
- **1.7**  Use caution as you cross a scree field.
- **1.8**  Arrive at a beautiful lookout to the waterfalls. Descend to the falls using the side trail to the left. Return the way you came.
- **3.5**  Arrive back at the trailhead.

## NEARBY HIKES

Cascade Springs, Mount Timpanogos, Timpanogos Falls

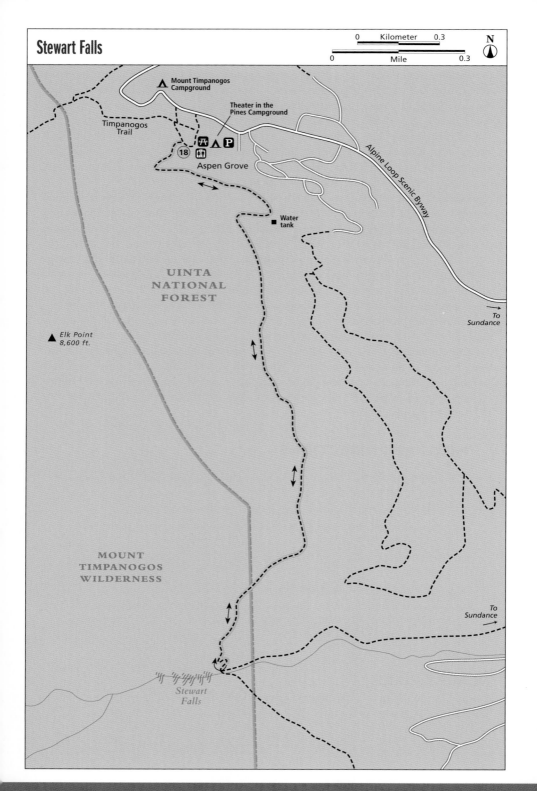

Stewart Falls

0 Kilometer 0.3
0 Mile 0.3

N

Mount Timpanogos
Campground

Theater in the
Pines Campground

Timpanogos
Trail

18

Aspen Grove

Water
tank

Alpine Loop Scenic Byway

To
Sundance

UINTA
NATIONAL
FOREST

Elk Point
8,600 ft.

MOUNT
TIMPANOGOS
WILDERNESS

To
Sundance

Stewart
Falls

## CREATURE COMFORTS

**Sundance Mountain Resort**, 8841 Alpine Loop Scenic Byway, Sundance; (801) 225-4107; www.sundanceresort.com. Sundance Resort is an upscale ski resort with an interesting history rooted in Hollywood and made famous by actor-producer-director Robert Redford. It is a beautiful area located in Provo Canyon on the Alpine Scenic Byway that connects with American Fork Canyon and Mount Timpanogos. The hotel is comfortable, with friendly staff and amazing grounds. There are on-site restaurants and attractions as well as easy access to the nearby hikes. There is a pet fee.

**The Tree Room and Foundry Grill, Sundance Mountain Resort**, 8841 Alpine Loop Scenic Byway, Sundance; (801) 225-4107; wwwsundanceresort.com. The Tree Room and Foundry Grill at Sundance Mountain Resort serve amazing country-chic food and beverages with options for many diet types and preferences. The Tree Room is an upscale spot with a unique atmosphere. Reservations are recommended. The Foundry Grill is more laid-back and offers wood-fired pizza and fresh ingredients. Great for brunch! No pups inside either restaurant, please.

# 19  BLOODS LAKE

## WHY GO?

Bloods Lake is a short and classic hike of the Wasatch that winds through the forest and ends at a beautiful tree-lined lake. This hike is used by many families and is a good hike for playful, friendly pups who enjoy a swim.

### THE RUNDOWN

**County:** Salt Lake
**Start:** Guardsman Pass
**Distance:** 1.0 mile out and back
**Hiking time:** About 1.5 hours
**Difficulty:** Easy but with a short steep section
**Trailhead elevation:** 9,686 feet
**Highest point:** 9,686 feet
**Best season:** Summer. Guardsman Pass is closed in winter.
**Trail surface:** Dirt, rocks
**Other trail users:** Hikers
**Canine compatibility:** Voice control
**Land status:** Bonanza Flats Conservation, Utah Open Lands
**Fees and permits:** None
**Trail contact:** Utah Open Lands, 1488 Main St., Salt Lake City, UT 84115; (801) 463-6156

**Nearest towns:** Park City and Salt Lake City
**Trail tips:** The parking area borders part of the Salt Lake watershed, which is off-limits to pups. To avoid this area, stick to the east side of the road. Do not go west out of the parking lot descending into Big Cottonwood Canyon with your dog. The parking area can get very busy on weekends. It's considered easy but has some steep sections, and water is available at the lake for your dog.
**Nat Geo TOPO! Map (USGS):** 7.5-Minute *Brighton, UT*
**Nat Geo Trails Illustrated Map:** *709: Wasatch Front North*

## FINDING THE TRAILHEAD

From the mouth of Big Cottonwood Canyon in Salt Lake City, head up Big Cottonwood Canyon Road for approximately 14 miles past Solitude Ski Resort. Across from the fire station, take a sharp left onto Guardsman Pass Road. Follow this road approximately 3 miles as it winds up the canyon to the summit. Park at the summit. The trail begins to the south above the basin. (**Note:** Dogs are not allowed in Big Cottonwood Canyon.)

From Park City, follow Marsac Avenue up through Deer Valley Ski Area to the roundabout at the Montage Resort. Take the roundabout exit that continues up Marsac Avenue as it winds up to a summit past the parking area for some mountain bike trails. Continue south until you reach the intersection of Guardsman Pass Road. Turn right onto Guardsman Pass Road and head west up the rough road until you reach the saddle and parking area at the top of Guardsman Pass.
**Trailhead GPS:** N40 36.382' / W111 33.314'

## THE HIKE

From the parking area, the trail begins to the south past the concrete barriers. There are two trailheads that begin from this area. To Bloods Lake, take the eastern trail, on the left. This trail contours the hillside for a bit rather than making an immediate climb. The trail is easy to follow and begins descending through the pines eventually dropping rather quickly to the quaint lake approximately 0.5 mile in. During your descent you will hike through quiet groves. Look for hawks looping over the meadow and wildlife snoozing or foraging below. Once at the lake, enjoy the scenery while your pup enjoys the water. It's a beautiful place occasionally populated by others enjoying their time away from the city. At your leisure return the way you came. The climb out can be a leg burner—for adult, child, and hound alike—but the views are stunning for the effort.

There are many stories to be told about Bloods Lake, but probably the most important is the effort that was made to protect this area. It is a classic story of the bulldozer verses the wilderness. So often the story is the same. The houses go up, the gates close, and the "no trespassing" begins. This time, however, the trees won, the moose won, the aspens won, and Bonanza Flats Conservation was created. The process was an arduous one and nothing less than heroic. The 1,390 acres encompasses lakes, migration routes, back-country ski runs, snowshoe trails, and numerous homes for the smaller and overlooked wildlife. Utah Open Lands and their mission to preserve open spaces around the state of Utah deserve a pat on the back, along with dozens of businesses, organizations, cities, and individuals that helped fund-raise for this property. For more information, please visit www.utahopenlands.org.

The hike to Bloods Lake is one way to celebrate the acquisition of such a beautiful place.

Martin posing by Bloods Lake.

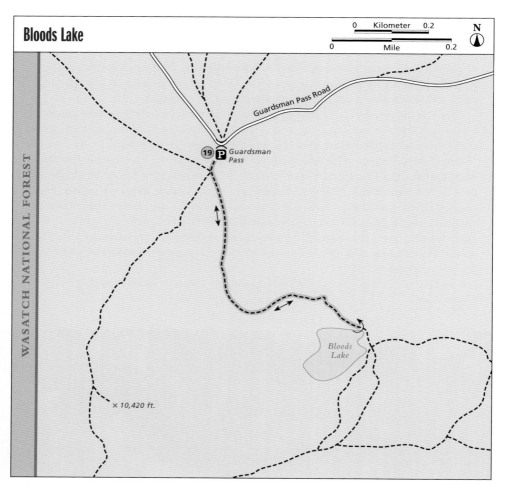

## MILES AND DIRECTIONS

**0.0** Walk south of the parking area to the trailhead. Take the left trail that parallels the hillside as opposed to climbing immediately, past the concrete barriers.

**0.5** Descend steeply. Bloods Lake will be visible to your right. Enjoy a walk around the lake and return the way you came.

**1.0** Arrive back at your car.

## NEARBY HIKES

Millcreek-area hikes, Run-a-Muk, Round Valley

## CREATURE COMFORTS

**Montage Deer Valley**, 9100 Marsac Ave., Park City; (435) 604-1300; www.montage hotels.com. The Montage is an upscale resort with beautiful grounds located among Park City's world-class trails. There are a variety of lodging options and packages available, and while this is a pricier option, there are typically great rates in the summer and fall. While you are here, enjoy the on-site spa and dining options as well as direct access to the famous Park City Mid-Mountain Trail (watch for bikes and runners!).

**High West Saloon**, 703 Park Ave., Park City; (435) 649-8300; www.highwest.com. High West is a Utah staple and a globally recognized distillery. They offer incredible food options including burgers, salads, and seasonal fare. There is typically live music on the weekends and a great patio (not pup-permitted yet).

# 20 **RUN-A-MUK**

## WHY GO?

Run-a-Muk is a 43-acre, fully fenced area in Park City, Utah, designated for off-leash dogs to run and play as their owners wander an easy trail that loops along the hillside. This is a perfect place to help dogs learn the rules of the trail and practice socialization and recall.

### THE RUNDOWN

**County:** Summit
**Start:** Run-a-Muk Trailhead
**Distance:** 1.0-mile loop with additional trail options
**Hiking time:** About 1 hour
**Difficulty:** Easy, with little elevation gain and well-established trails
**Trailhead elevation:** 6,438 feet
**Highest point:** 6,537 feet
**Best season:** Year-round
**Trail surface:** Dirt
**Other trail users:** Other hikers with their pups
**Canine compatibility:** Voice control
**Land status:** Public

**Fees and permits:** None
**Trail contact:** Basin Recreation, 5715 Trailside Dr., Park City, UT 84098; (435) 649-1564; www.basinrecreation.org
**Nearest towns:** Kimball Junction, Park City
**Trail tips:** It can get hot out in the sage flats, so bring water for your pups in the summer. And please clean up after your dog!
**Nat Geo TOPO! (USGS):** 7.5-minute *Park City UT, West*
**Nat Geo Trails Illustrated Map:** *709: Wasatch Front North*

### FINDING THE TRAILHEAD

From Kimball Junction heading south on UT 224, turn west (right) onto Olympic Parkway Drive toward the Olympic Park and the obvious ski jumps lining the mountain. Take the last exit of the roundabout up the road. The parking area for Run-a-Muk will be on your left. There is additional parking farther up the road on your right with tunnel access to the trails.
**Trailhead GPS:** N40 42.975' / W111 33.180'

## THE HIKE

There are few hikes in Utah that offer you and your dog the opportunity to run off-leash with full permission. Run-a-Muk is part dog park and part hiking trail, a rare and important combination in the introduction to hiking. This space allows you to enjoy watching your dog romp and play in delightful expression, learning trail manners with limited risk to some of the dangers you may encounter on a trail. The trail is simple and easy to follow without much elevation gain.

Walking the various unmarked trails in the Run-a-Muk area will allow you and your pup to weave along rolling sagebrush and wander through the aspen trees. This dog-friendly space allows dogs with high exercise needs to run as much as they would like with little risk. For social dogs, this is also a great place to find a playmate. Often you will see pups jumping and diving through the sage in fits of pure joy together. This space is made for you to practice voice control and recall training, allowing your dog's understanding of commands to be tested and refined during other hiking adventures you will have.

Millie and Juniper ready to run amok.
RACHEL WARNER

From the parking area, walk south toward the double set of gates. Once through this canine-containment system, walk south along the loop underneath the giant ski jumps and past the tunnel leading to the other parking area. Built for the 2002 Winter Olympics, these ski jumps, along with a bobsled track and other Olympic-inspired activities, are open year round for training and tourism.

Past the tunnel the trail continues its leisurely wander through clumps of young aspen trees and in and out of clearings. Depending on the time of year, you and your dog may find a small stream that you can easily step over. Once you see the big power poles, you'll find a junction. Turn right to complete a wider loop or take the left for a shortcut. There will be some spur trails leading up slightly into the hills, which is an alternative for extra-energetic dogs needing some additional elevation and added opportunity for exercise.

The trail will turn north. Follow it past the shortcut described above as it winds through the sage in sweeping serpentine patterns, climbing and descending mild rises as you go. Your dog and you will be meeting other dogs and people out enjoying their time together. From Great Pyrenees to Chihuahuas, this area is a popular social spot. The trail is wide and easy to follow with clear views of the path ahead, allowing you to keep a watchful eye on your pup running ahead.

You will weave your way down toward a neighborhood of condos. Here, you can follow the Downward Dog Trail to the east down to the field or continue on the main trail across a bridge and up some switchbacks. You'll climb slightly and the parking area will come into view. Do another loop if you and your pup need more, or call it quits and head for the gates. From the double gate, remember to leash your dog as the parking lot can be busy.

## MILES AND DIRECTIONS

**0.0** From the Run-a-Muk parking area, the trail begins through the double gates to the south.

**0.2** You will cross a stream, then shortly after, the trail splits. Veer right at the intersection near the power lines for a longer loop.

**0.5** Follow the main trail north, or loop toward the field.

**1.0** Arrive back at the trailhead.

## NEARBY HIKES
Glenwild, Ecker Hill Trails, Round Valley

## CREATURE COMFORTS
**Holiday Inn Express**, 1501 W. Ute Blvd., Park City; (435) 658-1600; www.ihg.com. The Holiday Inn in Kimball Junction is located just off the highway between Park City and Salt Lake City. This hotel has easy access to many of the Wasatch Front and high-country area hikes and is surrounded by many great restaurants and shopping. Pet fee applies.

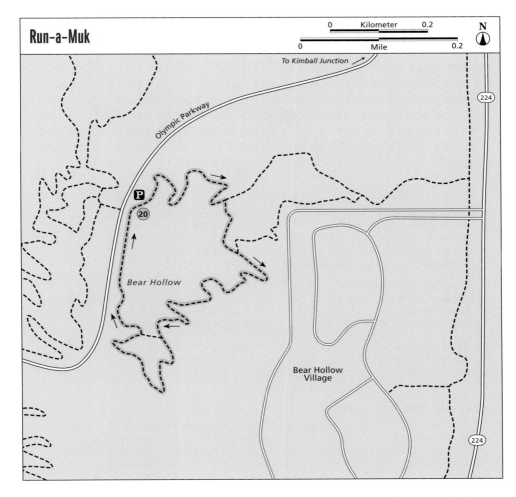

**Silver Star Cafe**, 1825 Three Kings Dr., Park City; (435) 655-3456. www.thesilver starcafe.com. The Silver Star Cafe is a contemporary American cafe offering from-scratch seasonal foods, live music, and beautiful views of the Park City area. They have a pup-permitted patio and amazing menu. They are also located at the base of the Armstrong Trail, a great bonus hike managed by Basin Recreation at Park City Resort.

# 21 WILLOW CREEK

## WHY GO?

A loop hike in beautiful backcountry with ample water and gorgeous views. During the fall the hills flame red as the scrub-oak leaves turn. Wildlife abounds in this space. Look for beaver dams, eagles, elk, and mule deer. Here, you are walking the hills of historic Utah sheep country. This is a great trail for the hiker and fisher. Be sure to acquire a permit before heading out if you want to fish.

### THE RUNDOWN

**County:** Wasatch
**Start:** Willow Creek Trailhead
**Distance:** 4.0-mile loop
**Hiking time:** 2–4 hours
**Difficulty:** Easy, with little elevation or exposure
**Trailhead elevation:** 7,920 feet
**Highest point:** 8,278 feet
**Best season:** Fall
**Trail surface:** Dirt trail, stream crossings
**Other trail users:** Hikers, horses
**Canine compatibility:** Voice control
**Land status:** National Forest

**Fees and permits:** None
**Trail contact:** Heber-Kamas Ranger District, 2460 S. Hwy. 40, Heber City, UT 84032; (435) 654-0470
**Nearest town:** Heber City
**Trail tips:** There are numerous stream crossings, so either wear shoes that can get wet or bring two pairs so you can switch them out.
**Nat Geo TOPO! Map (USGS):** 7.5-minute *Co-Op Creek*
**Nat Geo Trails Illustrated Map:** *709: Wasatch Front North*

### FINDING THE TRAILHEAD

From Heber City, continue south on US 40 through town toward Daniels Summit. US 40 will wind up through this beautiful canyon for approximately 25 miles. Continue past the Daniels Summit Lodge for approximately 2.8 miles, then look for the turnoff for FR 049. Turn left (north) onto FR 049, which is a very large dirt road with vault toilets. Turn right (east) onto FR 735 (GPS: N40 17.625' / W111 13.269'). Follow FR 735 for approximately 0.9 mile, past a camping spot to the parking area for Willow Creek. This is a popular area for equestrians, so please be mindful of vehicles pulling horse trailers. The trailhead is directly east of the parking lot.
**Trailhead GPS:** N40 18.329' / W111 12.598'

### THE HIKE

Willow Creek is a babbling stream and the trail offers a gorgeous hike that wanders through meadows and mountain forests, with plenty of chances for your pup to get a drink and cool off throughout the hike. From the trailhead, hike east. Shortly after you begin, you will cross Willow Creek. The trail curves east on a wider two-track trail with boulders, views into the dark timber, and beautiful grasses that sway in the wind. Willows grow all along the stream, providing habitat for birds and food for moose and elk. This is the stick to the lollipop-shaped hike. Watch the hills for deer as you go, and enjoy the views unfolding in front of you.

The next stream crossing is at mile 0.5 and is the most difficult crossing. It is wide and sometimes muddy from cattle use. If it looks difficult, try crossing farther north, upstream. Once on the other side, the trail splits in a loop around the mountain directly in front of you. You can take either route, but the north split is preferred.

The trail is obvious and crosses the creek occasionally. Your dog will love flopping in the gentle currents. At mile 0.9 the trail curves east, passing a tempting side canyon. "1910" is carved in an aspen or two up in that area, evidence that cowboys have roamed these hills for over a hundred years. As you head east again, look for wildlife on the far hills—elk herds and big bucks have been seen on numerous occasions while exploring this area.

Continue heading northeast. As the small valley narrows, look at the interesting geology off the main trail. As you continue, the small valley you have been walking through opens. There will be a trail heading north past some very old corrals at mile 1.8. Continue right, heading south to make the loop. It can get a little muddy here and the trail may not be perfectly clear, but head south. The trail will be very visible soon. Remember you are hiking a loop. Look back over your shoulder toward the rocky fins. The view is beautiful, an example of the incredible geology of the Uinta mountain range.

As you continue south, you will climb to the top of a small rise. At the top of this rise, the flora changes into more desertlike sagebrush with iron-rich soil and you'll see an occasional beaver dam. At mile 2.3 there is a side trail, which you may decide to explore, but the main trail continues south. Make sure you have a map if you decide to deviate from the main trail, especially if you haven't been to this area before.

The trail will continue the loop west and another creek will become accessible for your dogs. Watch for signs of beavers around 2.4 miles. The sun on this (south) side can

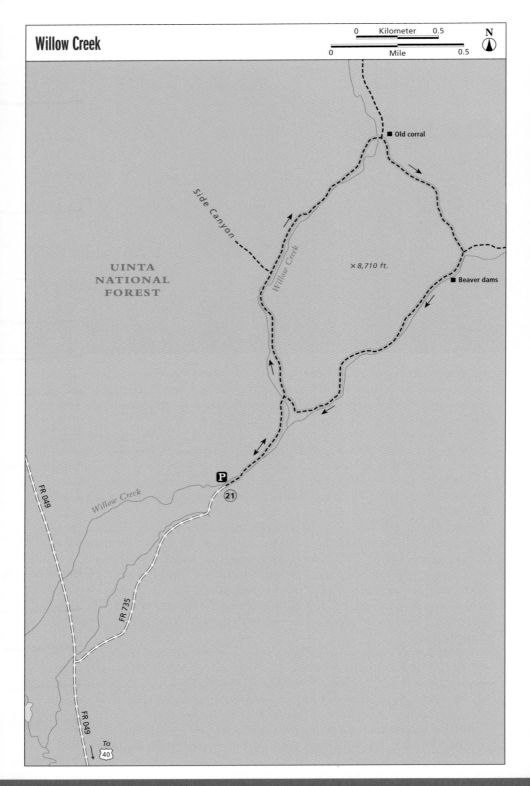

# Willow Creek

0 Kilometer 0.5

0 Mile 0.5

**N**

Side Canyon

Old corral

Willow Creek

UINTA
NATIONAL
FOREST

× 8,710 ft.

Beaver dams

**P**

㉑

FR 049

Willow Creek

FR 735

FR 049

To
㊵

be hot in the summer. As you round the bend, the valley opens up. Water is plentiful here and hot pups can get a drink as they please. As you continue you'll begin to see the trail you started on. At mile 3.4 you'll intersect the trail and complete your loop, heading west back to your vehicle.

## MILES AND DIRECTIONS

**0.0**  Follow the trail to the east of the parking area.

**0.1**  Cross Willow Creek.

**0.5**  Arrive at the junction for the loop, turn left, heading north.

**1.8**  Continue south past the trail split.

**2.3**  Continue south past the side trail.

**2.4**  Pass the beaver dam.

**3.4**  Complete the loop, then turn left heading west back to the parking area.

**4.0**  Arrive back at the parking area.

## NEARBY HIKES
Stewart Falls, Fifth Water Trail

## CREATURE COMFORTS
**Lodgepole Campground**, FR 113, Heber City, UT 84082; (801) 466-6411. Lodgepole is a popular campground in Daniels Canyon between Heber City and Strawberry Reservoir. Surrounded by pine, aspen, and fir trees, it is shady and a great spot during the summer. This campground has drinking water and flush toilets as well as group sites. No hookups for trailers, but a dump station is nearby. Reservations are recommended on www.recreation.gov.

**Lodge Pole Grill**, 17000 Highway 40, Daniels Summit Pass, Heber City. Lodge Pole Grill is located in the gorgeous Daniels Summit Lodge and offers rustic fare in a relaxed atmosphere. Their menu focuses on western-style mountain fare such as BBQ, burgers, and roasts, and they serve breakfast, lunch, and dinner. No pups, please.

# 22 NOBLETTS SPRING

## WHY GO?

Nobletts Spring is a short and sweet hike through the lush streamside ecology of the southern side of the Uintas. It is a family-friendly walk with plenty of water that is easy for older dogs.

### THE RUNDOWN

**County:** Summit
**Start:** Nobletts Trailhead
**Distance:** 2.0 miles out and back
**Hiking time:** 1–2 hours
**Difficulty:** Easy. This is a short hike with little elevation gain.
**Trailhead elevation:** 7,580 feet
**Highest point:** 7,814 feet
**Best seasons:** Summer, fall
**Trail surface:** Dirt trail, some tree root navigation, shale, stream crossing on logs
**Other trail users:** Horses, possible bikers
**Canine compatibility:** On leash (there are free-ranging sheep in the area)

**Land status:** National Forest
**Fees and permits:** None
**Trail contact:** Heber/Kamas Ranger District, 50 E. Center St., Kamas, UT 84036; (435) 783-4338; www.fs.usda .gov/gov/uwcnf
**Nearest towns:** Woodland, Kamas
**Trail tips:** The road between Francis and Hanna is closed during the winter.
**Nat Geo Topo! Map (USGS):** 7.5-minute *Soapstone Basin*
**Nat Geo Trails Illustrated Map:** *711: High Uinta Wilderness*

### FINDING THE TRAILHEAD

From Kamas, turn right (south) out of town toward Francis and Woodland on UT 32. At the four-way stop in Francis, turn left (east) toward Woodland onto UT 35. Continue for approximately 8 miles, then turn left at the sign into the Nobletts Spring Trail parking area.

This is a very large parking area and a building with toilets on the south end of the lot. The trailhead, with a "Nobletts" sign, begins to the northeast of the parking area and continues north toward the wetlands.
**Trailhead GPS:** N40 32.567' / W111 05.697'

## THE HIKE

From the parking area, follow the sign for Nobletts that begins as a dirt trail and heads north toward the wetlands and lush forest. The trail drops quickly toward a marsh with ponds where moose occasionally like to hang out. Moose are one of the more dangerous critters you will run into out on the trail in Utah. Unlike a deer or an elk, a moose will often turn and face an aggressor, real or not, and will charge if spooked. So keep a look out, and watch your dog, who will often clue you in to their presence. Moose are smelly, and a dog's nose will pick up on them right away.

After the more open feel of the wetlands, the trail becomes more narrow and the canyon feel begins. You will walk through eroded banks and tree roots, past deep pools and crystal-clear water. Continue up the canyon along the south side of Nobletts Creek. The trail is easy to follow and is speckled with columbine flowers. The hike continues

Columbines on the trail.

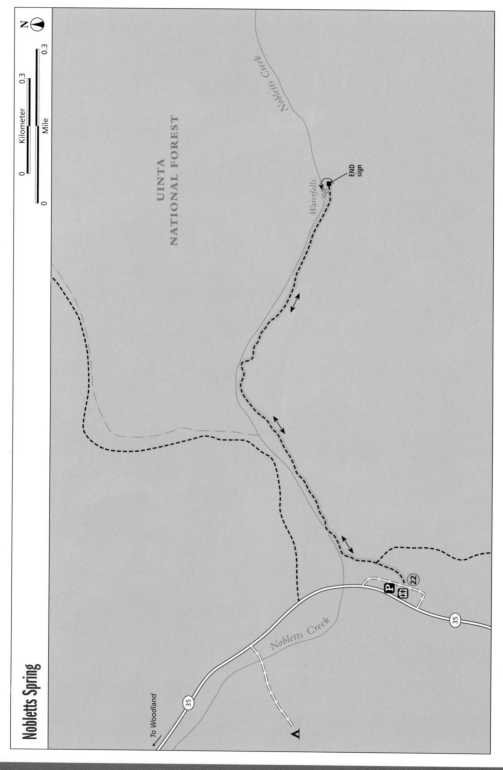

Nobletts Spring

UINTA
NATIONAL FOREST

Nobletts Creek

Waterfalls

END
sign

Nobletts Creek

To Woodland

35

35

22

N

Kilometer
0                    0.3

Mile
0                    0.3

upward, climbing and falling through little deviations in the trail. There are a handful of side trails, but stick to the main trail.

You will cross logs to avoid boggy sections of the trail and there are tree roots that add some small challenges to this trail. Continue following the clear path past the waterfalls and pools. There are plenty of spots to stop and sit, enjoying the air or view. Use caution. Waterfalls are dangerous for dogs if they fall in. Leash up if you have an overly curious pup.

The trail ends at the "End" sign after approximately 1 mile, although there is a trail that continues steeply up a talus hill that may be worth exploring. When you are finished at Nobletts Spring, return the way you came. This family-friendly hike is simple and beautiful.

## MILES AND DIRECTIONS

**0.0** Follow the trail indicated by the signs, heading northeast at the center of the parking area.

**1.0** Arrive at Nobletts Spring, where you will see an "End" sign nailed to a tree. Return the way you came. It is possible to continue farther up the trail, which will create a loop with Log Hollow.

**2.0** Arrive back at the Nobletts parking area.

## NEARBY HIKES

Log Hollow, Soapstone Basin

## CREATURE COMFORTS

**Woodland Farmhouse Inn**, 2602 E. State Hwy. 35, Kamas; (435) 783-2903; www .woodlandfarmhouseinn.com. Woodland Farmhouse is a must-visit if staying near the Uintas. This is a cute and cozy bed-and-breakfast built in an 1897 farmhouse with amazing views of the mountains and access to Kamas-area trails. They allow dogs in some rooms for a fee and serve a great breakfast. Reserve in advance as this is a popular spot for events.

**Woodland Biscuit Company**, 2734 E. UT 35, Woodland; (435) 783-4202; www .woodlandbiscuitcompany.com. Like many other Woodland accommodations and restaurants, the Woodland Biscuit Company is cozy, classic, and a worthy stop. They serve homemade country fare including home-style biscuits and gravy, sandwiches, soups, and other great options. The owners and staff are welcoming and kind. Look for the large metal "Cafe" sign on the old building with an outdoor, dog friendly patio.

# 23 FEHR LAKE TRAIL

## WHY GO?

The short walk to Fehr Lake gives families and elderly dogs a chance to get out into the Uinta Forest without too many obstacles. For those wanting more, the trail gets rougher and continues to three other beautiful high mountain lakes. With boardwalks over flowing streams, rocky descents, and beautiful surroundings, this trail provides a wonderful afternoon spent with your dog.

### THE RUNDOWN

**County:** Duchesne
**Start:** Fehr Lake Trailhead
**Distance:** 3.6 miles out and back
**Hiking time:** 2–4 hours
**Difficulty:** Easy. This hike follows boardwalks and has little elevation gain, but it is in high country.
**Trailhead/highest point elevation:** 10,369 feet
**Low point:** 9,928 feet
**Best season:** Summer
**Trail surface:** Boardwalks over marshes, dirt trail, and rocky trail especially on the trail to the lower lakes

**Other trail users:** Horses
**Canine compatibility:** On leash
**Land status:** National Forest
**Fees and permits:** Small 3-day-pass fee
**Trail contact:** Heber/Kamas Ranger District, 50 E. Center St., Kamas, UT 84036; (435) 783-4338; www.fs.usda .gov/gov/uwcnf
**Nearest town:** Kamas
**Trail tips:** No cell service
**Nat Geo TOPO! Map (USGS):** 7.5-minute *Mirror Lake*
**Nat Geo Trails Illustrated Map:** *711: High Uinta Wilderness*

### FINDING THE TRAILHEAD

In Kamas, Utah, turn right (east) onto the Mirror Lake Highway (SR 150). Travel 31 miles over Bald Mountain Pass to the Fehr Lake parking lot on the south side of the road. There is a small sign indicating the turnoff. If you reach the Moosehorn Campground, you have gone too far. The Fehr Lake Trail is on the south side of the parking lot.

**Trailhead GPS:** N40 41.566' / W110 53.515'

## THE HIKE

The hike to Fehr Lake and beyond to Shepard, Hoover, and Maba Lakes is a wonderful adventure into the beautiful high country. The trail is easy to follow and provides many opportunities for photograph taking, wild-strawberry picking, boardwalk crossing, trout fishing, eagle spotting, and life enjoying. On this trail it is possible to walk miles, but if a stroll for the short-legged, stiff-jointed, or low-elevation adjusted is what you need, this Uinta field trip is perfect for you and your dog.

From the parking area, head downhill to your right (south) toward the lake. This is one of the few hikes in the Uintas that has a downhill start. Travel down the rocky trail, and you will be at Fehr Lake in no time. The lake is nestled against the blocky cliffs, commonly found in the area and filled with crystal-clear water. If you have small children or elderly dogs, this is a nice place to spend an afternoon. Here, you can decide to turn around and return to your car or continue to other lakes farther along this trail.

Martin navigating the boardwalk.

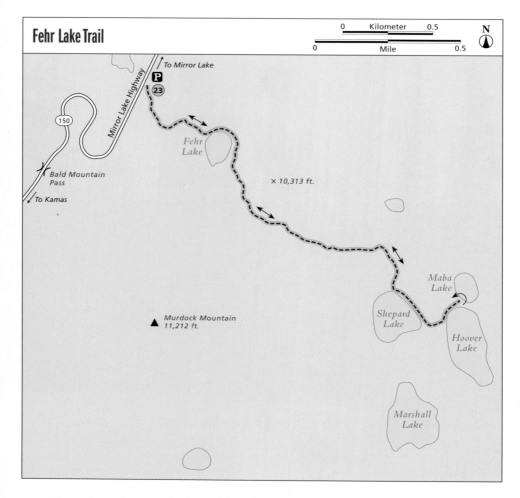

The trail continues to the lower lakes, skirting to the left (east) of Fehr Lake, arching elegantly south, and then disappearing in the trees. If you decide to continue beyond Fehr Lake, the hike to Shepard Lake continues south, passing through meadows and across boardwalks to avoid bottomless swamps. It is a common mistake for a dog to walk into these benign-looking mountain water pools only to end up completely submerged. In many of these pools, the undercut banks are steep. Encourage dogs to drink at the larger lakes and avoid a mishap in the water features in between them. The trail becomes rocky as it continues its descent toward Shepard Lake.

Shepard Lake is a popular place to camp and fish, and there are camping spots around the banks. The challenge, as always in the Uintas, is to find a place that isn't too rocky to make camp. After a break at Shepard Lake, the trail continues to the left (east), dropping down to the basin below. Here, you will also find places to camp, with Hoover Lake to the south. After a short walk past Hoover Lake, to the north you will find Maba Lake, speckled with lily pads. Either lake has great places to stop and enjoy lunch, especially after the first frost has eliminated the mosquitos. Make sure you look to the skies for the changing cloud formations. Uinta weather is always in flux. After an afternoon spent lakeside, you and your pup will be satisfied with miles hiked and sticks chased. Return the way you came, winding back north to your car or campsite.

## MILES AND DIRECTIONS

**0.0** Follow the trail south of the Fehr Lake parking area.

**0.3** Arrive at Fehr Lake. (**Option:** You can continue south toward Shepard Lake.)

**1.5** After a rocky descent you will arrive at Shepard Lake.

**1.7** After hiking around Shepard Lake and dropping down a small ridge, you will be on the banks of Hoover Lake.

**1.8** Maba is a small lake to the north of Hoover Lake. Return the way you came when you have finished enjoying the surroundings.

**3.6** Arrive back at the Fehr Lake parking area.

## NEARBY HIKES

Crystal Lake Loop, Trial Lake, Big Elk Lake

## CREATURE COMFORTS

**Holiday Inn Express Heber City**, 1268 S. Main St., Heber City; (844) 297-1379. The Holiday Inn Express in Heber is a great home base for accessing the high country and Wasatch Front–area hikes. There are kitchenettes in the rooms and helpful staff. There is a fee for pets.

**Mirror Lake Diner**, 35 S. Main St., Kamas; (435) 783-0110; www.mirrorlakediner.com. The Mirror Lake Diner is a classic country-style diner serving breakfast, lunch, and dinner, including hearty omelets, sandwiches, and chicken and waffles. They have a dog-friendly back patio.

# 24 CRYSTAL LAKE LOOP

## WHY GO?

This high-elevation Uinta Mountain hike tops out at 10,599 feet, making the view from the Notch breathtaking. You and your pup will hike some decent climbs to perfect views and will visit many varieties of water features along your way.

### THE RUNDOWN

**Start:** Crystal Lake Trailhead
**Distance:** 6.0-mile loop
**Hiking time:** 4–5 hours
**Difficulty:** Moderate due to high elevation and steep climbs
**Trailhead elevation:** 10,013 feet
**Highest point:** 10,599 feet
**Best season:** Summer
**Trail surface:** The Uintas are notoriously rocky; this trail has sections that live up to the rumors.
**Other trail users:** Horses
**Canine compatibility:** On leash
**Land status:** Uinta-Wasatch-Cache National Forest
**Fees and permits:** Small 3-day-pass fee
**Trail contact:** Heber/Kamas Ranger District, 50 E. Center St., Kamas, UT

84036; (435) 783-4338; www.fs.usda.gov/gov/uwcnf
**Nearest town:** Kamas
**Trail tips:** You can never be too prepared at high elevations. Bringing rain/snow gear is a must even in summer. Cell phone service is very minimal in the Uinta Mountains—always remember to tell someone where you are going and stick to your plan. There are restrooms at the trailhead. Bug spray is a *very* good idea.
**Nat Geo TOPO! Map (USGS):** 7.5-minute *Mirror Lake*
**Nat Geo Trails Illustrated Map:** *711: High Uintas Wilderness*

## FINDING THE TRAILHEAD

At the intersection of SR 248 and Main Street in Kamas, turn left (north) on Main Street. At the Chevron Station turn right (east) onto the Mirror Lake Highway (SR 150). The area's visitor center is to the right, shortly after the turn, if you're interested in gathering more information. Continue on Mirror Lake Highway for approximately 25 miles, stopping at the fee station at mile 6 to pay the fee if necessary. Turn left (north) onto the Trial Lake turnoff, FR 041, then keep left past the lake. Turn right (north) onto FR 038 toward the Washington Lake Campground, following the signs from Crystal Lake Trailhead until the road terminates at FR 488. The road is paved except for the last quarter mile; passenger cars should have no problem navigating it. The trail begins at the north end of the parking area.
**Trailhead GPS:** N40 40.901' / W110 57.766'

## THE HIKE

To complete the loop counterclockwise, the trail will head north from the northern end of the parking lot toward Wall Lake, a popular fishing spot. The trailhead is easy to see—the hike heads out into the forest on a wide, horse-friendly trail. This section is beautiful, pleasant, and gently winds through the pines. Pockets of water will appear and disappear through the trees. Your dog will be happy tromping through the water, the muddy bottoms turning your pup a different color.

Lilly Lakes can be seen shortly after beginning the hike and is a beautiful introduction to this land of lakes. At mile 1 Wall Lake, aptly named and located at the bottom of a majestic cliff, will be a welcome sight. After a small climb, views of the Notch loom large in the background and anglers line the banks. This short distance to the lake makes Wall Lake a popular place to fish.

Hike over the wooden bridge that spans the spillway to the north and continue toward the trail junction. You will take the Notch Trail, which turns left at the sign. This section is stunning, as the trail again skirts beautiful ponds and water features, eventually gaining elevation around mile 1.6. A couple of "Trail" signs encourage you through this green and beautiful wilderness. Next, the steep and rewarding switchbacks deliver you to a riveting lookout, only rivaled by the next one you will see, from the Notch itself. The trail continues north and then east, crossing marshes on long sweeping boardwalks. These hiker aides give the photographer a beautiful angle from which to shoot the features to the south.

At mile 2.3 the Notch Cut-Off Trail is well marked and continues north. This short and sweet little side trip gives a perspective of the area that is well worth the climb. From the Notch, the highest point on this trail, you can see Lovenia Lake and Ibantik Lake to the north. A trail continues down to these lakes (a backpacking trip option). To the south, a view of Mount Watson and a vast expanse is open and encourages gazing, cloudspotting, and daydreaming. This is a nice spot to prop yourself against the boulders, wonder about glaciers, and enjoy some lunch.

Fading trees are a sight that haunts almost every inch of the Uinta National Forest, or what is left of it. The remaining bleached bones still standing creak in the wind, an eerie sound to a solo hiker at dusk that makes finding a safe campsite a difficult thing to do. Over 2 million acres of forest in Utah have been ravaged by bark beetles. Small and adaptive, these tiny beetles have a foothold in the woods as they hunt for stressed trees, landing softy and burrowing into the phloem layer, just under the bark. As their feasting begins, a chemical reaction takes place in their own bodies, which is a green light for other beetles to join. Over the course of a season, the tree will be girdled, vital nutrients no longer able to travel through the destroyed layer, and death is imminent. Starting from the top, their green color fades to gray. Once this happens, there is nothing that can be done to save the tree. You'll notice pockets of these ghosts as you view out from the Notch.

When you are ready, continue back the way you came, this time veering right at the fork at the Notch Cut-Off Trailhead, toward Clyde Lake. The trail is easy to follow as it passes the shores of Twin Lakes to the north, then turns and heads south, climbing over a small hill. To your left in years past there has been a cairn art exhibit on the left, before you are able to get a visual of Clyde Lake. Once you descend to the shores of the lake, continue around the west and south sides following the trail. You will climb one last time over a short, steep, rocky incline, descending quickly and leaving Clyde Lake behind. The trail becomes very rocky as it falls quickly toward the beautiful Cliff Lake, passing Watson Lake, Petit Lake, and a few other beautiful water features along the way. At mile 5.1 you will arrive at Cliff Lake, and the trail swings to the north side, then continues dropping south toward the cutoff for the Smith and Morehouse Trail. This junction arrives quickly at mile 5.6. Go left at the junction, keeping Crystal Lake on your right, as you continue toward the parking lot. The trail will widen, and the ending is an easy stroll back to the parking area at mile 6.

> If you decide to camp in the Uintas, choose your campsite wisely. It is dangerous to set up your tent under dead trees because these trees are unstable and can easily fall down in the Uinta winds.

## MILES AND DIRECTIONS

0.0   Follow the marked trail to the north for Wall Lake.

0.3   Pass Lilly Lakes, the first of many small lakes on this hike.

1.0   Arrive at Wall Lake. Shortly after you will cross a bridge as you continue north.

1.2   Head left (north) at the junction.

1.6   Climb up the switchbacks.

2.3   Arrive at the Notch Cut-Off Trail heading north to the saddle.

2.6   Arrive at the Notch, a saddle between two peaks. Return back to the trail junction.

2.9   Stay west toward Twin Lakes and Clyde Lake.

3.5   Arrive at Twin Lakes. Continue around the lake, climbing a small hill that will drop you eventually into the Clyde Lake basin.

3.7   Arrive at Clyde Lake. Continue around the lake to the west, climbing slightly south.

5.0   Be careful on this very rocky descent.

5.1   Arrive at the picturesque Cliff Lake and follow the trail and boardwalks south.

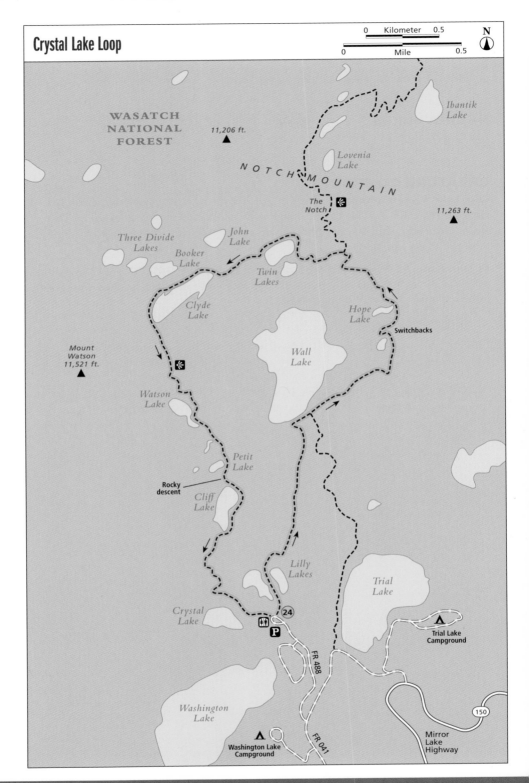

# Crystal Lake Loop

0    Kilometer    0.5

0    Mile    0.5

**N**

WASATCH
NATIONAL
FOREST

11,206 ft. ▲

*Ibantik
Lake*

*Lovenia
Lake*

N O T C H ░ M O U N T A I N

The
Notch

11,263 ft. ▲

*Three Divide
Lakes*

*John
Lake*

*Booker
Lake*

*Twin
Lakes*

*Hope
Lake*

*Clyde
Lake*

Switchbacks

*Mount
Watson
11,521 ft.* ▲

*Wall
Lake*

*Watson
Lake*

*Petit
Lake*

Rocky
descent

*Cliff
Lake*

*Lilly
Lakes*

*Trial
Lake*

*Crystal
Lake*

24

Trial Lake
Campground

FR 488

*Washington
Lake*

150

FR 041

Mirror
Lake
Highway

Washington Lake
Campground

**5.6** Veer left (east) at the trail junction, staying to the north of Crystal Lake. If you end up heading west, you are on the Smith and Morehouse Trail and need to retrace your steps.

**6.0** Arrive back at the parking lot.

## NEARBY HIKES

Fish Lake, Lofty Lake Loop, Bald Mountain

## CREATURE COMFORTS

**Lilly Lake Campground**, UT 150, Kamas, UT 84063. Located along the Mirror Lake Highway in the Uintas, Lilly Lake Campground is a beautiful spot to set up camp. There are toilets and drinking water available but no hookups. No reservations, so arrive during the week to get a prime spot.

**El Jalisciense #2**, 185 S. Main St., Kamas, UT 84036; (435) 783-7070; El Jalisciense is a popular Mexican restaurant in Kamas. They offer authentic Mexican food with great prices and quick service. No pups, please.

# 25 LOFTY LAKE LOOP

## WHY GO?

The Lofty Lake Loop hike can be a bit of a challenge for lowlanders, as the elevation never dips below 10,000 feet. The views, however, are worth the low oxygen levels. This darling of the Uintas offers meadow walkthroughs, wildflower viewing, incredible vistas, high mountain lakes, and plenty of water for your dogs.

### THE RUNDOWN

**County:** Summit
**Start:** Lofty Lake Trailhead (Pass Lake)
**Distance:** 4.3-mile loop
**Hiking time:** 2–3 hours
**Difficulty:** Moderate due to elevation
**Trailhead elevation:** 10,100 feet
**Highest point:** 10,900 feet
**Best seasons:** Summer–fall
**Trail surface:** Blocky granite, dirt trails, boardwalks, small stream crossings, rocky descents
**Other trail users:** Hikers
**Canine compatibility:** On leash, especially if your dog chases wildlife
**Land status:** National Forest
**Fees and permits:** Small 3-day-permit fee

**Trail contact:** Heber/Kamas Ranger District, 50 E. Center St., Kamas, UT 84036; (435) 783-4338; www.fs.usda .gov/gov/uwcnf
**Nearest town:** Kamas
**Trail tips:** The mosquitos can be thick up around these high mountain lakes. Bring a repellent, or plan to hike after the first frost. Always bring extra layers, a survival kit, and tell someone where you are going while traveling in the Uintas. Check the weather and try to hike early in the day rather than in the afternoon.
**Nat Geo TOPO! Maps (USGS):** 7.5-minute *Mirror Lake*
**Nat Geo Trails Illustrated Map:** *711: High Uinta Wilderness*

## FINDING THE TRAILHEAD

Lofty Lake Loop Trailhead is located at the Pass Lake Trailhead/Parking Area. From the intersection of SR 248 and Main Street in Kamas, turn left (north) on Main Street. At the Chevron Station turn right (east) onto the Mirror Lake Highway (SR 150). Continue on Mirror Lake Highway for approximately 32 miles, stopping at the fee station at mile 6 to pay the fee if necessary. Turn left (north) at Pass Lake Trailhead and continue to the parking lot. The trail begins at the north end of the parking area.
**Trailhead GPS:** N40 42.860' / W110 53.564'

## THE HIKE

This hike is a loop and can be hiked in either direction. The trailhead to go counterclockwise is easy to spot at the northeastern corner of the parking lot. You will see signs directing you toward Picturesque and Scout Lakes. The beginning of the trail begins with some rocky sections, as the high elevation gets your heart pumping right off the bat, and your pup will be able to find water almost immediately in small ponds off to the side of the trail.

At mile 0.5 it is possible to see Camp Steiner across Picturesque Lake. A short side trail to the east will make it easy for your pup to get a drink or splash in the lake. Continue on the main trail until you reach a junction at mile 0.8. There are idyllic meadows to

Wren making her way
to Kamas Lake.

the north that are beautiful, and your dogs will love a good roll in the deep grass. Keep to the main trail heading north. As you continue the trail will begin to arc west. Next you climb a series of switchbacks that are incredibly rocky and challenging. Watch your step as you negotiate this high-elevation obstacle. This section is the most difficult on the trail, with the steepness and the precise footing between Uinta boulders contributing to the challenge.

At the top of the climb, you'll find a trail to the northeast. That is the trail that will take you to Ruth Lake, a different adventure. From this crow's-nest-like perch, you can see views of various mountains. Of particular note is Mount Hayden to the east and Mount Marsell to the northwest.

Ignoring the side trail for Ruth Lake, continue hiking along this trail. At mile 1.5 you come to the descent for Lofty Lake. This pleasant dip in elevation is a nice respite from the climb. Once at the banks of this lake locked into a lovely valley, it is worth taking a deep breath. The glacial bowl of this valley with the clouds rolling overhead is certainly part paradise.

After enjoying the surroundings at the highest lake in the Uintas, Lofty Lake Loop continues descending through fields of yarrow, aster, and paintbrush to an overlook. At mile 2 you will arrive at a lookout with an expansive valley view. The closest lake is Cutthroat, farther on is Teal. Here, you can see the vast damage of the bark beetle as you look over the expansive forest in the distance. The valley incredibly vast and foreboding.

There are a few side trails that will beckon you and your dog to different lookout points to the north and east, but the main trail heads west. This can be a little confusing, but the trail stays parallel to the hill. Do not descend to Cutthroat Lake, unless you want to.

At this point the trail loop has reached its farthest point from the parking area and will begin swinging back southerly. At 2.5 miles you will reach Kamas Lake, backed up against the quintessential talus slopes so common in this area. The trail skirts the western edge of the lake, then heads south again, diving back into the forest. At 3 miles the trail leading to Cuberant Lake is on your right. "Cuberant" in the Ute language means "long." This area is worth exploring as part of a backpacking adventure, or you can add extra mileage to your day hike on a different trail day.

Next, you will cross the boggy terrain of Reids Meadow. Various boardwalks will keep you and your dog dry. During the summer the wildflowers are dazzling along this section. Current bushes and elephant's head flowers are especially a treat to see. Watch for views of Bald Mountain and Reids Peak as you skirt the meadows heading back to the car. There will be some other trail junctions that will tempt you west: the Weber River Trail and Pass Lake Trail. Stay left (east) on your loop, and you will have no problem getting back to the parking lot.

## MILES AND DIRECTIONS

**0.0**   Follow the trail to the north of the parking area.

**0.5**   Continue north. Picturesque Lake and Camp Steiner are visible through the trees.

**0.8**   Keep north past the small side trail to the water's edge.

**1.5**   Arrive at Lofty Lake after a pretty significant climb.

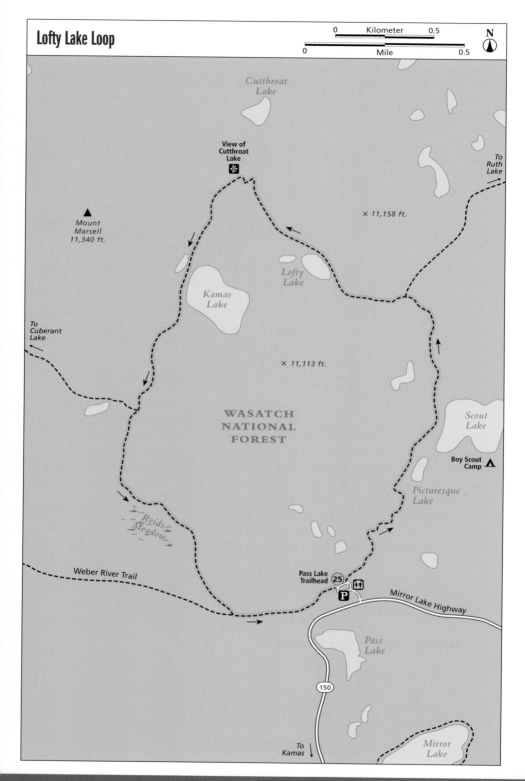

# Lofty Lake Loop

0  Kilometer  0.5

0  Mile  0.5

N

Cutthroat
Lake

View of
Cutthroat
Lake

To
Ruth
Lake

× 11,158 ft.

Mount
Marsell
11,340 ft.

Lofty
Lake

Kamas
Lake

To Cuberant
Lake

× 11,113 ft.

Scout
Lake

WASATCH
NATIONAL
FOREST

Boy Scout
Camp

Picturesque
Lake

Reids
Meadow

Weber River Trail

Pass Lake
Trailhead  25

P

Mirror Lake Highway

Pass
Lake

150

To
Kamas

Mirror
Lake

2.5   Pass Kamas Lake.

3.0   Stay left (east) at the trail junction with Cuberant Lake Trail.

3.3   Cross the boardwalks of Reids Meadow.

3.8   Stay left (east) past the Weber River Trail junction.

4.0   At the Pass Lake Trail junction, stay left (east).

4.3   Arrive back at the parking area.


## NEARBY HIKES

Crystal Lake, Naturalist Basin, Highline Trail


## CREATURE COMFORTS

**Moosehorn Campground**, Wasatch Cache National Forest, FR 105, Hanna UT, 84031; (877) 444-6777; www.recreation.gov. Moosehorn is a high-elevation, wooded campground at the base of Bald Mountain offering access to many of the Uinta hikes and lakes. All sites have fire rings and picnic tables and the campground itself has trash collection and vault toilets but no hookups. This is a highly recommended campground. Reserve on www.recreation.gov.

**Samak Smokehouse**, 1937 Mirror Lake Hwy., Kamas; (435) 783-4880; www .samaksmokehouse.com. Samak Smokehouse is a gourmet grocery store just outside Kamas as you head up the Mirror Lake Highway toward the Uinta-area hikes. It is a great spot to stop for snacks, groceries, camping essentials, and more. Their jerky is great!

# 26 RUTH LAKE

## WHY GO?

Ruth Lake is a lovely short walk for the beginning hiker to a beautiful basin. Wildflowers, mild stream crossings over quaint bridges, a beautiful lake, and not much in the way of elevation gain make this hike a great beginner's trail at high elevations. It is also a launching point for many backpacking adventures in the area. Although water is available for your pup on this trail, it is a good idea when going into the backcountry to bring food and water.

### THE RUNDOWN

**County:** Summit
**Start:** Ruth Lake Trailhead
**Distance:** 2.0 miles out and back
**Hiking time:** 1–2 hours
**Difficulty:** Easy. This is a short walk with little elevation gain.
**Trailhead elevation:** 10,045 feet
**Highest point:** 10,336 feet
**Best season:** Summer
**Trail surface:** Rocks, bridge crossings
**Other trail users:** Hikers, rock climbers
**Canine compatibility:** On leash
**Land status:** Uinta-Wasatch-Cache National Forest
**Fees and permits:** Small 3-day-permit fee
**Trail contacts:** Bear River Ranger Station, UT 150 Scenic, Evanston, UT

82930; (435) 642-6662; www.fs.usda.gov
**Nearest towns:** Evanston, WY; Kamas, UT
**Trail tips:** Like all Uinta excursions, be prepared for mosquitos and afternoon thunderstorms that can sneak up out of nowhere. There are also many other lakes to explore if you have navigational skills: Hayden and Naomi Lakes as well as the trail to the south that connects to the Lofty Lakes Loop trail. Be prepared with warmer layers, rain gear, water, and food.
**Nat Geo Topo! Map (USGS):** 7.5-minute *Mirror Lake*
**Nat Geo Trails Illustrated Map:** *711: High Uintas Wilderness*

### FINDING THE TRAILHEAD

From Kamas, Utah, travel along the Mirror Lake Highway to mile marker 35. Just past Butterfly Lake and Campground, you will see signage for Ruth Lake on the west side of the highway. There are pull-offs for parking on both sides of the highway.
**Trailhead GPS:** N40 44.027' / W110 52.055'

## THE HIKE

The hike to Ruth Lake is a beautiful sample of the great Uinta Wilderness. It's a great introduction to hiking or backpacking, an afternoon destination, or a longer adventure in the high mountains. This is a sweet hike with little mileage and elevation gain. The beauty that surrounds Ruth Lake is simply "Uinta-esque": rugged, unkempt, wild, and pristine. Although popular, this hike gives those who can't or don't want to tackle the elevation of the other Uinta "darlings" (hikes) of this area a chance to enter the wilderness more on their own terms.

The parking area and toilets are on the west side of the highway. The trailhead is well marked and easily spotted to the north or south. The trail starts out heading west. You

Wren enjoying
Ruth Lake.

climb slightly, making your way through some boulders on a path that is obvious and straightforward. The trail gains elevation at a gentle pace, but at over 10,000 feet, it may feel more challenging than it would be at lower elevations.

Rambunctious chipmunks with their notable racing stripes can be seen streaking across the trail. The prevalent wildflowers display their purples, pinks, and white hues. As you continue to hike, there will be opportunities to cross small streams over well-placed rock bridges, so you can keep your boots dry on this hike!

After mile 0.4 you will come to a Y junction. To your left is a trail for rock climbers. The cliffs to the southwest have available climbing routes. From Ruth Lake, you can watch climbers ascend the cliff, hand-over-hand all the way to the top.

Take the right fork and continue to Ruth Lake. As you walk west, you can stop and read the informative signs about the local area posted along the trail. Just before Ruth Lake, you will pass by a smaller lake that may entice your dog for a swim. Just a bit farther are the banks of Ruth. The trail will take you and your hound around the lake's perimeter. It is an ideal place to find a lunch spot, have a snack, and enjoy the surroundings. With navigation skills and a good map, it is possible to hike deep into the woods from here. For most, this gorgeous spot is good enough.

The Uintas are tricky to navigate through, and it is important to always let someone know where you will be traveling and when you plan to return. It is very easy to get turned around here. It is nearly impossible to find missing persons if there is no information on where they "should" be. This area with its volatile weather can make a simple hike into a dangerous one in a matter of hours. The seemingly docile nature of Ruth Lake is only a veneer. You are in the backcountry here. Be prepared with warmer layers, rain gear, water, food, and a panic-free disposition. When you are ready, follow the same trail back to the parking area.

## MILES AND DIRECTIONS

**0.0** Follow the signs for Ruth Lake, across the Mirror Lake Highway from the parking area.

**0.4** Stay right (west) at the signed Y intersection directing rock climbers left to the cliffs.

**0.9** You arrive at Ruth Lake. The trail continues around the perimeter.

**1.0** There are many lunch spots. Pick your favorite and enjoy your afternoon. Return the way you came.

**2.0** Arrive back at your car parked along the Mirror Lake Highway.

## NEARBY HIKES

Lofty Lake Loop, Crystal Lake

## CREATURE COMFORTS

**Butterfly Lake Campground**, FR 106 Mirror Lake Highway, Hanna, UT 84031; (435) 654-0470. Butterfly Lake Campground is another great campground just off the Mirror Lake Highway in the Uintas. It is a nice, quiet campground away from the road and not

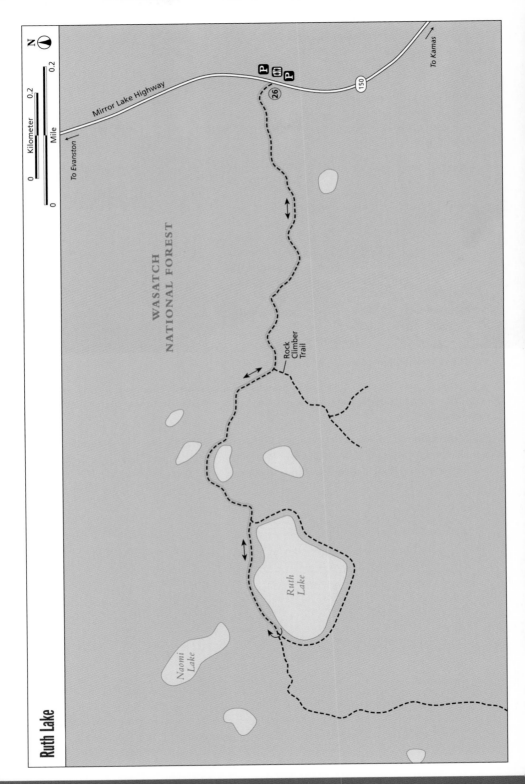

Ruth Lake

N

WASATCH
NATIONAL FOREST

Mirror Lake Highway

To Evanston

To Kamas

150

26

Rock
Climber
Trail

Ruth
Lake

Naomi
Lake

Kilometer  0.2        0.2

0    Mile

**Nicole and Wren at Ruth Lake**

as popular as many of the other campgrounds closer to Mirror Lake. It is mostly shaded with lake and trail access. Water and vault toilets are available, but there are no hookups or reservations.

**Hi-Mountain**, 40 N. Main St., Kamas, UT 84036; (435) 783-4466. Hi-Mountain is a popular burger joint in Kamas adjacent to a cute grocery store. They serve delicious burgers, fries, and shakes as well as soups, salads, and other special options.

# CANYON COUNTRY

*This is the most beautiful place on Earth. There are many such places. Every man, every woman, carries in heart and mind the image of the ideal place, the right place, the one true home, known or unknown, actual or visionary.*
—*Desert Solitaire,* Edward Abby

Canyon country with its vistas that last forever, with formations painted with colors of red, orange, purple, and blue, with its towering exposed geological wonders of Wingate and Navajo sandstone, all perched under an azure sky, is a paradise for the intrepid, curious, and rugged. From the car it is possible to see into these places of wonder, but to hike through them is extraordinary. To walk with your dog into the water-sculpted channels of the Colorado Plateau, to gaze in wonder on the barren peaks of the La Sals, and to see the Milky Way without light pollution comprise a rare and beautiful thing.

Southern Utah is a visual paradise and adventure mecca. With this area, though, comes very real cautions: heat exhaustion, flash floods, remoteness, and very little cell phone reception. Hikers and their dogs must be willing and able to be self-sufficient, prepared

Fergie surveying the hoodoos.

for elemental extremes, navigationally equipped, and brave. The rewards are great for those capable of challenge and hardship. A reliable 4x4 vehicle is also helpful.

There is usually too little or way too much water in the desert. With massive areas covered with sandstone, precipitation has little opportunity to infiltrate the soil during a rainstorm. This water becomes runoff, sometimes traveling miles down smaller canyons and washes, collecting and gaining volume with each added tributary dumping what they have into the larger canyons downstream. Given enough rain, a small stream can turn into massive displays of erosional fury, doing its best to carve out the canyons just a little more. Rain overhead may not be as dangerous as rain in the drainages upstream, so make sure you check the weather and check in with the ranger stations before attempting narrow or slot canyons in the slickrock canyon country.

The desert in summer is hot, which can impact your dog negatively. Know your particular dog's needs and tolerances when it comes to heat, and choose to hike in these remote areas during the cooler months of the year.

The San Rafael Swell has wild and desolate places. With a rich mining history and huge geological displays, from mighty uplifts as in the San Rafael Reef to the erosional forces that sculpted the Little Grand Canyon, and surrounding buttes, plateaus, and mesas, this area is stunningly beautiful and feral. Dinosaur tracks, petroglyphs, and pictographs can be found throughout the area, making it mysterious and inspiring. Moab, too, just beyond the hustle and bustle of Main Street, can offer views unlike anywhere else on earth. A person could spend a lifetime in the La Sals and Moab area exploring and be constantly amazed. Remember that dogs are not allowed in the national parks, so some of the iconic Utah images will not be possible to witness with your pup. But there are many options that whisper to the intrepid to visit. For many, once you've heard it, it will be hard not to return again.

The hikes in this area are a mix of everything from popular to remote. Some offer signed navigation and others have none at all. Some of these hikes require skills with navigation and a strong set of legs, while others are straightforward and stunning. Make sure you pick the ones that are appropriate for you and your dog, considering heat, the weather, mileage, navigation, remoteness, and lack of services nearby. Sandstone can be hard on a dog's paws, so be vigilant about your dog's well-being and health.

# 27 GRANDSTAFF CANYON TO MORNING GLORY NATURAL BRIDGE

## WHY GO?
Wedged between national parks, Moab does not immediately come to mind as a dog-friendly destination. The meandering stream and soaring Wingate-sandstone features of Grandstaff Canyon, concluding at the overhead 263-foot natural bridge, begs a dog owner to reconsider Moab as dog friendly.

### THE RUNDOWN

**County:** Grand
**Start:** Grandstaff Trailhead (previously Negro Bill Canyon Trailhead)
**Distance:** 4.8 miles out and back
**Hiking time:** 2–3 hours
**Difficulty:** Easy, with little elevation gain and straightforward navigation
**Trailhead elevation:** 3,970 feet
**Highest point:** 4,384 feet
**Best season:** Year-round
**Trail surface:** Sandy trail, sandstone travel, river crossings
**Other trail users:** Hikers
**Canine compatibility:** Voice control
**Land status:** Bureau of Land Management
**Fees and permits:** None
**Trail contact:** BLM Field Office Moab, 82 E. Dogwood, Moab, UT 84532; (435) 259-2100; www.blm.gov/office/moab-field-office
**Nearest town:** Moab
**Trail tips:** There are many stream crossings on this trail—wearing shoes that you can get wet will make it easier. Watch out for poison ivy and keep an eye out for trail arrows that mark the way. Also, avoid this hike during the heat of the day, as the sand can burn paws. Remember, the desert surrounding Moab is fragile, so stay on the trail! Restrooms are available at the trailhead.
**Nat Geo TOPO! Map (USGS):** 7.5-minute *Moab*
**Nat Geo Trails Illustrated Map:** *500: Moab North*

## FINDING THE TRAILHEAD

From downtown Moab, drive north on US 191. Just before you cross the Colorado River, turn right on SR 128 toward Castle Valley. Drive 3 miles and the signed parking lot for Grandstaff Trailhead is on the right-hand side of the road.
**Trailhead GPS:** N38 36.603' / W109 32.018'

## THE HIKE
It is up for debate about what is more legendary, the beauty of this canyon or its namesake, William Grandstaff, who is said to be immortalized in the rock itself. In a certain light, on a certain day of the year, the sun will supposedly hit a particular feature just right and give stage to what is said to be old Bill himself. Watch closely . . . who knows who or what you might see.

Mr. Grandstaff was born as a slave in Alabama in 1846, arriving in Moab around 1877 with a man named Frenchie. Soon after arriving he began a life of prospecting, ranching,

Wren navigating the trail.

farming, and most notably distilling whiskey. In the 1800s towns grew—just as they do now—and Grandstaff decided it was time to find someplace with fewer people. With his acquired cattle herd, he stumbled into a canyon and no doubt saw the beauty and the resources it could provide his herd and set up camp. With the perennial stream, and the immense diversity of vegetation, gold could not have been more valuable to a cattleman. In the desert, water is queen. Because of a series of troubling events related to Grandstaff's means of income, Grandstaff left the area and ultimately ended up in Colorado, where he died a very well-respected man in 1901.

Like Grandstaff, the geology in this area offers lasting memories. Bend after bend offer the eyes soaring walls to climb, imagining routes in and out of the canyon. This area boasts the magnificence of the Morning Glory Natural Bridge, or Morning Glory Alcove Arch, which spans 243 feet, making it one of the largest "bridges" in the world.

Your trail begins to the south of the parking area following the signs along the shoulder of Grandstaff Creek. It is well marked and well traveled. After a mile the trail crisscrosses the water, making for enjoyable problem-solving and minor route finding. These family-friendly aquatic interludes offer wonder and beauty every step of the way. Coyote willows, the invasive Russian olive, and poison ivy call the canyon home. Be careful of thorns, oils, and stickers as you make your way along the trail to the box canyon with Morning Glory arching above.

At the end of your hike, you will find a spring, which is a wonder all its own. Because sandstone is porous, water can filter down through the layers until a more impermeable layer of rock is reached. Water's nature is to follow the path of least resistance, so it moves along this barrier and arrives back at the surface once more, eroding the rock as it moves.

After enjoying the spectacle of the arch, return the way you came.

## MILES AND DIRECTIONS

**0.0**   Follow the well-marked trail south from the parking area.

**1.0**   Continue on the trail as it crosses the creek occasionally.

**1.5**   Watch for the poison ivy hazard as you cross the creek again.

**1.8**   Continue south as the trail splits.

**2.0**   Arrive at the first view of Morning Glory Natural Bridge.

**2.4**   Arrive at Morning Glory Natural Bridge and spring. Return the way you came.

**4.8**   Arrive back at the parking area.

## NEARBY HIKES
Onion Creek, Corona Arch, Faux Falls

# Grandstaff Canyon to Morning Glory Natural Bridge

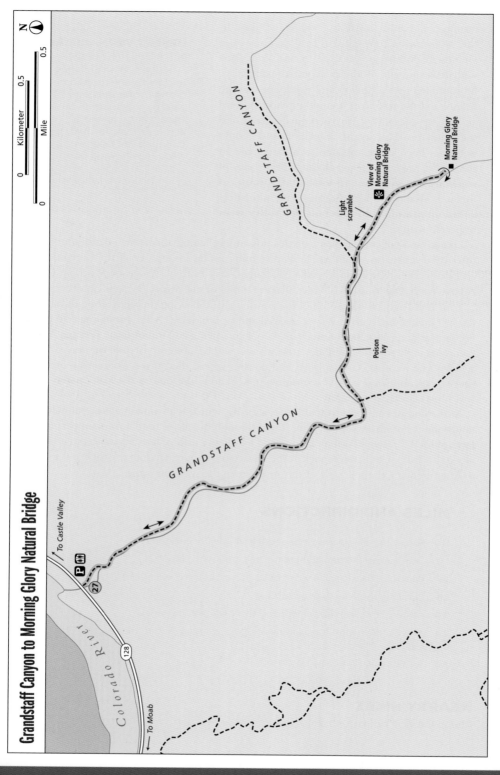

N

Kilometer
0          0.5

Mile
0          0.5

Colorado River

To Moab

128

27

P

To Castle Valley

GRANDSTAFF CANYON

GRANDSTAFF CANYON

Poison ivy

Light scramble

View of Morning Glory Natural Bridge

Morning Glory Natural Bridge

## CREATURE COMFORTS

**Gonzo Inn**, 100 W. 200 South, Moab, UT 84532; (435) 259-2515; www.gonzoinn.com. The Gonzo is a southwestern-style eclectic hotel located in the heart of Moab. The rooms are bright and colorful with kitchens and views of the red rock surrounding town. Breakfast is included and pets are welcome with a pet fee.

**Milt's Stop and Eat**, 356 Mill Creek Dr., Moab, UT 84532; (435) 259-7424; www .miltsstopandeat.com. Milt's is Moab's oldest restaurant and serves classic burgers and shakes as well as more gourmet options. They use fresh, grass-fed meats and local vegetables. Their buffalo burgers are great and even better paired with their classic malts.

# 28 **CORONA ARCH**

## WHY GO?

This southern Utah short hike traverses into stellar national-park-worthy landscapes. Much of the area around Moab is off-limits to dogs, but this stunning arch is dog friendly and very accessible to folks and pups wanting a short and sweet photographic adventure. It can get hot out there on the desert slickrock for pups and people, so use your judgment to decide when to do this hike and bring plenty of water for all travelers.

---

### THE RUNDOWN

**County:** Grand
**Start:** From Corona Arch Trailhead
**Distance:** 2.5–3.0 miles out and back, depending on how close you get to the arch
**Hiking time:** 1–1.5 hours
**Difficulty:** Moderate due to some technical spots
**Trailhead elevation:** 3,941 feet
**Highest point:** 4,379 feet
**Best seasons:** Winter, spring
**Trail surface:** Slick rock, sand
**Other trail users:** Hikers only
**Canine compatibility:** On leash
**Land status:** Bureau of Land Management
**Fees and permits:** None
**Trail contact:** BLM Moab Office, 82 E. Dogwood, Moab, UT 84532; (435) 259-2100; www.blm.gov/office/moab-field-office
**Nearest town:** Moab
**Trail tips:** Sand and sandstone can burn paws. Please be aware of the surface temperature as you enjoy the desert. Use your hand to judge the temperature throughout your hike to ensure a safe trip for your pup. Always bring plenty of water when walking, even on the easiest of desert routes. Stay on the trail to avoid crushing fragile cryptobiotic soil.
**Nat Geo TOPO! Map (USGS):** 7.5-minute *Gold Bar Canyon UT/Moab UT*
**Nat Geo Trails Illustrated Map:** *501: Moab South*

---

## FINDING THE TRAILHEAD

From Moab, travel north on US 191 toward Arches National Park. You will cross over the Colorado River and continue for 1.3 miles, then turn left (south) at the sign for Potash Road (UT 279). Potash Road, or "Wall-Street" to rock climbers, parallels the Colorado River on the west side. If you reach the Arches National Park entrance, you have gone too far. Drive 10 miles on Potash Road, past the two campgrounds, pictographs, and petrified dinosaur tracks. The drive is spectacular. The parking lot for Corona Arch is on the right-hand side of the road, immediately before the Gold Bar Campground.
**Trailhead GPS:** N38 34.465' / W109 37.942'

## THE HIKE

After parking, the trailhead is at the south end of the parking lot heading up a rocky slope toward Bootlegger Canyon. Soon, you will cross the railroad tracks of the old Potash Railway. These tracks were laid in 1964 as part of the Union Pacific Railroad, Cane Creek Branch. After exiting the 7,050-foot Bootlegger Tunnel, these rails continue downstream to Potash.

Potash, the namesake of the road that brought you to the trailhead, is named after the potash that is mined not far from the parking area. Potash is a potassium-salt mixture that is a main component of modern fertilizer. The deposits of potash in the Moab area are layered more than 3,900 feet below ground in the Paradox layer. The layer became rich in sodium and potassium as a result of ancient inland seas and/or lakes flooding and evaporating over and over again. There are different ways to mine this substance, but in Moab, water is injected into the earth to dissolve the salt, creating a brine. This brine is pumped out into evaporation pools, and Moab's 300 days a year of sunshine goes to work on the pools, evaporating the water. The remaining substance is then moved by railcar to be processed.

After crossing the tracks you will see graffiti and mock-petroglyphs scratched into the side of the rock wall. Don't be fooled by the work of contemporary vandals. Continue on the old jeep track, which narrows and climbs up a rocky drainage. There are many cairn trail markers. These small stacks of rocks will keep you on track as the route winds east. After 0.8 mile you will see a cable bolted into the rock. Use this handline to help with safety as you skirt the lip of the Bootlegger Canyon.

As you round the bend at mile 0.9, you will get your first view of the crown, or Corona Arch. Hike carefully along the sandstone to the second cable, which is more challenging than the first. Use the "moki steps," footholds pecked into the rock, and make your way carefully up the rock.

If you are traveling in a group of more than one, it is recommended that one person climb up the rock and then calls your dog while another person supports the dog as he climbs. Once you have scaled the obstacle, look for a small metal ladder to the north. While you will not want to use the ladder, which is on the main trail, to climb with your

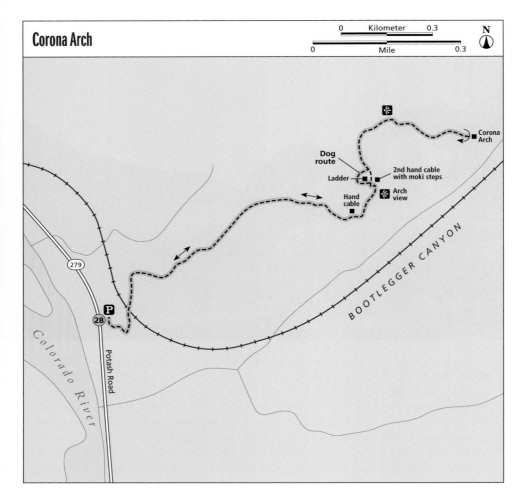

dog, it is possible to hike with your dog to the left (west) around this obstacle. There is a slight incline and a short traverse to meet back up with the main trail.

From this ladder, the route toward the arches and their beautiful desert-varnish display is obvious and splendid. Depending on the light, the best view is looking back at Corona after striding under the archway. After taking in this desert beauty, return the way you came.

## MILES AND DIRECTIONS

**0.0** Park at the Corona Arch parking area. The trail begins at the southern end.

**0.3** Cross the railroad tracks of Bootlegger Canyon.

**0.8** Hold on to the handline.

**0.9** Use the second handline and "moki steps" to get up the obstacle and hike around the ladder to the left. After rounding the bend you will get your first view of Corona Arch.

| 1.1–1.5 | Arrive at Corona Arch and explore the area. Return the way you came. |
| 3.0 | Arrive back at the parking area. |

## NEARBY HIKES
Hunter Canyon, Hidden Valley Trail, Grandstaff

## CREATURE COMFORTS
**The Virginian Motel**, 70 E. 200 South, Moab, UT 84532; (435) 259-5951; www.virginian motelmoab.com. The Virginian is a cute motel with affordable prices and friendly staff. The rooms are modest but comfortable, and the on-site amenities such as BBQ grills and picnic tables are a plus. Pet fee required.

**Moonflower Community Cooperative**, 39 E. 100 North, Moab, UT 84532; (435) 259-5712; moonflower.coop. Moonflower is a community-run natural-foods grocery store with great prepared foods to take on the go. Their foods are fresh, organic, and local when possible, and their prepared-food selection has options for everyone. Be sure to pick up some Nunn Better Jerky—great for picnics!

## WHY GO?

Hunter Canyon is a streamside walk through a beautiful red rock canyon. This hike includes mild scrambling and trail finding, gorgeous alcoves, and cottonwoods in all shapes and sizes as it winds its way toward Hunter Arch.

### THE RUNDOWN

**County:** Grand

**Start:** Hunter Canyon Trail and Campground

**Distance:** 5.8 miles out and back

**Hiking time:** 2–3 hours

**Difficulty:** Moderate due to the occasional scramble and longer mileage

**Trailhead elevation:** 4,224 feet

**Highest point:** 4,237 feet

**Best season:** Year-round

**Trail surface:** Sand, dirt, some slickrock travel, a few boulder scrambles

**Other trail users:** Possibly horses

**Canine compatibility:** Voice control

**Land status:** Bureau of Land Management

**Fees and permits:** None

**Trail contact:** Moab Field Office, 82 E. Dogwood, Moab 84532; (435) 259-2100

**Nearest town:** Moab

**Trail tips:** This hike is at risk for flash flooding. Check the forecast or with the BLM before attempting.

**Nat Geo TOPO! Map (USGS):** 7.5-minute *Moab*

**Nat Geo Trails Illustrated Map:** *501: Moab South*

### FINDING THE TRAILHEAD

From Main Street (US 191) in Moab, travel south through town past the City Market. Turn right (west) on Kane Creek Boulevard, just before the McDonald's. If you pass the Moab Brewery on Main Street, you have gone too far. Continue west on Kane Creek Boulevard past 500 West heading toward the Colorado River. Kane Creek Boulevard will veer south, following the Colorado River. Stay on Kane Creek Boulevard for 4 miles—the pavement will end and road will become Kane Springs Road, but continue another 3.1 miles on the well-maintained dirt road through winding, sometimes steep switchbacks. Use caution as there are a lot of cyclists and dirt-bike traffic as you make your way to the trailhead. There is signage for Hunter Canyon Campground. The trailhead begins just east of the parking area past the vault toilets.

**Trailhead GPS:** N38 30.594' / W109 35.797'

## THE HIKE

Hunter Canyon is a spectacular example of Utah's infamous red rock canyon country. The creek has water year-round, but be cautious during flash flood season. This hike has continual access to water, making it fun and safe for your dog.

The trail begins as a sandy walk with many trails braiding their way upstream through the walk-in Hunter Canyon Campground. To minimize impact in the canyon, stay on the most-used trail. After 0.5 mile be on the lookout for Hunter Arch high up along the south wall.

Hunter Canyon hosts some unusually shaped Fremont cottonwoods (*Populus fremontii*). Cottonwoods are common in the West, lining waterways as they need lots of water to thrive. "There this riparian tree is forever being swept into the stream as the braided channels shift and eat at their banks. But forever the tree comes back, undismayed and determined." (Donald Culross Peattie, *A Natural History of North American Trees*, 2007). The Fremont cottonwood bark is deeply furrowed, and its heart-shaped leaves make identification easy. Mature trees often reach heights of 100 feet, and although they are not particularly long-lived, they continue to reseed to maintain their presence. During the spring the cottonwood's small hanging seed pods burst open to release their cotton puffs, which swirl around and hang in the air until finally floating to the ground, looking just like a winter dusting of snow.

Throughout your walk up Hunter Canyon, take note, too, of the debris left from the last flash flood. Tree roots, boulders, bones, and, in fact, whole trees lay in dis-

Wren cooling off in Hunter Canyon.

arrayed piles, attesting to the strength of water moving in flood stage. Coyote willow, showy milkweed, and cattails also line the creek as the trail follows the meanders of the stream. The long, narrow leaves and flexible shafts of the coyote willow allow them to bend with the force of fast-moving water without snapping, another example of natural adaptation. Flood debris finds stable footing at the base of the willow's tangle of small trunks, and the webs of black widow spiders can be seen attached to the canyon wall as you travel up Hunter Canyon. This shy but venomous spider is common in the desert, hiding in the cracks of the sandstone and waiting for their thick webs to ensnare insects. For your safety, don't disturb the spiders, and keep your fingers out of dark cracks and holes as they may be occupied!

At mile 1.3 there is a lovely spot for lunch, complete with refreshing pools for dog water recreation, and a couple shade trees for their human companions. Many hikers turn around here and head back to the trailhead, but continue on—you will not regret it. There are fewer hikers the farther up the canyon you walk.

Soon, you'll approach a minor rock scramble that adds a fun challenge to the adventure. There are endless ways to negotiate across a boulder field. Pick a route, but if the way seems too difficult, look around for other options that may be better suited for you and your dog.

At mile 1.7 there is a sandstone monolith feature and a cheerful grouping of cattails. It is easy to let your mind ponder the origin of such a cattail patch. These plants were

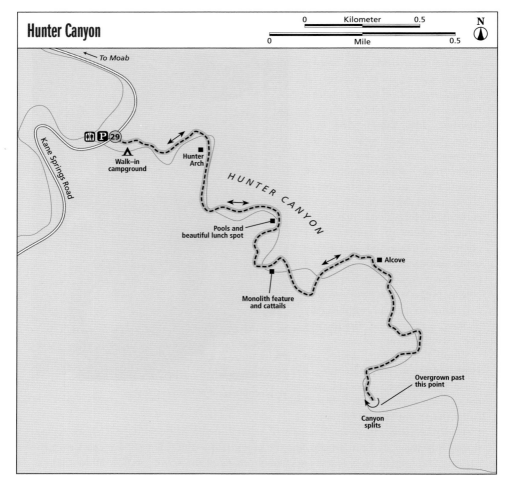

To Moab

Kane Springs Road

P 29

Walk-in campground

Hunter Arch

HUNTER CANYON

Pools and beautiful lunch spot

Alcove

Monolith feature and cattails

Overgrown past this point

Canyon splits

hugely important natural resources to the Fremont and Anasazi cultures as a source of food as well as materials for basket making and sandals. Was this patch of cattails cultivated and tended to by the Fremont peoples, or would this cache be visited year after year?

Pack rat nests or midden piles can also be found along the way. These nests are often used generation after generation—some for thousands of years—making them incredibly valuable for researching the past. Not much escapes the clutches of the pack rat; arrowheads, woven belts, plants, seeds, and bones are all of interest to these hoarders, again providing clues to the past climate, human residents, and fauna of the area.

As you continue, at mile 2.5 there is a very large alcove on the north wall of the canyon, an example of the way erosion chews through cliffs in this desert. At mile 2.9 the canyon forks. Neither way is easily traveled, so it is best to turn around here and enjoy the walk back to the trailhead.

## MILES AND DIRECTIONS

**0.0** Head into the canyon via the trail just east of the parking area.

**0.5** Pass Hunter Arch high up on the south side of the canyon.

**1.3** Pass some pools of water.

**2.5** Pass a beautiful alcove.

**2.9** The canyon splits, and both ways are very overgrown. It's best to turn around here.

**5.8** Arrive back at the trailhead.

## NEARBY HIKES

Corona Arch, Onion Creek, North Fork of Mill Creek

## CREATURE COMFORTS

**Hunter Canyon/Spring Canyon Camping Area**, Kane Creek Boulevard, Moab, UT 84532; (435) 259-2100; www.blm.gov/visit/hunter-canyon-campground. Hunter Canyon Campground is located just outside Moab, with easy access to hiking and other recreation in the area. There are walk-in and trailer sites but no hookups. Vault toilets are available, but plan to bring your own water. Much of the campground is shaded. This is a popular spot and there are no reservations so plan to arrive early.

**Eddie McStiff's**, 57 S. Main St., Moab, UT 84532; (435) 259-2337; www.eddiemcstiffs .com. McStiff's is a well-known Moab restaurant with a pup-friendly patio. They serve American fusion fare including burgers, sandwiches, and salads, and refreshing drinks including cocktails and brews.

# 30 **ONION CREEK NARROWS**

## WHY GO?

Onion Creek is an easy stroll through a beautiful canyon, where water is readily available and the geology is mind-blowing. This walk follows a creek and is excellent for older dogs, families, and for adventure days you just want to take it easy.

### THE RUNDOWN

**County:** Grand
**Start:** Onion Creek
**Distance:** 2.0 miles +/- out and back
**Hiking time:** About 1 hour
**Difficulty:** Easy
**Trailhead elevation:** 4,557 feet
**Highest point:** 4,557 feet
**Best season:** Year-round
**Trail surface:** River bottom, water crossings
**Other trail users:** Horses
**Canine compatibility:** Voice control
**Land status:** Bureau of Land Management
**Fees and permits:** None

**Trail contact:** Moab Field Office, 82 E. Dogwood, Moab, UT 84532; (435) 259-2100
**Nearest town:** Moab
**Trail tips:** The road to Onion Creek Narrows is windy and fords the creek many times. It is best suited with a high-clearance 4x4 vehicle. Canyon country roads can become very slippery when wet. Bring appropriate footwear for stream crossing, and do not attempt this hike during stormy weather.
**Nat Geo TOPO! Map (USGS):** 7.5-minute *Fisher Towers*
**Nat Geo Trails Illustrated Map:** *500: Moab North*

## FINDING THE TRAILHEAD

From Moab, drive north toward Green River/Arches National Park on Main Street (US 191). Before you cross the bridge over the Colorado River, turn right (east) onto SR 128 toward Castle Valley. You will be on the east side of the Colorado River, driving along some of the most beautiful byway you can imagine. Between mile markers 21 and 22, turn right (south) on Onion Creek Road (BLM 100). If you pass Lower Onion Creek Campground or Fisher Towers Road, you have gone too far. From Onion Creek Road, you will pass the Onion Creek Trailhead and Equestrian Trail.

Continue on Onion Creek Road toward the narrows as it begins its adventure crossing in and out of Onion Creek. Flash flooding is a very real risk in this canyon, so do not attempt this hike if it's raining or rain is forecasted. There are a few exposed sections on the road with drop-offs that could be intimidating to the four-wheel-drive equivalent of a tenderfoot. The views of the drive are absolutely worth it.

Just after an unmistakable modern bridge, travel until you can find a place to park along the road that also gives you access to the river. The trail travels in the streambed back toward the main highway through the narrows.

**Trailhead GPS:** N38 42.402' / W109 18.240'

## THE HIKE

Onion Creek Narrows is short, sweet, and completely worth the long drive from Moab. It is not rugged or abounding with trials. Instead it offers a glimpse into the simple journey of water, erosion, and the beautiful formations that capture the imagination. Look

Wren
in the
narrows.

for surrounding features with names like Totem Pole, Mongoose Tower, and Stinking Spring. Try to pick them out!

Down Onion Creek there are old stories told by the river cobbles cemented high above the current water level. The Onion Creek Narrows have an array of interesting and ancient geology: the red rocks of the Triassic Moenkopi Formation, which is 245 million years old; and the rust-colored mudstone, sandstone, and conglomerate of the Permian Cutler Formation, which is 290 million years old. There are new stories too: the ones of mule deer and side canyon secrets, and showcases of time, sand, wind, and water. What makes Moab and Castle Valley special is the amount of rock and rock layers exposed. You are able to see the sediments from the ancient inland seas and immense sand dunes millions of years old and giant red rock formations that were once vast sand dunes that covered much of southern Utah. There are dinosaur bones and petrified wood in the hills and streambeds. The past is big in Moab.

The way down Onion Creek is easy and straightforward. Walk downstream heading west. As you travel downstream, enjoy the views of the towers and old formations above. The trail will twist and turn along the canyon bottom following the creek. Your dog will enjoy the echoing of conversations and the chance to run in the shallows. The narrows walk ends when you make it to Onion Creek Road, about a mile or so downstream. Turn around when you are ready and walk back up the stream to the car. Be on the lookout for beautiful stones, animal tracks, and apparent butterflies, and of course, look up as you travel: The rock sculptures above the creek bed are astounding.

## MILES AND DIRECTIONS

**0.0** Park on the side of the road past the bridge and find your way down to the creek bed.

**0.1** Walk downstream, passing under the bridge.

**1.0** Arrive at Onion Creek Road. Return the way you came.

**2.0** Arrive back at the car.

## NEARBY HIKES

Grandstaff, Fisher Towers

## CREATURE COMFORTS

**Upper Onion Creek Campground**, BLM 100, Moab, UT 84532; www.recreation .gov. Onion Creek Campground is a beautiful spot with views of the Colorado River, Castle Valley, and the La Sal Mountains. This site has fire grates, tables, toilets, and shade shelters. There are no hookups or water. This is a popular spot for equestrians, so use caution if your pups haven't been exposed to horses. Reservations can be made on www .recreation.gov. This location is 40 minutes from Moab so plan to stock up on food beforehand. Bring water and shade shelters as this spot can get hot in the summer.

**Moonflower Community Cooperative**, 39 E. 100 North, Moab; (435) 259-5712; moonflower.coop. Moonflower is a community-run natural-foods grocery store with great prepared foods to take on the go. Their foods are fresh, organic, and local when

# Onion Creek Narrows

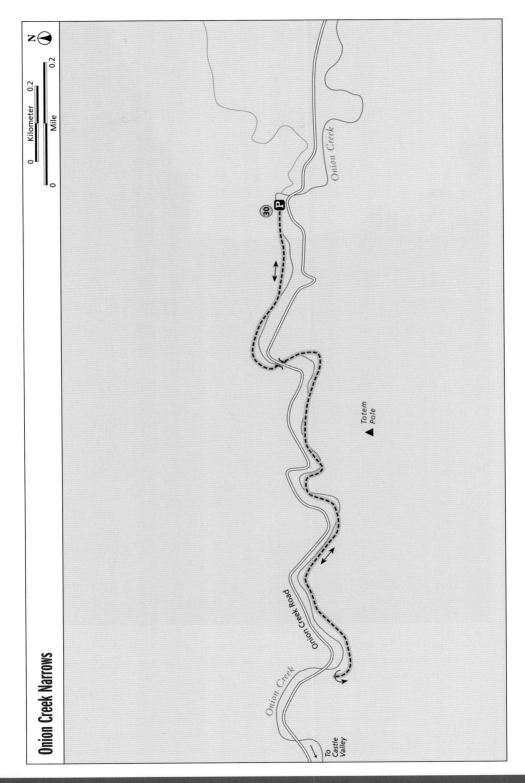

Onion Creek

possible, and their prepared-food selection has options for everyone. Be sure to pick up some delicious Nunn Better Jerky for trail snacks. It's great for picnics and a great spot to pick up groceries before camping near Moab.

# 31 MOUNTAIN VIEW VIA MINERS BASIN TRAIL

## WHY GO?

The Mountain View and Miners Basin Trails are located in the La Sal Mountains near Moab, just north of the Warner Lake Campground. The trail to Mountain View climbs through the shady pines and ends at a spectacular view. From there, your hike can be combined with other trails in the area if desired.

### THE RUNDOWN

**County:** Grand
**Start:** Miners Basin Trailhead
**Distance:** 4.0 miles out and back
**Hiking time:** 2–3 hours
**Difficulty:** Moderate due to higher elevation and steeper sections
**Trailhead elevation:** 9,442 feet
**Highest point:** 10,093 feet
**Best seasons:** Summer, fall
**Other trail users:** Hikers
**Canine compatibility:** Voice control. On leash around wildlife.
**Land status:** Manti-La Sal National Forest
**Fees and permits:** None
**Trail contacts:** Moab Ranger District, 62 E. 100 North, Moab, UT 84532; (435) 259-7155. Monticello Ranger District, 496 East Central, Monticello, UT 84535; (435) 587-2041.
**Nearest town:** Moab
**Trail tips:** This is a hunting area in the fall. If you hike at that time of year, you and your pup should wear orange and be aware of those around you. Although only 30 miles or so from Moab, the Warner Lake Trailhead will take even the most ambitious drivers an hour to get to. The roads are graded dirt for part of the way. Four-wheel drive is recommended.
**Nat Geo TOPO! Map (USGS):** 7.5-minute *Warner Lake*
**Nat Geo Trails Illustrated Map:** *Manti-La Sal National Forest 703*

## FINDING THE TRAILHEAD

From Moab, drive south 7.8 miles on Main Street (US 191). Turn left (east) on Country Road/Old Airport Road as you pass Spanish Valley and continue for 0.6 mile. Turn right (south) onto La Sal Mountain Loop Road/Spanish Valley Drive and continue for 14.2 miles. Turn right onto FR 063 toward Warner Lake Campground. Continue for approximately 5 miles, where there will be a wooden sign and a trail heading north before the Warner Lake parking area. Continue to the parking area, then hike back south along the road. The trailhead is on the north side of the road, indicated by a trail register and gate.
**Trailhead GPS:** N38 31.229' / W109 16.581'

## THE HIKE

The trail begins heading north, climbing gently up toward Shuman Gulch through a grove of aspens. At mile 0.2 the trail will T-junction with an old road. Turn right and continue northeast along the trail, climbing steadily while paralleling the road. Just beyond this you will pass an old fence, but stay to the right of the sign and continue. The trail will become very steep and rocky at times, with large trail obstacles to maneuver around as you ascend. There will be water available for your dog down in the gully to

What a great hike for photographers!

the north. At mile 0.8 you will arrive at the Mountain View Trail junction, which turns right (south). There are other options from here to explore at a later date, including Golden Throne.

On the Mountain View Trail, the scenery is drastically different than other hikes in the area. With its deep ravines and tall conifers, the mood is somber. On this shaded trek you will be able to see, smell, and feel water collecting in gullies to the south. There will be muddy places for your dog to get a drink. These pools are frequented by elk. You most likely will be able to smell the wafting "gamy" aroma of a bull elk as you pass by. This side of the forest is definitely elk country, with places for whole herds to disappear. Elk are most active during the early morning and later afternoon or evening times, while they wander around to feed. During the day they will bed down while it is hot, chewing their cud and napping. If you pay attention, you can see antler rubs on the trees from the bull elk as they prepare themselves for the rut. These displays are unmistakable, with the bark of trees stripped away and whole willow clumps mowed down. This behavior has been speculated as a show of masculine prestige. If you are lucky to be in this area during the rut, you may hear the sound of a bull elk bugling, a sound so eerie and wild that it may make the hair on your arms stand up. With dogs' keen sense of smell, they can detect these large animals long before we can, making it fun to learn their body language when they detect a wild animal. Often dogs' behavior will change with different animal detections. Try to see, smell, or hear what they do. Elk, like mule deer, have a keen sense of smell and rely on it heavily as part of their prey drive. They will flee at the slightest detection of human scent. Learning to pay attention to the way wind shifts and moves through a forest will help you see more animals, if that is your goal.

Continue on the Mountain View Trail as it steeply climbs following the left side of the drainage. There are sections that are fairly difficult and require some thoughtful foot

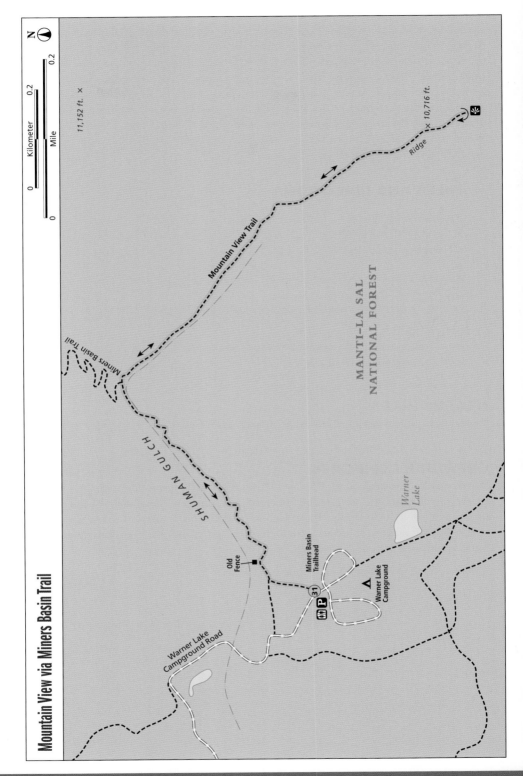

# Mountain View via Miners Basin Trail

N

Kilometer
0    0.2

Mile
0    0.2

11,152 ft. ×

Ridge × 10,716 ft.

Mountain View Trail

Miners Basin Trail

SHUMAN GULCH

MANTI-LA SAL
NATIONAL FOREST

Warner
Lake

Old
Fence

Miners Basin
Trailhead

31 P

Warner Lake
Campground

Warner Lake
Campground Road

placement. The trail will then cross above the now shallow drainage and head south. At mile 1.5 the light begins to peek out from the top of the ridge and the anticipation of the view begins to grow. At mile 1.8 there is a small opening of the trees on the ridge and the view east toward Manns Peak is spectacular. Follow the ridge south a little farther to the end of the ridge and enjoy the views of the La Sals, Canyonlands, and beyond. On the rocky top of this bare ridge, it is possible to have unobstructed views of the faraway horizons. It is a beautiful spot to rest and enjoy your accomplishment. When you are finished, return the way you came, and watch for elk tracks through the open corridors in the aspens.

## MILES AND DIRECTIONS

**0.0** Park at the Warner Lake parking area, then walk down the road until the signs for the trailhead.

**0.2** Stay east on the dirt road. Pass the old fence, then veer right following the trail.

**0.8** Arrive at the junction for Mountain View and Miners Basin. Head south for Mountain View.

**1.5** The drainage ends and the trail turns to the south.

**1.8** Climb the ridge.

**2.0** Arrive at the summit, and return the way you came.

**4.0** Arrive back at the trailhead.

## NEARBY HIKES

Warner Lake, Squaw Spring, Clark Lake Loop

## CREATURE COMFORTS

**Warner Lake Campground**, FR 036, Moab, UT 84532; www.recreation.gov. Adjacent to the beautiful Warner Lake, the Warner Lake Campground has tent, RV, and cabin sites with a variety of amenities. Reservations should be made early on www.recreation .gov, especially for the cabin sites. Drinking water and vault toilets are available and all campsites include fire pits and parking.

This is a remote area, so stock up on food and water.

# 32 WARNER LAKE TO DRY CREEK

## WHY GO?

The Warner Lake Trail to Dry Creek is a challenging hike with incredible elevation gains through aspen groves and conifer forests. Not for the faint of heart, this trail is for the salty trail dog and her rough-and-tumble human. With Herculean efforts, it is possible to earn a view that begins among the bold La Sals and ends flirting with Mount Ellen, the highest peak in the Henry Mountain range. In between, Utah's canyon lands and its unique geology can be seen.

### THE RUNDOWN

**County:** Grand
**Start:** Warner Lake Trailhead
**Distance:** 8.0 miles out and back
**Hiking time:** 3–4 hours
**Difficulty:** Strenuous due to longer mileage and elevation gain
**Trailhead elevation:** 9,390 feet
**Highest point:** 11,543 feet
**Best season:** Early summer
**Trail surface:** Dirt trail, shale, rocky sections
**Other trail users:** Mountain bikers
**Canine compatibility:** On leash recommended
**Land status:** National Forest
**Fees and permits:** None
**Trail contacts:** Moab Ranger District, 62 E. 100 North, Moab, UT 84532;

(435) 259-7155. Monticello Ranger District, 496 East Central, Monticello, UT 84535; (435) 587-2041.
**Nearest town:** Moab
**Trail tips:** Be prepared for the 2,153 feet of elevation gain and loss on this hike. It is outlandishly beautiful and also difficult at times. Make sure to bring extra layers, food, and water for all hikers.
**Nat Geo TOPO! Map (USGS):**
7.5-minute *Warner Lake, Mount Waas*
**Nat Geo Trails Illustrated Map:** *703: Manti-La Sal National Forest*
**Other map:** *Latitude 40° East Map Recreation Topo Map: Moab East*

### FINDING THE TRAILHEAD

From Moab, drive south 7.8 miles on Main Street (US 191). Turn left (east) on Country Road/Old Airport Road as you pass Spanish Valley and continue for 0.6 mile. Turn right (south) onto La Sal Mountain Loop Road/Spanish Valley Drive and continue for 14.2 miles. Turn right onto Forest Road 063 toward Warner Campground. Continue for approximately 5 miles—there will be a wooden sign and a trail heading north before the Warner Lake parking area. The trail begins southeast of the parking area.
**Trailhead GPS:** N38 31.155' / W109 16.514'

## THE HIKE

From the Warner Lake Trailhead, you will enjoy a view of Warner Lake and the 11,641-foot Haystack Mountain beyond that will surely astound. During the splendor of autumn with the aspens showing off, there are very few places that can rival the view. The trail heads southeast. If you begin early, before the fishermen line the banks, this place is as peaceful as it gets. Hike along the trail past a green gate in the trees. At mile 0.2 there are signed junctions with Oowah Lake Trail, but continue south until you reach a fork at mile 0.3. Veer left at the sign (033), traveling through the forest and intermittent meadows.

Wren and Warner Lake.

Aspen trees are part of the Poplar family. They have round-shaped leaves, which attach to the leaf stem by a petiole. What is unique about *Populus tremuloides* is that the petiole is flat instead of round like other trees. It is attached at 90-degree angle, allowing it to twist and flutter in the slightest breeze. This construction also gives the leaf a better chance of remaining intact during high-velocity winds. Another interesting fact is aspens are usually clones or offshoots of one another. Pando, or "trembling giant," is a colony of quaking-aspen trees near Fish Lake, Utah, that is estimated to be around 80,000 years old.

As you continue under stunning aspen trees, you'll pass an old fence at mile 0.6, and soon a view of Haystack Mountain will emerge through the leaves. If you are quiet, you may hear a mule deer or two in the thicket. Look for bear signs as you travel down the trail, marked by perfect claw marks scarred over on the white trunks of the aspens.

Mule deer, named after their mule-like (big) ears, are indigenous to North America. They rely heavily on their sense of smell to avoid predators. Often hikers and their dogs will send these incredibly agile creatures pronking, a stiff four-legged springing movement that allows the deer to sail over obstacles and see over thickets and through the woods. These creatures are most active during the early morning and at dusk. Throughout the La Sals, the mule deer population is concentrated and they are spotted frequently. Overall, the population of the mule deer, or "muleys" as they are affectionately known, is declining mostly due to habitat loss. There are other theories, but without room to roam and food to eat, animals cannot survive.

As you continue hiking you will arrive at the junction with the famous Whole Enchilada mountain bike trail at mile 1.2. This is a shuttled downhill trail and is likely to be busy, so plan to leash up your pup for a while. Follow the Whole Enchilada (W.E.) up against the mountain bike traffic until you reach the signed Dry Fork Trail junction at mile 1.9. This will be on your left.

Take the Dry Fork Trail north, pausing to let your dogs get a drink. Dry Fork is appropriately named, and there will not be available water until this same spot on your return trip. At this point the trail will head northeast as you climb steadily and steeply through the petering out of aspens and into the conifers. Bear signs and elk are prevalent.

Follow the drainage up toward a natural and imposing amphitheater. The mountains on either side will close in as you approach the switchback trail that will take you to the saddle. During summer the columbines and purple-blue larkspurs highlight the beauty of this area.

At mile 3.4 the switchbacks begin, and begin they do. The shaley hillside packs a punch, and if you look up as you are climbing, the views will take the rest of your breath away. Use caution and take breaks, as it can get warm on the ascent.

You'll reach the saddle at mile 4. From here, Beaver Basin is to your east, and your view to the west extends all the way to the Henry Mountains, looking over canyon lands and the deep deserts of the Needles District. Manns Peak looms large at the exposed saddle. Be prepared because the wind can be biting.

It is possible to continue trekking, but the trails are not as visible from the saddle, and proficient orienteering skills are needed. When you are ready, head back the way you came, being extra careful on the way down.

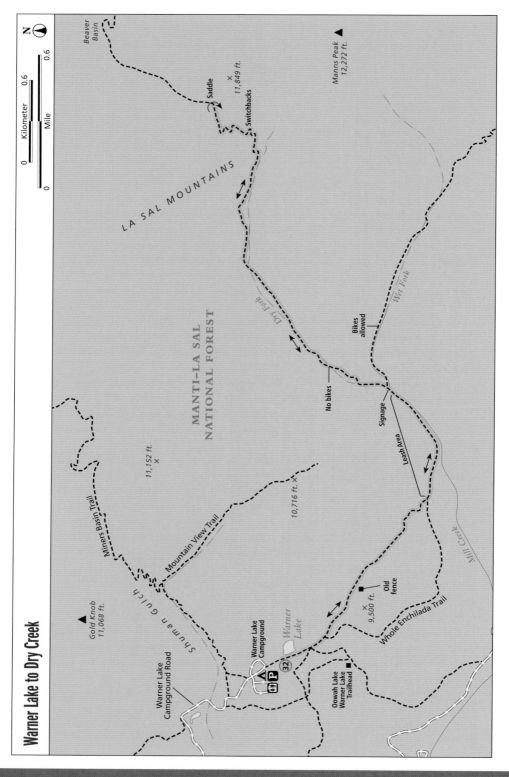

# Warner Lake to Dry Creek

Beaver Basin

Saddle

11,849 ft.

Switchbacks

LA SAL MOUNTAINS

Manns Peak
12,272 ft.

Dry Fork

Wet Fork

MANTI–LA SAL
NATIONAL FOREST

No bikes

Bikes allowed

Signage

Leash Area

Miners Basin Trail

11,152 ft.

Gold Knob
11,068 ft.

Shuman Gulch

Mountain View Trail

10,716 ft.

Old fence

9,500 ft.

Mill Creek

Whole Enchilada Trail

Warner Lake
Campground Road

Warner Lake
Campground

Warner
Lake

32

Oowah Lake
Warner Lake
Trailhead

N

Kilometer
0        0.6

0        0.6
Mile

## MILES AND DIRECTIONS

**0.0** Follow the trail to the southeast of the parking area.

**0.2** Stay left at the trail junction with Oowa Lake Trail.

**0.3** Turn left at the fork indicated by the sign (033).

**0.6** Pass an old fence.

**1.2** Leash your pups as you merge with the Whole Enchilada mountain bike trail, heading opposite the cyclists up the trail.

**1.9** The signed Dry Fork Trail cutoff trail heads north.

**3.4** Begin climbing the steep switchbacks.

**4.0** Arrive at the saddle, and return the way you came.

**8.0** Arrive back at the car.

## NEARBY HIKES

Miners Basin, Oowah Lake, Warner Lake Loop

## CREATURE COMFORTS

**Warner Lake Campground**, FR 036, Moab, UT 84532; www.recreation.gov. Adjacent to the beautiful Warner Lake, the Warner Lake Campground has tent, RV, and cabin sites with a variety of amenities. Reservations should be made early on www.recreation.gov, especially for the cabin sites. Drinking water and vault toilets are available, and all campsites include fire pits and parking.

This is a remote area, so stock up on food and water.

# 33 LITTLE GRAND CANYON

## WHY GO?

Little Grand Canyon is a beautiful backpacking trip through the San Rafael Swell along the San Rafael River. As a point-to-point hike through canyon country, this area requires all the gear and knowledge associated with backcountry travel. Beautiful and remote, this trail follows and crosses the San Rafael River many times. It winds its way through beautiful high-walled geology and riparian desert ecology. This is a remote destination. This hike requires a shuttle car.

### THE RUNDOWN

**County:** Emery
**Start:** Fuller Bottom
**End:** San Rafael Bridge
**Distance:** 16.0 miles +/- point to point
**Hiking time:** About 2 days
**Difficulty:** Strenuous due to stream crossings, overnight, rough terrain, and remoteness
**Trailhead elevation:** 5,220 feet
**Trail end elevation:** 5,128 feet
**Best seasons:** Fall, early summer
**Trail surface:** Sand, rock, water crossings, water travel
**Other trail users:** Horses
**Canine compatibility:** Voice control
**Land status:** Bureau of Land Management
**Fees and permits:** None

**Trail contacts:** BLM Price Field Office, 125 S. 600 West, Price, UT 84501; (435) 636-3600. Emery County Sheriff, (435) 381-2404. Wayne County Sheriff, (435) 836-2789.
**Nearest town:** Huntington
**Trail tips:** Full backpack regalia and trekking poles for extra stability can be helpful during water crossings. Consider heat, river levels, and flooding when planning this trip. Monsoon season is in late summer. Check the weather.
**Nat Geo TOPO! Map (USGS):** 7.5-minute *Buckhorn Reservoir, Sids Mountain, Bottleneck Peak, Bob Hill Knoll*
**Nat Geo Trails Illustrated Map:** *712: San Rafael Swell*

### FINDING THE TRAILHEAD

This hike requires a shuttle vehicle. The hike begins at Fuller Bottom and ends at the San Rafael Bridge.

**To San Rafael Bridge:** From the town of Huntington, head south on UT 10 for 7 miles. Turn left (east) on the Green River Cutoff Road (road 401). Continue east for approximately 13 miles until you see a road junction with some interpretive signage and a restroom on the right. You'll pass Fuller Bottom Road on the right, which will be where the hike will start. Continue on the Green River Cutoff Road for 2.1 miles and follow it past the nondescript Wedge Cutoff Road. Cross over a small bridge and take the next right onto Buckhorn Draw Road (road 332), then continue for approximately 10 miles until you reach the San Rafael Bridge. Cross the bridge and continue past the campground, taking your first right (west) onto an unnamed road. Follow this for approximately 0.8 mile until you reach a turnaround with some corrals. This is the end of the hike.

**To Fuller Bottom:** From the takeout, follow your steps back until you reach the Green River Cutoff Road. Follow this west for 2.1 miles and turn left onto Fuller Bottom Road. Veer right (south) at the split with Wedge Road to continue on Fuller Bottom Road. Continue on Fuller Bottom Road for another 5 miles until you reach the signage for the San Rafael River. Park at the pull-off to the left of the road.

## THE HIKE

After arriving take a moment to enjoy the view of Fuller Bottom and the view east toward Little Grand Canyon. If you are lucky, you will hear a pheasant or two calling in the tamarisk thicket. After parking your vehicle at the pullout, next to the metal SAN RAFAEL RIVER sign, begin your hike, packs on, with a short descent to the sandy Fuller Bottom Road. It is important to remember in this section to hike east toward the obvious canyon beginning. How you do this is not critical. There is not one trail. You will be on the Fuller Bottom Road briefly, leaving its confines for the flatlands that lay to the east. This section is difficult only in that there are cattle trails that seem promising but then peter out, leaving you in a tamarisk thicket.

Tamarisk, also called "salt cedar," is an invasive shrub that was introduced in the 1900s and promoted as a solution for riverbank erosion control and windbreaks. Since its introduction, tamarisk has flourished—perhaps too well—choking out the native cottonwoods and willows throughout the West. The densely populated tamarisk make the trudge to the mouth of the Little Grand Canyon challenging. Make your way the best you can.

Once you enter the canyon, the trail becomes visible and meanders in and out of the riparian zone along the river. Use the river and the canyon as your directional guide—cross when you need to cross, hike the benches when you can hike the benches. This type of hiking is dynamic and ever-changing, making it exciting and at times challenging.

The A-team at Fuller Bottom.

Hiking with your dogs down canyons such as this is a challenging yet rewarding experience. But it is important to be cognizant of each crossing and gauge if your dog will need assistance. If your dog is not a strong swimmer, I would not recommend this hike. The San Rafael River is not exceedingly deep—1 to 3 feet during the slow outflow—but depending on your dog, helping them across would be a safe choice. Helping a dog may look a few different ways: holding on to the dog's harness or life vest as you walk across the stream; sending someone to scout the best way up the bank on the other side of the river, then calling your dog; or it may be best to cross the river diagonally. If the current seems swift, hike up- or downstream to find a more tranquil wide crossing. Take a little extra time to be safe considering your dog's ability.

On this hike you will always be hiking downstream. Do not be dismayed during this short and challenging beginning. It is helpful to keep the San Rafael River in sight and again hike downstream. As you make your way downstream, notice the honeycomb weathering in the sandstone along the side walls. At mile 2.9, just past a nameless side canyon, heading north you will find petroglyphs on the northern wall. Common theories hold that the Fremont people, a sort of catchall category of the ancient peoples that lived in this area around 2,000 years ago, most likely authored these stories. The terrain you are hiking through is beautiful now, with high streaked walls of sandstone and the healthy glow of the coyote willows. For the most part there is a substantial and obvious trail. It is helpful to have a trekking pole to gauge the depth of the river at each crossing. If it is too deep, travel up- or downstream a little ways to find a more appropriate crossing point.

After mile 4.8 Salt Wash will be visible to the south. Along the way you will begin to see lots of signs of beaver life: chewed-down trees and places where they maneuvered the logs into the river to construct their dams. Beavers and their importance to western riparian zones are part of an ongoing conversation happening throughout Utah, from the northern Bear River range to the southern Escalante River. Grandcanyontrust.org has many articles advocating for the beaver and its vital influence on the health of our water systems.

At mile 7 the trail takes you through an old juniper grove, which seems out of place. And around mile 9 there are places to make a safe camp out of the drainages. In the desert the weather can change seemingly in an instant, and weather miles away may have grave consequences. The sandstone acts almost like a bobsled run for water, as very little rain can create a lot of pour-off. Camping in a place with the potential to flood is a dangerous decision. Always camp on the benches out of harm's way.

The backcountry ethics of positive impact are important in areas as beautiful as the Swell. The scars left by fire rings and giant pits of coals is unsightly, as is toilet paper that was left behind. There are simple things that help preserve the pristine feel of an area, such as burning small sticks if you have a fire, as this reduces the coals left behind, which are unsightly. At the Boulder Outdoor Survival School, we were taught to grind our coals, sprinkling the coal dust on plants in the area. With these strict codes, the areas used for teaching for over 40 years look virtually untouched.

In the morning continue your hike downstream (east). At mile 11.7 Good Water Canyon is to the north, named for the "good water tanks" at the head of the canyon. According to Owen McClenahan in Steve Allen's *Utah's Canyon Country Place Names*, 2012, the water here was used to make whiskey during the Prohibition era.

At mile 12 you will pass by an old fence, worse for wear. Shortly after that, at 12.5 miles, Cane Wash comes in from the south and is navigationally significant because the next

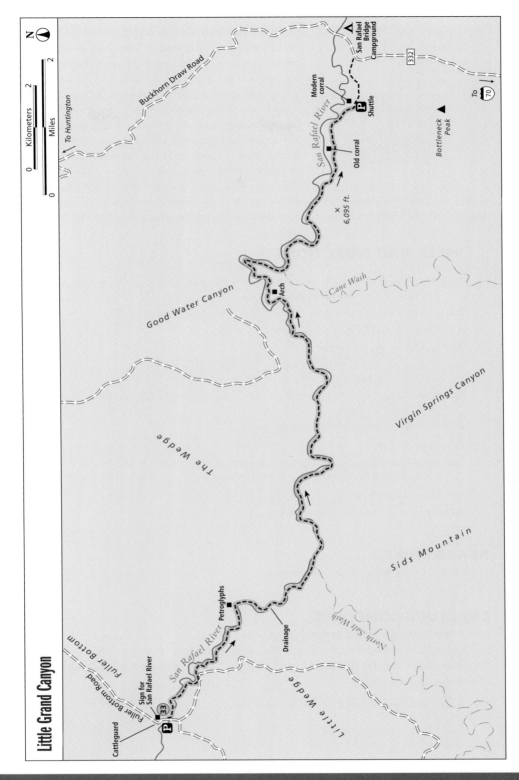

# Little Grand Canyon

**N**

| 0 | Kilometers | 2 |
| 0 | Miles | 2 |

Buckhorn Draw Road

To Huntington

San Rafael River

San Rafael Bridge Campground

332

To 70

Modern corral

Shuttle

**P**

Old corral

× 6,095 ft.

Bottleneck Peak

Good Water Canyon

Cane Wash

Arch

Virgin Springs Canyon

The Wedge

Sids Mountain

Petroglyphs

Drainage

North Salt Wash

San Rafael River

Little Wedge

Fuller Bottom

Fuller Bottom Road

Sign for San Rafael River

33

**P**

Cattleguard

San Rafael River

> On the way to the shuttle car drop-off on Buckhorn Draw Road, you can find beautiful pictographs called the Buckhorn Panel. Their style is similar to the "Great Gallery" in Horseshoe Canyon in Canyonlands National Park.

large drainage you come to will signal you to climb out of the river basin onto a horse trail above the river. The views of the high plateaus of this section of the river are gorgeous. At mile 14.5, just past a large wash entering the canyon from the south, the trail heads up to the previously mentioned horse trail bypassing some wild tamarisk thickets. At mile 15 an old empty corral rests propped up under a rather large boulder, signifying the final mile of the hike. No doubt a place to hole up for a day or two while moving cattle through the canyon. As you round the final bend, enjoy the incredible views of the surrounding valley. At mile 16 your car will be visible near the more modern corrals on the bench above the river.

## MILES AND DIRECTIONS

**0.0** Walk down one of the many cattle trails heading east into Fuller Bottom past the sign for the San Rafael River.

**2.9** Look up on the north wall—you will be able to see some petroglyphs.

**4.8** Continue east past Salt Wash to the right (south).

**7.0** Wind through the juniper grove.

**9.0** There are many camp options along this hike. Remember: Always camp out of danger of flash floods in canyon country.

**11.0** Continue east past Good Water Canyon, a significant drainage coming in from the north (left).

**12.0** Pass by an old fence and continue east.

**12.5** Pass Cane Wash coming in from the south.

**14.5** As you pass a significant drainage on the south side of the canyon, follow the trail south up the ridge to a horse trail above the river and continue east.

**15.0** Pass an old corral.

**16.0** Arrive at the San Rafael Bridge.

## NEARBY HIKES
The Wedge, Good Water Rim, Calf Canyon

## CREATURE COMFORTS
**San Rafael Bridge Campground**, Buckhorn Draw Road, Green River, UT 84525; (435) 636-3600; www.recreation.gov. This campground is a small spot with only six campsites at the takeout for Little Grand Canyon. There are toilets but no water or amenities, and a fee applies.

This is a remote area, so stock up on food and water.

# 34 CHUTE CANYON

## WHY GO?

Chute Canyon is a fairly remote canyon in the San Rafael Swell. This hike offers the beauty of high sandstone walls and battleship features as it wanders through the twists and turns of the narrows. On your hike you will witness true beauty in this wild place. Bringing water is imperative.

---

### THE RUNDOWN

**County:** Emery
**Start:** Chute Canyon Trailhead
**Distance:** 7.2 miles out and back
**Hiking time:** 2-4 hours
**Difficulty:** Moderate due to length and remoteness
**Trailhead elevation:** 5,132 feet
**Lowest point:** 4,828 feet
**Best seasons:** Spring, fall
**Trail surface:** Wash bottom, sand, gravel
**Other trail users:** Hikers
**Canine compatibility:** Voice control
**Land status:** Crack Canyon Wilderness Area, Bureau of Land Management
**Fees and permits:** None

**Trail contact:** BLM Price Field Office, 125 S. 600 West, Price, UT 84501; (435) 636-3600
**Nearest town:** Hanksville
**Trail tips:** This hike is located in a remote area of Utah. There are no amenities available and 4x4 driving is required. It is imperative to bring water, food, maps, GPS, and a compass. No cell service. Plan to fill up your vehicle's fuel tank in Hanksville.
**Nat Geo TOPO! Map (USGS):** 7.5-minute *Horse Valley*
**Nat Geo Trails Illustrated Map:** *712: San Rafael Swell*

---

## FINDING THE TRAILHEAD

From I-70, head south on UT 24 and take exit 149 toward Hanksville. Travel on UT 24 until signage directs you west (right) on Temple Mountain Road, approximately 24 miles. If coming from Hanksville, heading north on UT 24, the turnoff for Temple Mountain Road is shortly after mile marker 136. Continue west for 5 miles, passing the turnoff for Goblin Valley State Park and Bell Canyon/Little Wild Horse Canyon, other iconic San Rafael Swell hikes that are dog friendly and worth checking out. Pass the Temple Mountain Wash pictograph panel and continue as the pavement ends. You will see Temple Mountain Campground on your right. Veer left (south) onto Behind-the-Reef Road, a primitive road heading south, as it winds its way around the curves of the canyon foothills. There are plenty of pull-offs for camping if you are prepared to stay out for a couple days. After about 7 miles Behind-the-Reef Road will drop you off at the trailhead for Chute Canyon. The road sharply turns past the signed trailhead and parking area, climbing steeply, and it is very rough. From the parking area, head southeast toward the canyon. The Nat Geo Trail Illustrated Map and Google Earth are recommended for perspective.
**Trailhead GPS:** N38 37.741' / W110 45.798'

## THE HIKE

The San Rafael Swell was scoured by the various mining booms from the late 1800s through the 1950s. Copper Globe, Muddy Creek, Lucky Strike, Tomsich Butte, and Little Susan are historic uranium mines of this area. The uranium miners and their hearty

Entering the canyon.

spirits gave more than their backs and sweat to the Swell. They made their living off the highs and lows of the market, skill, and probably luck. Their history unites in the present as the mining roads that ushered them from claim to claim are the contemporary trails we use today. *Mining on the Swell* on YouTube is a great introduction to some of the miners and their stories from this area. As mentioned in the film, keep a look out for milkvetch, a plant known for growing on patches of uranium. Chute Canyon, no doubt, had its part in the boom.

You'll begin your hike down Chute Canyon from the parking area to the southeast. You will wander down on a dirt road, crossing the streambed a time or two. At mile 1 a sign will indicate no more vehicles allowed. The vehicle tracks fade away, and little rippling pockets of water lead you downstream. Throughout your hike you will witness incredible examples of the geologic layers. Keep a lookout for the beauty of the sand-stone, clay layers, and honeycomb shapes. These honeycomb shapes are called "tafoni" or "stone lace" and are found throughout the Reef. They are beautiful and otherworldly.

In the wash it is possible to find petrified wood. If you should be so lucky as to find anything of the sort, please leave it where you found it. These rare treasures belong in the desert.

Depending on the light or the time of day, spirals, eroded by the wind, appear high up on the canyon walls. On the way back they may seem to have vanished. This disappear-ing act is part of the magic of the desert. By mile 2.6 the canyon narrows to around 6 feet from wall to wall. At mile 3.6 the canyon widens up into a desert badlands, marking the end of this out-and-back trail. Return the way you came.

## MILES AND DIRECTIONS

**0.0**  Follow the dirt road southeast down the canyon as it crisscrosses the creek bed.

**1.0**  Continue past the "Closed to motorized vehicles" sign.

**2.6**  Continue down the canyon as it narrows.

**3.6**  The canyon widens again, making this a good turnaround point. Return the way you came.

**7.2**  Arrive back at the trailhead.

## NEARBY HIKE
Goblin Valley

## CREATURE COMFORTS
**Temple Mountain Campground**, Temple Mountain Road near Hanksville, Utah; www.recreation.gov. Temple Mountain Campground is located just off Behind-the-Reef Road. There are no reservations and early arrival is recommended, however, this is a great spot to camp while exploring the San Rafael Swell and nearby areas. There are tent sites and RV sites available for free and they include fire pits, toilets, shelters, and tables.

This is a remote area, so stock up on food and water.

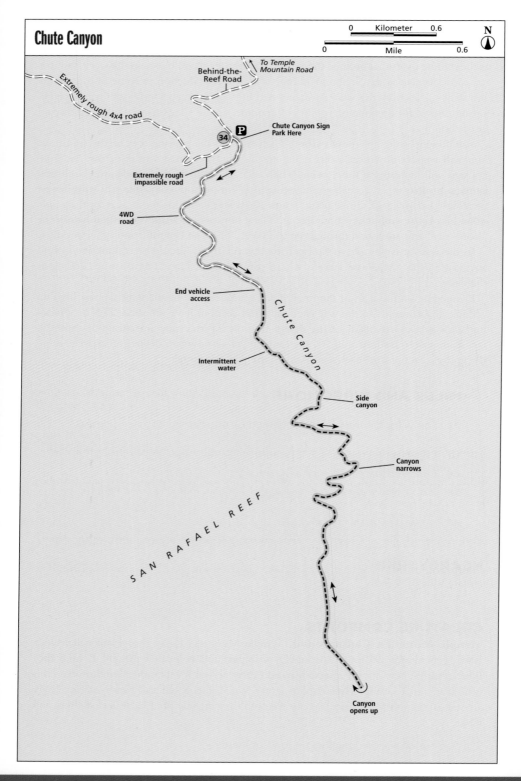

# Chute Canyon

Kilometer 0 0.6
Mile 0 0.6

N

To Temple
Mountain Road

Behind-the-
Reef Road

Extremely rough 4x4 road

34 P

Chute Canyon Sign
Park Here

Extremely rough
impassible road

4WD
road

End vehicle
access

Chute Canyon

Intermittent
water

Side
canyon

Canyon
narrows

SAN RAFAEL REEF

Canyon
opens up

Martin and Wren enjoying canyon country.

**Tamarisk Restaurant**, 1710 E. Main St., Green River, UT 84525; (435) 564-8109; www.tamariskrestaurant.com. The Tamarisk is a great restaurant on the Green River serving breakfast, lunch, and dinner to hungry hikers and other recreation enthusiasts traveling to Moab or the San Rafael Swell. They have delicious omelets, salads, and sandwiches as well as western-style entrees. No pups please.

# 35 WILD HORSE CANYON

## WHY GO?

The beautiful Wild Horse Canyon hike follows the dry bed of Wild Horse Creek in the San Rafael Reef. Look for large and small arches as you travel down this canyon—there are quite a few! A couple small slots makes this canyon a family-friendly affair with lots of sculptured twists and turns to explore. There is no reliable water in Wild Horse Canyon, so please bring plenty for hikers and dogs alike. **Note:** This is different than the well-known Little Wild Horse Canyon. *Do not attempt if rain is forecasted!*

### THE RUNDOWN

**County:** Emery
**Start:** Wild Horse Parking Area sign
**Distance:** 6.2 miles out and back
**Hiking time:** 2–3 hours
**Difficulty:** Moderate due to longer mileage, wash walking, and remoteness
**Trailhead elevation:** 5,525 feet
**Lowest point:** 5,197 feet
**Best seasons:** Spring, fall, winter. Flash floods possible.
**Trail surface:** Wash bottom, some sandstone walking
**Other trail users:** Hikers
**Canine compatibility:** Voice control
**Land status:** Bureau of Land Management, Crack Canyon Wilderness Area (BLM)
**Fees and permits:** None
**Trail contacts:** BLM Price Field Office, 125 S. 600 West, Price, UT 84501; (435) 636-3600. Wayne County Sheriff, (435) 836-2789.

Emery County Sheriff, (435) 381-2404.
**Nearest town:** Hanksville
**Trail tips:** This is a remote area. It is important that you are self-sufficient: Maps (both TOPO and Illustrated), water, food, compass, and GPS are *not* optional. There are no services nearby and no cell service. There is not any reliable water in Wild Horse Canyon, so bring plenty. A morning or evening hike through Wild Horse Canyon would be best, as it could get very hot during the day. Flash floods are common in these slot canyons, so use caution! Four-wheel drive is required and high-clearance vehicles are recommended.
**Nat Geo TOPO! Map (USGS):** 7.5-minute *Temple Mountain*
**Nat Geo Trails Illustrated Map:** *712: San Rafael Swell*

## FINDING THE TRAILHEAD

From I-70, head south on UT 24 and take exit 149 toward Hanksville. Travel on UT 24 until signage directs you west (right) on Temple Mountain Road, approximately 24 miles. If coming from Hanksville, heading north on UT 24, the turnoff for Temple Mountain Road is shortly after mile marker 136. Continue west, passing turnoffs for Goblin Valley State Park and Bell Canyon/Little Wild Horse Canyon at 5 miles, which are other iconic San Rafael Swell hikes that are dog friendly and worth checking out. Continue west on Temple Mountain Road beyond the end of the pavement and the Temple Mountain Campground, which has vault toilets but no water. Turn left (south) onto Behind-the-Reef Road. It is important to pay attention because there are no signs on Behind-the-Reef Road directing you to Wild Horse Canyon. Instead you will need to watch for the first significant drainage on your left (east) and turn into the drainage following the tire tracks that form the road. Drive toward the canyon, passing a half dozen campsites on either side of the dirt road you are on. You will see the sign for Wild Horse, with a small parking area. The views from

Beautiful canyon country.

this small parking lot are incredible so take a moment to look at the giant features known as the Reef, hence the name Behind-the-Reef Road. Looking on Google Maps will also help you find this area.
**Trailhead GPS:** N38 39.237' / W110 42.600'

## THE HIKE

From your turn off of UT 24 onto Temple Mountain Road, the adventure begins. So vast are the vistas out here in the Swell, so bright are the purples, blues, and reds that it is difficult to imagine what the words "canyon country" mean before you see it.

Today, mining has all but disappeared here, replaced by the sounds of ATVs in some sections of this vastness. But Wild Horse Canyon is an outlet for walkers, with a chance to see and explore with your dog a world ripped apart and put back together by geologic forces. This area is also incredibly rich in minerals, historical significance, archaeology, and without a doubt first-rate beauty.

After 6.2 miles on Temple Mountain Road, there is a small dirt road on your right that will take you to see petroglyphs and some imposing pictographs done in the Barrier-Canyon style, before your turnoff to Behind-the-Reef Road. Take a minute on your drive to pause and look out over the south-central Utah landscape.

From your parked 4x4 vehicle, hike down the dirt road heading into the sweeping embrace of this lovely canyon. From the parking area, the way forward is simple to find. Head south into Wild Horse Canyon. Arches peek out from each side of the high sand-stone walls. Some arches are only visible for a brief moment, some are flush against the wall. Look for light, which indicates the arches' whereabouts.

There are a couple well-used campsites down the canyon that are not very private. The 0.9-mile mark is the "no-more vehicles point." Here, the trail narrows some as you continue south, walking through some flood-sculpted formations and large boulders. The trail heads sharply east. The walls get taller to the south. To the north is the San Rafael Reef, an example of an anticline. An anticline is layers of rock that have been pushed up over millions of years. Take a moment to consider the forces required to push the land upward.

When talking about central Utah, it is important to consider wild horses, commonly referred to in the West as mustangs. The word *mustang* comes from the Spanish word *mesteño*, meaning wild or stray, and certainly mustangs have remained as wild as humans will allow. The iconic image of wild horses roaming the valley and gorges of the still wild places of this country is becoming harder to find.

In the 1800s traders brought horses to this part of the country while using the Old Spanish Trail, which connected northern New Mexico to southern California. This trail was considered to be one of the most perilous of the trade routes that crisscrossed the country during this time. Horses were often being herded through the area to be sold or traded in California. Mishaps were unavoidable for many horse wranglers, and escapees began to populate the area. Today, thousands of horses stand in holding facilities, having been rounded up and placed in corrals, families separated and sold off or kept in captivity indefinitely. The Swell and around Wild Horse Canyon is one of those special places that a lucky person may get a glimpse of a herd of wild horses or burros.

# Wild Horse Canyon

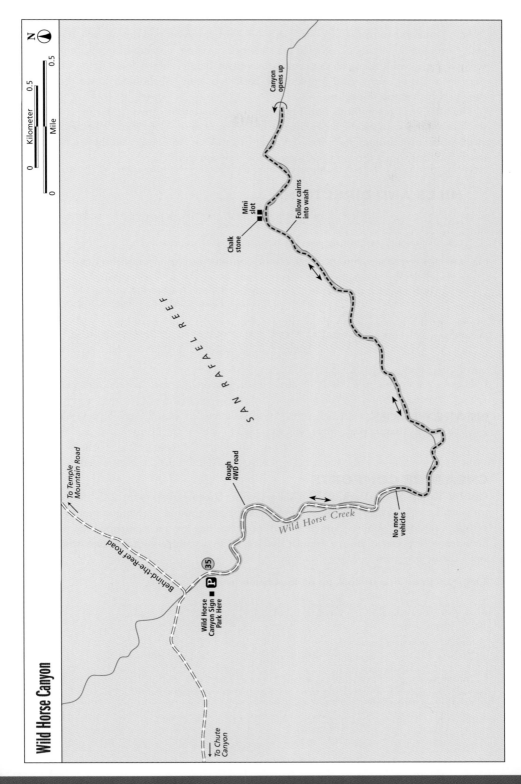

To Temple
Mountain Road

Behind-the-Reef Road

To Chute
Canyon

Wild Horse
Canyon Sign
Park Here

35

Rough
4WD road

*Wild Horse Creek*

No more
vehicles

S A N   R A F A E L   R E E F

Chalk
stone

Mini
slot

Follow cairns
into wash

Canyon
opens up

Kilometer

Mile

N

At 1.4 miles the trail splits at a small pour-off—either way around this obstacle is walkable. Continue downstream, enjoying the slickrock traveling, a respite from the sand. You will stay high, avoiding a small slot canyon, eventually being ushered down to the canyon floor by a trail of cairns. At 2.5 miles look back over your left shoulder to see the slot canyon, which is fun to explore.

The little slot canyon heads north through the eroded mini-canyon, offering you the slot-canyon feel without the scrambling. When the trail in the slot canyon ends at a large chalk stone, turn around and hike back south to mile 3. Here, you can enjoy a hearty snack and some quiet canyon time. Return the way you came.

## MILES AND DIRECTIONS

**0.0**  Follow the dirt road to the south of the parking area.

**0.9**  Only nonmotorized vehicles are permitted past this point.

**1.4**  You will pass a small pour-off. Walk to the north or south around this trail obstacle.

**2.5**  From a ledge, you will hike down to the wash floor. A small slot canyon will be visible back north, which is fun to explore as a small out-and-back deviant from the main trail.

**3.1**  This is a good place to turn around, but you are welcome to continue farther to explore the canyon. Hike back the way you came when you are explored out.

**6.2**  Arrive back at your car.

## NEARBY HIKES

Chute Canyon, Goblin Valley, Little Wild Horse

## CREATURE COMFORTS

**Goblin Valley State Park**, Goblin Valley Road, Green River; (435) 275-4584; state parks.utah.gov/parks/goblin-valley. Goblin Valley Campground is a unique spot located among sandstone "goblins" and hoodoos. Reservations are recommended via www .reserveamerica.com as this is a popular site. It is ADA accessible with hookups, showers, and a nature program.

This is a remote area, so stock up on food before entering.

# 36 THUNDER MOUNTAIN

## WHY GO?

This trail offers incredible views of hoodoos, the Aquarius Plateau, and nearly endless miles for hiker and hound. There are other hikers, equestrians, and mountain bikers on this trail.

### THE RUNDOWN

**County:** Garfield
**Start:** Thunder Mountain Trailhead
**Distance:** 8.0 miles out and back (to White Point)
**Hiking time:** 3–4 hours
**Difficulty:** Moderate due to some elevation and mileage
**Trailhead elevation:** 8,107 feet
**Highest point:** 8,329 feet
**Best seasons:** Spring, fall, winter (weather permitting)
**Trail surface:** Dirt
**Other trail users:** Horses, mountain bikers

**Canine compatibility:** On leash
**Land status:** Dixie National Forest
**Fees and permits:** None
**Trail contact:** Red Canyon Visitor Center, Highway 12; (435) 676-2676
**Nearest town:** Panguitch
**Trail tips:** Bring water for your dog and only hike this area in the cooler weather.
**Nat Geo TOPO! Map (USGS):** 7.5-minute *Wilson Peak, UT*
**Nat Geo Trails Illustrated Maps:** *219: Bryce Canyon* and *705: Paunsaugunt Plateau, Mount Dutton, Bryce Canyon*

### FINDING THE TRAILHEAD

From Bryce Canyon, turn west on UT 12. After 6 miles look for Coyote Hollow Road (FR 113), a dirt road heading south. This dirt road will lead you through the Coyote Hollow Equestrian Campground, then it continues winding its way to its terminus at the Thunder Mountain Trailhead. Park along the pullout. The trail begins at the west side of the parking area, indicated by signage.
**Trailhead GPS:** N37 42.162' / W112 16.769'

## THE HIKE

Thunder Mountain has become a place of worship for the geologist, mountain biker, ultra-runner, endurance horse rider, and hiker. This place is one of a kind. The trail is easy to follow and clearly visible, with few obstacles to White Point. Water is not available, and with little-to-no shade, the trail can get very hot during the summer and early fall.

From the parking area, the trail begins with an informational sign about the Red Canyon area. As you begin you'll follow the trail in and out of drainages along "fins" formed by ice and other weather. They are hoodoos in the making. Their unearthing will occur perhaps millions of years from now. Big Pine Draw can be seen to the south around mile 0.8, as you continue surrounded by ponderosa pines and shrubby manzanitas (hearty plants with smooth rust-colored stems). Each rise offers you more beauty as the brilliant orange rock becomes closer with each step. Experiencing the contrast between the red and white earth, the majestic green ponderosas, and an incredibly blue sky is a treat for the senses. Your dog will enjoy this hike as there is a wonderful feeling of space and horizon.

At 2 miles the view to the north over the flats to the uplifts and the toothy canyons of the Aquarius Plateau holds the secrets of pristine wilderness. One can easily imagine

The girls enjoying the view.

the ghosts of outlaws on horseback seeking refuge in the rough country. At 3.4 miles the remains of an old outhouse and hitching post can be seen on your left, a likely remnant of an old forest service outpost. The trail continues to climb into the orange rocks with more noteworthy views beginning at mile 3.6. The hoodoos and their iconic poses will hold your gaze. Be sure to include your pup in a photo of the landscape and views. Continue walking until you reach the sign indicating White Point and enjoy the view before heading back the way you came.

## MILES AND DIRECTIONS

**0.0**  Follow the signs for the trail at the west side of the Thunder Mountain parking area.

**0.8**  Look south for Big Pine Draw.

**3.4**  Pass the outhouse and hitching rail.

**3.6**  Enjoy the views.

**4.0**  Arrive at the signs for White Point. Return the way you came, or continue on as you wish.

**8.0**  Arrive back at the trailhead.

## NEARBY HIKES
Kodachrome Basin State Park, Losee Canyon, Red Canyon

# Thunder Mountain

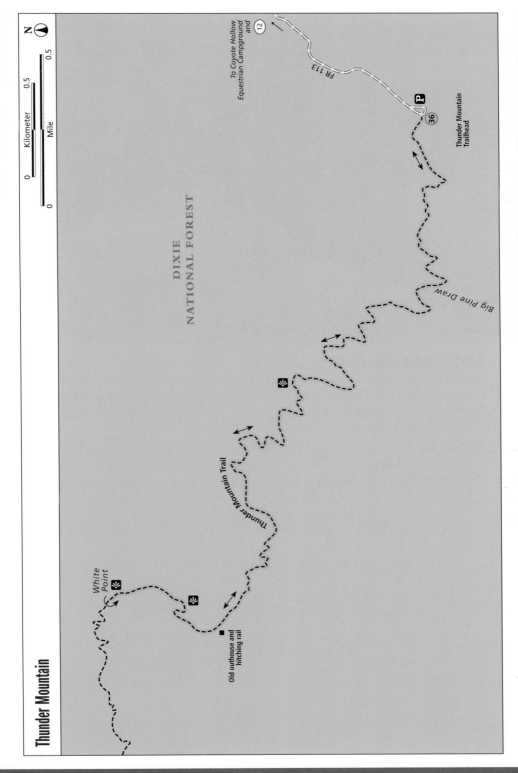

To Coyote Hollow
Equestrian Campground
and

(12)

FR 113

P

(36)

Thunder Mountain
Trailhead

Big Pine Draw

DIXIE
NATIONAL FOREST

Thunder Mountain Trail

White
Point

Old outhouse and
hitching rail

N

Kilometer

0        0.5

0        0.5
Mile

Hoodoos country

## CREATURE COMFORTS

**Ruby's Inn and Ruby's Inn Campground and RV Park**, 1280 S. H63, Bryce Canyon, UT 84764; (435) 834-5301. Ruby's is a lodge and campground located just outside Bryce Canyon. The lodge has western-chic rooms and the RV park has full hookups and amenities as well as convenient access to area restaurants.

**Cafe Adobe**, 16 N. Main St., Hatch, UT 84735; (435) 735-4020. Cafe Adobe is a cute cafe in Hatch that offers salads, nachos, sandwiches, and more as quick bites to-go or via fast service in their main dining room. One of the few great restaurants on US 89.

# 37 LOSEE CANYON

## WHY GO?

Losee Canyon offers beauty similar to Bryce Canyon without the popularity of a national park. This hike is an adventure through the hoodoos that make this area of the world iconic. The mixed conifer forests and neon-colored rocks leave a lasting impression. Bring lots of water. The desert heat can feel relentless if you are not prepared.

### THE RUNDOWN

**County:** Garfield
**Start:** Losee Canyon Trailhead
**Distance:** 5.3 miles out and back
**Hiking time:** 2-3 hours
**Difficulty:** Easy. Despite its length, this is an easy hike through a dry wash.
**Trailhead elevation:** 7,204 feet
**Highest point:** 7,672 feet
**Best seasons:** Spring, fall, winter
**Trail surface:** The trail follows a dry wash. The terrain is primarily sand, gravel, and dirt.
**Other trail users:** Horses, hikers, mountain bikers
**Canine compatibility:** On leash advised due to horses and bikes

**Land status:** Dixie National Forest
**Fees and permits:** None
**Trail contact:** Red Canyon Visitor Center, Highway 12; (435) 676-2676
**Nearest town:** Panguitch; amenities available at the entrance of Bryce Canyon
**Trail tips:** Potential flooding. Could be hot during noontime travel. The light is beautiful in the evening during the fall. *Bring lots of water* as the desert is relentless.
**Nat Geo TOPO! Map (USGS):** 7.5-minute *Casto Canyon*
**Nat Geo Trails Illustrated Map:** *705: Paunsaugunt Plateau, Mount Dutton, Bryce Canyon*

### FINDING THE TRAILHEAD

From US 89, drive 2 miles east on Scenic Highway 12 toward Bryce Canyon. Look for signage for Losee and Casto Canyons. After turning north (right) on Losee/Casto Canyon Road, drive approximately 2 miles on a dirt road to the parking area and trailhead. From Bryce Canyon, drive west on UT 12 toward Red Canyon. After the visitor center for Red Canyon, there will be signage for Losee and Casto Canyons. Turn right (north) and follow the dirt road for 2 miles to the trailhead and parking area.
**Trailhead GPS:** N37 46.174' / W112 20.016'

## THE HIKE

According to Steve Allen, author of *Utah's Canyon Country Place Names*, "Lossee," the proper spelling of Losee Canyon, was named after the Isaac Lossee family, who settled in Panguitch, Utah, during the 1800s. Like many places in Utah, pioneer lineage wrote this canyon's name tag. It is not difficult to imagine what the first eyes on this area would have seen, and perhaps what the first hearts would have felt riding a good horse through this canyon to the east after having spent a little time wandering in Losee. Little has changed in a good many years. What you might tell someone after having been in this canyon is simply how awe is described, or how wonder sounds when said aloud. Every memory holds power—from the trees to the powdery dust kicked up by running dogs to the spring-filling small depressions in an otherwise dry wash.

Follow the sign!

This hike is family friendly, especially in the cooler months. The many formations along the way lend themselves to entertaining games of the imagination. There are many "faces" hidden in the eroded formations along the trail and imaginary creatures to be discovered in ancient cemented wash banks.

From the trailhead or parking area, the trail begins to the east and heads up through the juniper trees into the wash. You will snake through this canyon as the trail winds upstream. Sometimes the trail is unclear through the gravel of the wash bottom, so keep an eye on the far bank to uncover the whereabouts of the trail upstream. If you miss a cutoff, continue hiking up the wash looking for artifacts and rejoin the trail farther on. Take the time you need to enjoy the spectacular scenery that surrounds you. As you weave in and out of the dormant waterway, your company will be woody-stemmed manzanita and ponderosa and maybe Jeffery pines, eventually convening with the hoodoos.

The spire-like formations we call "hoodoos" range in height from a few feet to hundreds, and they line the trail as you walk through the wash up the canyon. The formations are unique and created by the amazing properties of water. In winter, snow falls and settles on the limestone, siltstone, and dolomite top layer of the forming hoodoo. During the warmer hours of the day, the snow melts slightly on top of the fin. The melted water trickles down into the rock, and as the temperature drops below 32 degrees F, the water freezes and expands, forcing cracks in the rocks. Over time this effect causes a "window" to form in the fin, and eventually the roof of this gap collapses, forming the hoodoo shape. If you are curious, Ranger Poe of Bryce Canyon has informative geology lessons on YouTube.

As you get nearer to the junction with Casto Canyon, the trail gets steeper. If hiking in the evening, the canyon will begin to glow as the light reflects off the orange formations. At mile 2.7 up the canyon, you arrive at the four-way trail junction. Take a pause.

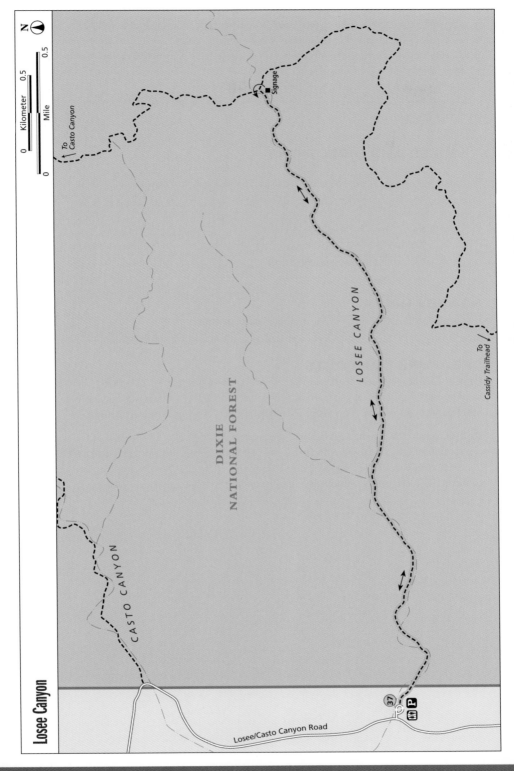

Losee Canyon

N

Kilometer
0          0.5

Mile
0          0.5

To
Casto Canyon

CASTO CANYON

DIXIE
NATIONAL FOREST

LOSEE CANYON

Signage

To
Cassidy Trailhead

Losee/Casto Canyon Road

37

It is possible that an outlaw or two stood where you are standing, debating which escape route to take. This is a wild place—it is worth your time to explore this tough, gorgeous place and its neighboring canyon trails. It is possible to hike north and back down Casto Canyon. *Note:* This route is open to off-highway vehicles. In the less popular times, this option is suitable for the mile-seeking hiker and fit pup.

If the Casto Canyon route is not appealing, when you are finished convalescing, head back the way you came.

## MILES AND DIRECTIONS

**0.0**  Park at the Losee Canyon Trailhead. The trail begin to the east.

**1.8**  Continue east up Losee Canyon past the small side canyon coming in from the north.

**2.7**  Climb to the junction of Casto Canyon, the Cassidy Trail, and Red Canyon, with signage directing the adventurous onward. Return the way you came.

**5.4**  Arrive at the parking area for Losee Canyon.

## NEARBY HIKES

Kodachrome Basin, Thunder Mountain, Red Canyon

## CREATURE COMFORTS

**Bryce Canyon Pines**, Highway 12, Bryce, UT 84764; (435) 834-5441; www.bryce canyonrestaurant.com. Bryce Canyon Pines offers a variety of lodging options including hotel rooms and cabins. The attached restaurant serves great home-style food.

**Red Canyon RV Park**, 3279 UT 12, Panguitch, UT 84759; (435) 676-2243; www.red canyonvillage.com. Red Canyon is just off of Highway 12 and is a great RV park offering small cabins, tent sites, and RV sites all with access to BBQ grills, fire pits, and shower facilities. Reserve online and reserve early during the peak summer season.

# SOUTHERN UTAH

*There are no words that can tell the hidden spirit of the wilderness, that can reveal its mystery, its melancholy, and its charm.*

—Theodore Roosevelt

The desert tortoise and her decline around the area of St. George, Utah, has prompted a massive overhaul of public land and conservation. If you plan on visiting southern Utah, you will hear about the Red Cliffs Desert Reserve and the miles of trails that crisscross through the area with small step-overs and field fences to keep these gentle beasts protected against the world of cars, construction, and development. A rugged place that feels accessible, the Red Cliffs area offers hikers, bikers, and equestrians access to enjoy the desert fully.

The unpredictability of water in southern Utah is an issue. This area is more exposed, with overall hotter temperatures, than other areas of Utah. It is best to hike here in the winter, spring, or late fall to help minimize heat stress on your dog. There are oases, of

Martin in the desert.

course. Water Canyon, for one, offers respite from the parched world with running water and the emerald-green leaves of lush cottonwoods.

The flowing rivers and big drainages in the dog-friendly Kanab is a wonderland of geology to travel. From world-famous slots to backcountry canyon hiking to flowing rivers and hoodoos, each hike offers something new and different to explore. With that being said, there are dangers associated with some of these areas as well. The Paria River and the narrows are spectacular and frequently flash-flooded during the rainy months and require a diligence from the hiker and their dog, so this area may not be for you. It is imperative that you be able to take care of your dog as well as yourself and monitor your surroundings as you make your way through these remote areas. Cell phones are not reliable out here, and it is a challenging set of circumstances that will present themselves as you hike.

It is also important to understand that some of the hikes in these areas require long approaches or high-clearance 4x4 drives through sand and river bottoms. Understanding that the roadways will turn to a very slick clay, making them not only dangerous but impassable during a rainstorm, is important to know and consider while planning your visit to this wonderland.

But what is to be gained from this unique area of the world is without question priceless. Geologically diverse from the iron-rich Red Reef cliffs to views of the jaw-dropping Navajo sandstone and Zion Canyon from the Eagle Crags Trail to the deep wilderness of Kanab, there are hundreds of miles of trails to explore in this area alone.

Remember that there are dog restrictions in Snow Canyon and Zion National Park, and be prepared to be amazed.

# 38 EAGLE CRAGS

## WHY GO?
Eagle Crags is an easy-to-follow hike just outside Zion National Park. As US national parks do not allow dogs, this hike will provide you and your pup a wonderful glimpse, from the vantage point of a nested eagle, into the mysteries of Zion Canyon and the surrounding landscape.

### THE RUNDOWN

**County:** Washington
**Start:** Eagle Crags Trailhead
**Distance:** 5.2 miles out and back
**Hiking time:** 1.5–2 hours
**Difficulty:** Moderate. The climb is steep up to the view of the crags, and it can get hot.
**Trailhead elevation:** 4,348 feet
**Highest point:** 5,235 feet
**Best seasons:** Spring, fall, winter (weather permitting)
**Trail surface:** Sand, rock
**Other trail users:** Hikers
**Canine compatibility:** Voice control
**Land status:** Bureau of Land Management

**Fees and permits:** None
**Trail contact:** St. George BLM Field Office, 345 E. Riverside Dr., St. George, UT 84790; (435) 688-3200
**Nearest town:** Springdale
**Trail tips:** A high-clearance vehicle is needed to get to the trailhead. Do not attempt when wet. It's very important to bring water, and don't forget your camera.
**Nat Geo TOPO! Map (USGS):** 7.5-minute *Springdale West*
**Nat Geo Trails Illustrated Map:** *214: Zion National Park*

### FINDING THE TRAILHEAD
From Rockville, Utah, turn south on Bridge Road and cross the Virgin River over the one-way bridge. Continue south—do not turn east on Grafton Road/250 East. Stay south on 200 East for 1.3 miles as it becomes dirt, climbs the plateau, and passes through a remote neighborhood. Keep to the main road, avoiding the signed private roads, until you reach the parking lot for Eagle Crags. There are restrooms and signage at the trailhead.
**Trailhead GPS:** N37 08.845' / W113 01.866'

## THE HIKE
This hike, as you climb to the crag, will reward you and your pup with spectacular panoramic views. You will catch glimpses of Mount Kinesava, which was named after a moody and unpredictable god, guarding the entrance to Zion National Park, and Parunuweap Canyon, popular for canyoneering, commanding the scene from the east. Johnson Mountain peeks in from the north, and the Virgin River glimmers as it snakes along the bottom. This hike is well worth the effort. You and your pup will be afforded an eagle's view perched high at the base of the crags as you scan the landscape below.

Depending on the time of year you visit, the emerald-green or brilliant yellow hue of thirsty Fremont cottonwoods is visible below you, mirroring and matching the Virgin River.

**Nice view of Zion Canyon.**

As you climb, clusters of ephedra, or "Mormon tea," shrubs will be visible, with their slender segmented green stems and noticeable fragrance. Like many things this medicinal plant is long on lore and short on facts. It gets its nickname because it was said that pioneering Mormons used it as a tea. It is said to give the consumer a bit of a kick. The taste is not extraordinary, and if gnawed on raw, the astringent properties make it difficult to enjoy. Nonetheless, it adds green to this dry bench and has survived a very long time in the deserts of the Southwest. You can also see yucca, rabbitbrush, sand sage, Engelmann prickly pear, and hedgehog-like cacti holding council in groups on the trail's edge.

If your pup is a wanderer, leashing is advised. There is quite a bit of cryptobiotic soil, a biological crust that holds soil in place, found in this area, and it is important not to disturb it. The junipers and piñon pines give little shelter as the trail climbs up toward the talon-like formation of Eagle Crags. A "crag" is a very steep and rugged rock face or cliff, and one can easily imagine an eagle soaring gracefully over this landscape. These cliffs were also labeled as the Virgin Temple by the Powell Expedition in 1871–1872.

The trail itself is very easy to follow. After 0.5 mile there is a small lookout trail spurring off to the north, which is fun to follow for a few strides to get an unobstructed view down Zion Canyon. The main trail continues east. At 0.7 mile there is an old fence that has weathered its many seasons honorably. Continue climbing until mile 2, where you'll find another spectacular view into the throat of Zion Canyon. Shortly after winding through seemingly precariously balanced house-size boulders, the most difficult climb on the hike begins. After switchbacking up the incline to the base of the crags, the trail levels and peters out to wandering game trails heading north. If it isn't too hot, this is a wonderful place to stop and relax, looking out over the big country to the north. Return the way you came.

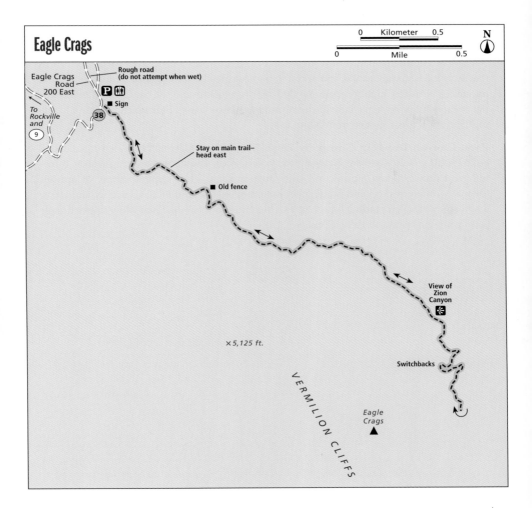

Eagle Crags

0 — Kilometer — 0.5
0 — Mile — 0.5

N

Rough road (do not attempt when wet)

Eagle Crags Road 200 East

P ⚿ ■ Sign

To Rockville and 9

38

Stay on main trail— head east

■ Old fence

View of Zion Canyon

× 5,125 ft.

Switchbacks

VERMILION CLIFFS

Eagle Crags ▲

## MILES AND DIRECTIONS

**0.0**   The trail begins to the east of the parking area near the signs.

**0.5**   Continue past the trail spur, or take it for a good view. Follow the main trail east.

**0.7**   Pass the old fence.

**1.9**   Look to the north for a beautiful view of Zion Canyon.

**2.6**   Climb to the base of the crags. Return the way you came.

**5.2**   Arrive back at the parking area.

## NEARBY HIKES

Pa'rus Trail (the only dog-friendly hike in Zion), Hurricane Cliffs Trails

## CREATURE COMFORTS

**Driftwood Lodge**, 1515 Zion Park Blvd., Springdale, UT 84767; (435) 772-3262; www.driftwoodlodge.net. The Driftwood is a great hotel with big, pet-friendly rooms that have kitchenettes, patios, and access to a grassy area behind the hotel (dogs permitted on leash). This is a highly recommended spot near Zion and the St. George area hikes, but it can fill up fast, especially in the summer, so book early. The attached King's Landing Bistro is a great spot to grab a bite too.

**Zion Canyon Brewing Company**, 2400 Zion-Mount Carmel Hwy., Springdale, UT 84767; (435) 772-0404; www.zionbrewery.com. Zion Brewery is a local favorite offering great brews, many options, and large portion sizes. They serve a variety of options for many different diets and preferences including salads, sandwiches, burgers, and tacos. Their spicy chicken sandwich is great and big enough for two. They allow dogs on their patio near the river and Pa'rus Trail.

# 39 RED REEF AT RED CLIFFS RECREATION AREA

## WHY GO?

Red Reef at Red Cliffs Recreation Area is a short walk with undertones of the conservation efforts being made to protect this historically, geologically, and biologically significant area. Family friendly and beautifully simple, this hike is a must-do if in the area. Bring plenty of water.

### THE RUNDOWN

**County:** Washington
**Start:** Red Cliffs Trailhead
**Distance:** 1.5 miles out and back
**Hiking time:** 1–1.5 hours
**Difficulty:** Easy—this is a short hike with few obstacles and little elevation gain.
**Trailhead elevation:** 3,211 feet
**Highest point:** 3,305 feet
**Best seasons:** Fall, winter
**Trail surface:** Sand, slickrock, water crossings if creek is flowing
**Other trail users:** Hikers
**Canine compatibility:** On leash
**Land status:** Red Cliffs Recreation Area (BLM)

**Fees and permits:** Small day-use fee
**Trail contacts:** Washington County HCP Administration, 10 N. 100 East, St. George, UT 84770; (435) 634-5759; www.redcliffsdesertreserve.com. BLM St. George Field Office; (435) 688-3200; www.blm.gov/office/st-george-field-office.
**Nearest town:** St. George
**Trail tips:** Parking is limited and the trail can get very busy on weekends.
**Nat Geo TOPO! Map (USGS):** 7.5-minute *Harrisburg Junction*
**Nat Geo Trails Illustrated Map:** *715: St. George, Pine Valley Mountain*

## FINDING THE TRAILHEAD

From I-15 near St. George, take exit 22 toward Leeds, then head south on Old Highway 91. Continue south for approximately 2.1 miles, then turn right (west) at the sign for Red Cliffs Recreation Area and Campground. You will proceed under the freeway through a narrow tunnel (not recommended for RVs). Continue for 1.5 miles, past the fee station, to a parking area located on the right side (east) of the road. The trailhead will be to your northwest before the road loops to the north over a bridge.
**Trailhead GPS:** N37 13.463' / W113 24.376'

## THE HIKE

Red Reef Trail is located in the Red Cliffs Recreation Area, part of the Red Cliffs Desert Reserve. The Red Cliffs Desert Reserve is a conservation area, with its focus on saving the desert tortoise, a reclusive beast whose decline is largely responsible for the creation of this and other protected areas near St. George.

If you are lucky enough to see a tortoise while exploring in this area, it is imperative to their health and well-being that they are left alone. While living in dry, harsh desert environments, these amazing animals have developed the ability to store about 40 percent of their body weight in liquid. The tortoise then reabsorbs the stored liquid through-out the dry summer months. If carelessly picked up, their defense mechanism activates,

which is the release of their stored water, leaving the tortoise without reserves. There are guidelines at www.redcliffsdesertreserve.com/wildlife/desert-tortoise. Being informed of appropriate protocol is important while in desert tortoise habitat. If while in the area, you see a tortoise in a life-threatening situation, please call (435) 688-1426.

The creation of Red Cliffs around the value of conservation and recreation has allowed for multiuse spaces to exist with public access to hundreds of miles of trails. The Red Cliffs Recreation Area and the Red Reef hike is part and parcel of this vision. Aesthetically, the Red Reef area is incredible. The color of the rocks in the canyons surrounding this hike are unmatched. This short walk through the desert is very special for folks looking for a hike that is beautiful, family friendly, straight forward, and rewarding. While on leash, you and your pup can explore the sights and smells of a desert ecosystem unique to this area.

From the parking lot, the trail begins by heading north on a sandy path. As you continue, there are many formations, wild exposed root art, and hidey-holes to experience. This area has a variety of fauna to look for as well, from the water-loving cottonwoods crowding Quail Creek to the shy globe mallow and flashy cholla on the dry benches. There are other creatures that are worth watching out for as well, including Great Basin rattlesnakes, sidewinders, and gila monsters (although rare).

At mile 0.2 there is a side canyon coming from the west. Continue north along the trail. At 0.4 mile a bench is located down the trail. At 0.5 mile there is also a beautiful alcove that is worth exploring. The trail dips and climbs a little rounding the bend and heads more westerly up the wash. As you enter Quail Creek, you will hike among the twisted cottonwood trees and the ecosystem of the desert. You will find a few hiking options, including up and around boulders or straight up the wash through the sand. The trail continues up the wash, and depending on the time of year, the amount

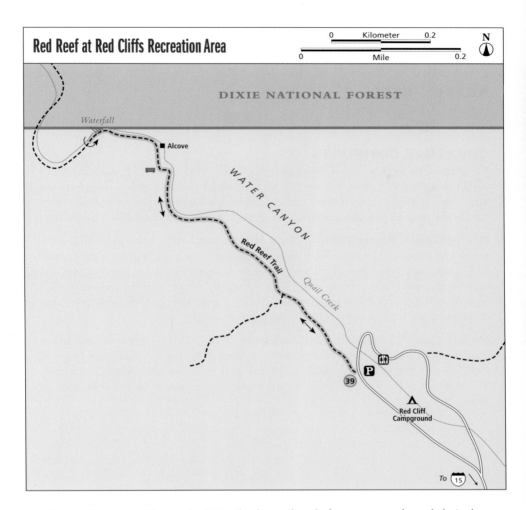

0   Kilometer   0.2

0   Mile   0.2

N

DIXIE NATIONAL FOREST

Waterfall

■ Alcove

WATER CANYON

Red Reef Trail

Quail Creek

39

P

Red Cliff
Campground

To 15

of water features will vary. At 0.7 mile the trail ends for most people and their dogs at the moki steps, which are chipped steps into the sandstone on the north side of the pour-off. Attempting to get your dog over this obstacle without proper equipment could prove dangerous. Be cautious when crossing the pools, if there are some. The sandstone can get quite slippery and there is always the threat of flash floods in desert canyons, especially in monsoon season. After enjoying the area, return the way you came.

## MILES AND DIRECTIONS

**0.0**   Head east along the sandy trail signed for Red Reef.

**0.2**   There is an optional side canyon to the south of the trail.

**0.4**   Pass the bench and enjoy the beauty.

**0.5**   Pass an alcove, a possible side trip across Quail Creek to the north.

**0.7**  Arrive at the moki steps and return the way you came.

**1.4**  Arrive back at the parking area.

## NEARBY HIKES

Silver Reef Trail, Anasazi Trail

## CREATURE COMFORTS

**La Quinta La Verkin**, 101 E. 500 North, La Verkin; (435) 635-3111; www.laquintala verkin.com. The La Quinta in La Verkin is a newly built hotel centrally located between St. George and Springdale. It is pet friendly, allowing up to three pets in a room, with a fee for pets over 45 pounds. The rooms are large and clean and the staff is friendly.

**Red Mountain Resort (Ivins)**, 1275 Red Mountain Circle, Ivins; (435) 673-4905; www.redmountainresort.com. Red Mountain Resort is located in the foothills above St. George, away from town. It is a wellness-focused resort with a spa, fitness center, and outdoor recreation activities on-site. There is a nightly pet fee, pets are welcomed with organic treats, and pet dishes are provided. This is a great spot for a vacation near many of the southern Utah–area hikes. You won't want to leave!

**MeMe's Cafe**, 975 Zion Park Blvd., Springdale; (435) 772-0114; www.memescafezion .com. MeMe's is a cute cafe offering healthy options in Springdale, near Zion National Park. They highlight local ingredients and have menus for breakfast, lunch, and dinner. The staff is friendly, and their patio is a great spot to relax under the towering walls of Zion.

# 40 WATER CANYON

## WHY GO?

High canyon walls and vibrant cottonwoods line the creek as Water Canyon opens up into a true desert oasis. Ferns, patinas, and fluted sandstone waterways ensure this walk will be remembered.

### THE RUNDOWN

**County:** Washington
**Start:** Water Canyon Trailhead
**Distance:** 3.0–5.0 miles out and back, depending on route
**Hiking time:** 2–4 hours
**Difficulty:** Moderate. The hike to the fluted box canyon is moderate, with short steep ascents and boulders to scramble over. Beyond the box canyon, the trail continues but becomes strenuous and technical and should be attempted with caution. This description does not include hiking beyond the box canyon.
**Trailhead elevation:** 5,241 feet
**Highest point:** 5,548 feet
**Best seasons:** Fall, winter, spring. Summer is not recommended due to high temperatures.
**Trail surface:** Sand, slickrock, mossy sandstone

**Other trail users:** Hikers, canyoneers
**Canine compatibility:** Voice control
**Land status:** Bureau of Land Management
**Fees and permits:** None
**Trail contact:** BLM, St. George Field Office; (435) 688-3200; www.blm .gov/office/st-george-field-office
**Nearest towns:** Hildale, Hurricane, St. George
**Trail tips:** No cell service! There are options on this trail. The map provided is just to the fluted-water-abundant box canyon. The trail continues up to the left, if you are interested in other options. Flash flooding is possible, so use caution.
**Nat Geo TOPO! Map (USGS):** 7.5-minute *Hildale*
**Nat Geo Trails Illustrated Map:** N/A

## FINDING THE TRAILHEAD

Water Canyon is located about an hour east of St. George, very close to the Arizona border. From St. George, head north on I-15 for approximately 6 miles, take exit 16 for Hurricane (pronounced HUR-i-kin), and turn right (east) on Route 9. Follow Route 9 for approximately 9.7 miles to the town of Hurricane. Turn right (south) onto 100 East, then left (east) at the first cross street onto SR 59 (UT 59). Follow UT 59 for approximately 21.8 miles past Apple Valley to the town of Hildale. In Hildale turn left (east) onto Utah Avenue. The town of Hildale is only a couple blocks from the Arizona border. If you see the "Welcome to Arizona" sign, you have gone too far and will need to turn around. Follow Utah Avenue as it becomes Canyon Street. Continue on Canyon Street as it heads north for approximately 0.8 mile up to the Y intersection. Veer right onto Water Canyon Road and continue north onto the dirt road for approximately 1.8 miles. The road may be rough so high-clearance 4x4 is recommended. Do not attempt this road if rain is imminent. There are vault toilets at the trailhead.
**Trailhead GPS:** N37 02.281' / W112 57.325'

## THE HIKE

Upon arrival, the awe of Water Canyon is almost tangible. The essence of time, water, and life all converge in Water Canyon. It is an understatement to suggest that this place

Wren isn't afraid of brambles.
Watch for thorns!

is merely "special." Water Canyon seems to have a soul of its own. The cliffs surrounding the parking lot rise over hundreds of feet from the creek below. Cottonwoods make an early appearance, and during autumn their golden hue adds to the sensory overload.

From the parking area just past the restrooms, the small "step-over" marks the beginning of the trail, which continues south along the bench deeper into the canyon. There are many routes to pick from, human trails zigging and zagging through the stands of box elder trees, with occasional campsites unfortunately marked by giant unsightly fire rings. As you wind up through the sandy hillside, keep an eye out to see the arch high on the west wall. Approximately 0.3 mile into the hike, you'll enter blackberry thickets: These gnarly brambles are beautiful in a tangled, messy kind of way. Keep your pups close to avoid stepping on thorns.

As you continue up the trail, many options are presented for bypassing trail obstacles. Try not to create new trails, but depending on which route you take, your pup may need assistance climbing over and around the sandstone boulders. Keep the creek to your right (west) and travel upstream into the canyon. The trail dips and plunges through the Jurassic-age sandstone, carved out by the small stream below.

As you round the final bend into the box canyon, you will find a beautiful wall streaked with desert varnish that almost glows in the soft light. The sound of water gently calls to the seeps high above, dripping on the rows of ferns interrupting the red rock with a vibrant green vein. The continual presence of moving water is carving yet another slot canyon. Here, geology, erosion, and time collide to create a spot of near perfection. This box canyon is a stunning spot to sit, contemplate, and listen to water bouncing off the walls from above, rushing below you into hidden chambers, and spilling out toward the valley below. Canyon wrens can be heard trilling their songs in this surreal and beautiful place.

From this point, it is possible to climb higher to see waterfalls and other slot canyons, but the route is more technical. As you move up the canyon, this trail climbs left out of the drainage. Follow the only route that is possible along the east wall up and continuing south.

If you decide not to continue, enjoy taking pictures, share a snack, and take some time to relax before returning the way you came. You may return via the creek itself, but you will be in and out of the water. This route requires some boulder hopping and nontechnical canyoneering. Remember: Never go down something you can't get back up! This way is more dangerous than the trail. Make the right choice for you and your dog.

## MILES AND DIRECTIONS

**0.0** Head north past the restrooms at the parking area for Water Canyon toward the step-over.

**0.1** There will be many trails. Pick your route as you hike south.

**0.3** There are blackberry bushes on either side of the trail.

**0.5** Look to the west side of the canyon. High on the wall there will be an arch.

**0.9** On the canyon wall to your left (east), there will be a beautiful example of desert varnish.

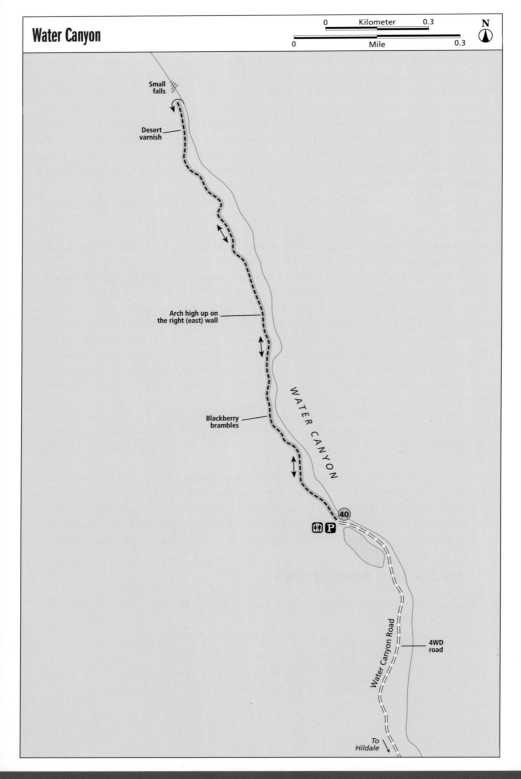

Water Canyon

0    Kilometer    0.3
0    Mile         0.3

N

Small falls

Desert varnish

Arch high up on the right (east) wall

Blackberry brambles

WATER CANYON

40

Water Canyon Road

4WD road

To Hildale

**1.5** Arrive at the small waterfalls and box canyon that is the iconic view of Water Canyon. To continue up Water Canyon, the primitive trail begins on the southeast side of the canyon in the Water Canyon box canyon. If you choose to continue up, you will need a topo map and a skill set to navigate ledges, scrambles, and trailless landscapes. When you are finished soaking in the beauty, return the way you came or down the creek bed if light canyoneering techniques are more for you and your dog.

**3.0** Arrive back at the parking area.

## NEARBY HIKES

Eagle Crags, Red Reef at Red Cliffs, the Beehive

## CREATURE COMFORTS

**Glamping Near Zion**, Water Canyon Road, Hildale, UT 84737; www.airbnb.com/rooms/19436986. This site near the Water Canyon Trailhead offers guests 10-by-12-foot wall tents with a queen bed, access to a public restroom, and water available at a nearby spring. Pets are allowed at tent sites but not allowed in the tents.

It is a good idea to be stocked on the things/food you need before Hildale/Colorado City. Nearest restaurants are in Hurricane.

# 41 YANT FLAT

## WHY GO?

Yant Flat is a short, sandy hike to a playground of colors and shapes. You will experience gorgeous views of sandstone rocks, shaped into flares and spirals of all different designs.

### THE RUNDOWN

**County:** Washington
**Start:** Yant Flat Trailhead (no sign)
**Distance:** 3.0 miles +/- out and back
**Hiking time:** About 2+ hours
**Difficulty:** Easy. Yant Flat follows a sandy wash briefly but is short and with little elevation gain.
**Trailhead elevation:** 4,588 feet
**Best seasons:** Spring, fall
**Trail surface:** Sandstone and sand
**Other trail users:** Horses
**Canine compatibility:** Voice control
**Land status:** National Forest
**Fees and permits:** None
**Trail contact:** Pine Valley Ranger District, 196 E. Tabernacle, Suite 38,

St. George, UT 84770; (435) 652-3100
**Nearest town:** St. George
**Trail tips:** Morning or evening light will make your Candy Cliffs experience that much more beautiful. If you are a photographer, plan to arrive early. Once in the Candy Cliffs, there isn't a trail, just open slickrock to wander on.
**Nat Geo Topo! Map (USGS):** 7.5-minute *Harrisburg Junction*
**Nat Geo Trails Illustrated Map:** *715: St. George, Pine Valley Mountain*

## FINDING THE TRAILHEAD

From St. George, drive north on I-15 to Leeds/Silver Lake (exit 22). Turn left (north) onto Main Street. After mile 1.5 turn left (west) and take Silver Reef Road. Silver Reef Road will turn into Oak Grove Road. This is where the pavement ends. Keep south on FR 031 for approximately 7 miles along the rough road as you wind around, passing many tempting turnoffs. Take the turnoff on the left just after the forest service road (FR 903) to a small parking area. The trail begins to the east of the parking pullout.
**Trailhead GPS:** N37 14.074' / W113 28.615'

## THE HIKE

After parking in the pullout, the trail begins just to the east. There are forest service markers to indicate the beginning of a trail, and strategically placed boulders to keep motorized vehicles out of the area. The walk is pleasant, weaving in and out among the juniper trees and prickly pear cacti. On a frosty morning, footprints of mice and rabbits crisscross the trail, hints to their goings-on. You will hike past juniper and piñon pine trees, which provide food and protection for many desert creatures. The trail is easy to follow, and it is mostly possible to walk side by side with your hiking buddy.

Yucca with their brandished swordlike leaves line the trail. The endpoints of these little daggers can be quite unpleasant if contact is made. These plants have many purposes, much like cattails. Cordage can be made with their fibers. Yucca are high in saponin, and their roots and materials from their leaves can be worked into a soapy lather to provide a cleaning agent. Their valuable stalks can be used for a hand drill spindle oftentimes without having to do much work to straighten them.

   As the trail continues the anticipation of the view into the Candy Cliffs increases after you reach each small rise. When the moment comes, it is unmistakable. As soon as the sand turns into its compressed and weathered cousin, sandstone, then the valley opens up in front of you. What lies beyond the sandy lip of the valley to the south is a playground of spirals, pillows, or reptilian-skin parodies. Here, you witness a limitless potential for wonder. Climb up for a vantage point and look around, including looking back north on the vortex wall. It is a wonderland of shapes, features, and colors worthy of exploration. Take time to sit and survey this place.

   When walking on the sandstone, there isn't a marked trail. Dogs will get the opportunity to try their balance and problem-solving skills. Be careful and know your and your dog's limits. Friction is the key to walking on sandstone. Keep your center of gravity over your feet to give your feet/shoes the best chance to stick to the rock. It is difficult to judge the steepness and integrity of footing on bowls, such as the Yant Flat north wall. It is easy to get oneself in a pickle on sandstone if you aren't careful. Following cracks and seams helps keep everyone safe. Pups may not have the necessary intuition, so practice on less steep sections or blaze a safe trail, then call your dog up the same way you went. The "butt-scoot" is also a perfectly reasonable reaction to steep pitches. Remember, the more points of contact on the sandstone you have, the more friction there is.

   Rain can drastically change the surface friction on the rock, so be very careful. Also, sandstone can be very hard on paws, especially the "tenderfooted" or "green" pup. Sandstone can be like sandpaper to the pads, with added heat causing abrasions quickly. After your tailored adventure through this remarkable land, return the way you came.

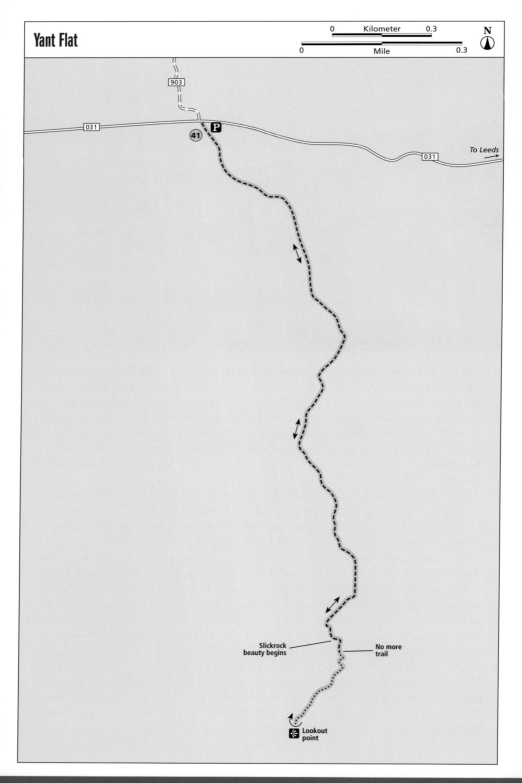

Yant Flat

031

903

41 P

To Leeds

031

Slickrock
beauty begins

No more
trail

Lookout
point

N

0 Kilometer 0.3

0 Mile 0.3

## MILES AND DIRECTIONS

**0.0**  Head southeast on the trail just east of the parking pull-off.

**1.5**  Approach the slickrock where the trail ends and explore. Just remember your route and return the way you came.

**3.0**  Arrive back at the trailhead.

## NEARBY HIKES

Red Cliffs, Yellow Knolls, Anasazi Trail

## CREATURE COMFORTS

**Oak Grove Campground**, FR 032, Pine Valley, UT 84781; (760) 788-0250; www
.recreation.gov. Oak Grove is a shady walk-in campground with fire pits, toilets, and a nearby creek. It is a great spot near St. George and the nearby hikes with incredible views. No reservations so plan to arrive early.

Camping is allowed on Forest Service land. Please leave no trace and bring your own water.

**Cafe Allure**, 661 E. St. George Blvd., St George, UT 84770; (435) 767-9727; www
.cafeallure.net. Cafe Allure is a St. George favorite serving a diverse menu of wraps, salads, and sandwiches. Definitely try a smoothie! Great for taking food to-go as a picnic to Yant Flat.

# 42 BAY BILL AND MERWIN CANYONS

## WHY GO?

With a long approach, the hike to the Bay Bill and Merwin Canyons is not well traveled. If you are up for adventure, each of these slot canyons offers challenge, adventure, and beauty. The walls of the sandstone cliffs are majestic and untainted. This area still runs wild. Bring ample water for you and your dog.

### THE RUNDOWN

**County:** Kane
**Start:** From the fenced entrance to the wash leading up to Bay Bill and Merwin Canyons, along the East Fork of the Virgin River
**Distance:** 3.0 miles +/- out and back
**Hiking time:** 2+ hours
**Difficulty:** Difficult. This includes walking in sand/wash, river crossings, and a lot of mileage.
**Trailhead elevation:** 4,976 feet
**Highest point:** 5,118 feet
**Best season:** Fall
**Trail surface:** Sand
**Other trail users:** ATVs for approach, after fence, horses, backpackers
**Canine compatibility:** Voice control
**Land status:** Parunuweap Canyon Study Area (BLM)

**Fees and permits:** None
**Trail contact:** Kanab Field Office, 669 S. US 89A, Kanab, UT 84741; (435) 644-1272; www.blm.gov/office/kanab-field-office
**Nearest towns:** Kanab, Mt. Carmel Junction (for gasoline), Orderville for minor supplies.
**Trail tips:** The last reliable water that you will have is before you leave the East Fork of the Virgin River on your approach in. Allow your pup to drink, and make sure you have full water bottles. If camping and water runs short, it is a pleasant walk to the river after making camp.
**Nat Geo TOPO! Map (USGS):** 7.5-minute *Mount Carmel*
**Nat Geo Trails Illustrated Map:** N/A

## FINDING THE TRAILHEAD

From Kanab, Utah, drive 16.1 miles north on US 89, and turn left (west) onto an unnamed, unpaved road. The road is obvious and is 0.5 mile south of Mount Carmel Junction. If you get to the gas station, you've gone too far. This road parallels the East Fork of the Virgin River and is popular with off-highway vehicles. About 0.5 mile after the turnoff, you will pass the Barracks Corrals, a good place to park if you have a vehicle not suitable for off-road. From here, the road is sandy and goes in and out of the river. It is possible to drive it with a high-clearance 4x4 vehicle to get closer to the trailhead, but it is *difficult*. If you do not own a vehicle capable of off-roading, park at the Barracks Corrals, walk in, and spend the night out near Bay Bill and Merwin.

From the corrals, it is about 4.5 to 5 miles to the beginning of Bay Bill Canyon wash, and then 1.2 miles up the wash to the beginning of the slot canyon. This will make for a long day if you can't get your vehicle closer to the trailhead. It is important to stay on the road because there are private property parcels along the way. About 2 miles from the corrals, the road stays on the bench. Then 2 miles beyond that, the road descends to the Virgin River Basin toward a gate and the private property sign "Foot Ranch." After another 0.5 mile, on your left (south) you'll approach the entrance to Bay Bill Canyon. The trailhead is the third canyon to the north indicated by an "Entering Wilderness Study Area" sign. As always in canyon country, there is a risk

Exploring the slot.

of flash flooding especially while traveling in slot canyons. Check the weather before heading into the backcountry.

**Trailhead GPS:** N37 10.808' / W112 44.605'

## THE HIKE

The Parunuweap Wilderness Study Area contains a large portion of the East Fork of the Virgin River and eventually butts up against the mighty Zion National Park boundary. The approach to these canyons seems long and could be defined as a "slog." Once you're walking up Bay Bill Canyon, though, you will likely not care. The sights are breathtaking. Rocks seem to flow and move as the light changes. You can hear the clatter of mule deer, their hoofed feet sticking to tiny seams in sandstone, a reminder of a wilder time. From the Wilderness Study Area gate at the confluence of the dry Bay Bill Canyon and the East Fork of the Virgin River, the walk south will be flat and sandy. Hike on the cattle trails along the bank of the wash when a trail is evident. This will make your walk slightly easier and more direct. To save energy, you will want to avoid following the serpentine wash. As always in canyon country, there is a risk of a flash flood, especially while traveling in slot canyons. Check the weather before heading into the backcountry.

Piñon pine trees line the bank and are responsible for the piñon pine nut, which are a staple food for many species, including the brilliant piñon jays. These birds are relatives of the raven and cache their food for the winter much like the Clark nutcracker. Studies have shown these birds to retain 95 percent of these cached seeds. The remaining 5 percent they leave is almost a symbolic gift, a thank you, a reseeding arrangement that benefits many. Pine nuts have an enormous caloric output of 3,000 calories per pound, making them a staple food crop for the ancient peoples in the Southwest. If you are lucky enough, you may collect some for yourself.

After mile 1 you'll come to a Y intersection, providing the different canyon options: Bay Bill or Merwin. Bay Bill Canyon continues southwest, and Merwin, the smaller of the two, heads southeast.

If taking the Merwin fork, follow the wash on your left. Continue for a couple sweeping turns in the wash until you see what looks like a box canyon. But as you approach, it will become clear that what looked like a box canyon is actually a vaulted room with Merwin Arch above. Once inside, look up at the graceful lines of Merwin Arch. Head toward the back side (south) of the alcove, and you'll be excited to find the slot, which is not immediately noticeable. Step inside the roofless tunnel of the slot canyon. Hike as far as you would like, returning the way you came back to the Y junction between the canyons.

Bay Bill Canyon is another option from the Y junction. With fluted sandstone sidewalls, this hike narrows more gradually than Merwin. The carved pockets and tiny amphitheaters eroded by floods give this narrow canyon a more spacious feel. It is always wide enough to ride a horse through, making it popular with equestrians, so plan to share the trail. You can walk as far as you'd like down Bay Bill Canyon exploring, but keep in mind that the way back is still in deep sand and a bit of a challenge.

When you are finished exploring, make camp in a safe place high out of the drainage or head back to your vehicle. Eventually return to the nonmotorized-vehicle gate, and then back to your vehicle.

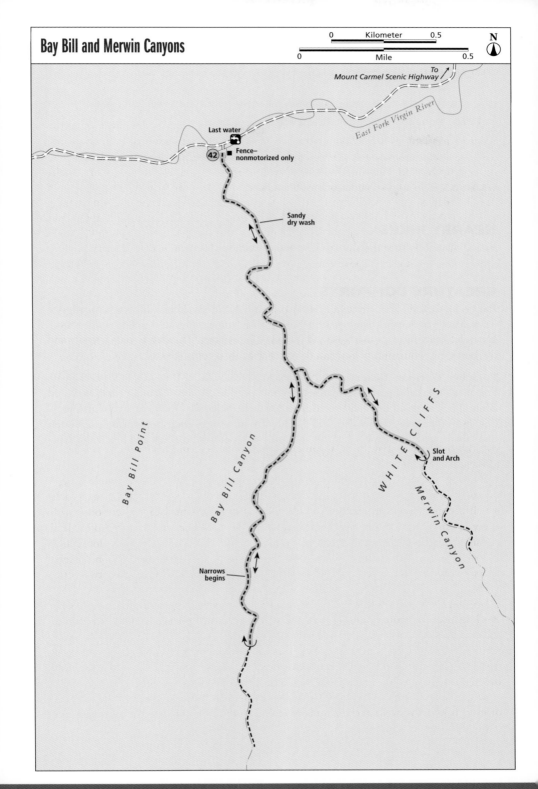

# Bay Bill and Merwin Canyons

0    Kilometer    0.5

0    Mile    0.5

**N**

Last water

Fence—
nonmotorized only

Sandy
dry wash

To
Mount Carmel Scenic Highway

East Fork Virgin River

Bay Bill Point

Bay Bill Canyon

WHITE CLIFFS

Slot
and Arch

Merwin Canyon

Narrows
begins

## MILES AND DIRECTIONS

**0.0** Begin south into Bay Bill Canyon Wash past the nonmotorized-vehicle-only gate.

**0.9** Arrive at the Y junction with Bay Bill to the right and Merwin to the left.

**1.5** **Option:** Head left (southeast) into Merwin Canyon.

**1.5** **Option:** Head right (southwest) into Bay Bill Canyon.

After you have had your fun exploring the slots and narrows of these lesser known canyons, hike back out the way you came.

**5.0–8.0** Arrive at the nonmotorized-vehicle gate.


## NEARBY HIKES

Paria River, Toadstools, Wahweap Hoodoos, Wiregrass Canyon


## CREATURE COMFORTS

**Parry Lodge**, 89 E. Center St., Kanab, UT 84741; (888) 289-1722; www.parrylodge .com. Parry Lodge is a landmark in Kanab with vintage digs and pet-friendly rooms. Extended-stay suites are available and include kitchenettes. The staff is very friendly and the breakfast, while not included, is delicious. Highly recommended!

**Forscher German Bakery**, 110 N. State St., Orderville, UT 84758; (435) 648-3040. Forscher's is an authentic German bakery just outside Mount Carmel near Kanab and Zion. They serve all the delicious German classics including bratwurst, liverwurst, pretzels, and other great sandwiches and pastries. Be sure to try their homemade sourdough that's made using their special starter and process. Open for breakfast and lunch and typically closes for the off-season in early October.

# 43 **TOADSTOOLS**

## WHY GO?

This is an easy walk to a collection of toadstool hoodoos. This hike is family friendly and incredibly fun as a leg stretcher between adventures or as a destination in and of itself.

### THE RUNDOWN

**County:** Kane
**Start:** Toadstool Trailhead
**Distance:** 1.5 miles + out and back
**Hiking time:** About 1 hour
**Difficulty:** Easy. This is a very short hike on clear trails.
**Trailhead elevation:** 4,495 feet
**Highest point:** 4,572 feet
**Best seasons:** Spring, fall
**Trail surface:** Wash, dirt, hoodoo dust
**Other trail users:** Hikers
**Canine compatibility:** On leash due to patches of cryptobiotic soils and fragile rock formations

**Land status:** Bureau of Land Management
**Fees and permits:** None
**Trail contact:** Paria Contact Station, 2040 Long Valley Rd., Kanab, UT 84741; (435) 644-1200; www.blm .gov/visit/paria-contact-station
**Nearest town:** Kanab
**Trail tips:** This hike has very little shade and no water. Bring a camera!
**Nat Geo TOPO! Map (USGS):** 7.5-minute *West Clark Bench*
**Nat Geo Trails Illustrated Map:** *859: Paria Canyon, Kanab Vermillion Cliffs National Monument Escalante National Monument*

### FINDING THE TRAILHEAD

From Kanab, take US 89 east, driving 44.5 miles until you reach the turnoff for the Paria Ranger Station to the south of the road. Continue east 2 miles and watch for signs for the Toadstool Hoodoos. Turn left (north) into the parking area. The trail starts north of parking area.
**Trailhead GPS:** N37 06.079' / W111 52.391'

## THE HIKE

The Toadstool Hoodoos are endearing formations that prove geology has a sense of the whimsy. Their sturdy little capstones, like their mushroom counterparts, are suspended in the air, held aloft on dwindling necks of stone, which make them downright cute. These features are darling, mysterious, and wonderful to visit. This is a short and sweet hike that is easy to follow.

You can access the trailhead through a fence on the center north side of the parking area. Head north overland to shallow winding washes, across the rim rock, with its variety of colors, up to the base of the hoodoos. From the parking area, you can catch a glimpse in the distance of the Toadstools, so just follow the trail heading north. You may notice a small power line as you walk and wonder why it's there, but try to ignore its intrusion as you head to the Toadstools.

The final climb from the wash bottom to the toadstool formation reveals a fanciful display of hoodoos. Have fun walking around the hoodoos and looking at them from every side, as the necks of the hoodoos reveal their true shapes. The Toadstools are fragile, so

even though tempting, please don't climb them. It is best to enjoy from a short distance away.

Like the features in Bryce Canyon, these hoodoos have been eroded by the desert elements over thousands of years. The theory is that the wind whips up particles from the base of the hoodoo that gradually etch away the softer rock layers grain by grain. As the wind pulls sand particles from the ground up the spire of the hoodoo, it begins to lose force as it rises, eroding the lower areas of the feature much faster than the upper layers. As the rock erodes, more sand particles get blown around causing more erosion. Notice how fine the sand is as you walk. This sand comes from the Entrada sandstone and is responsible for many of the formations in the San Rafael Swell and southern Utah canyons.

You'll notice the "ribs," or layers, of sandstone along the spires of the Toadstools. These ribs are indicated by varying colors and densities of rock, typically with the very top layers, or "caps," being much larger and harder than the layers below it, resulting in the appearance of pedestaled goblins. This red sandstone is contrasted against the white coves of the Dakota sandstone cliffs. It is easy to understand why the Paria River is a chalky brown color, as it is thick with the sediment gleaned from the layers of white and red sandstone.

Along the way, observe the patches of cryptobiotic soil, or biological soil crust. Please do not tread upon and do not allow your pup to walk through these patches. It takes a very long time for these crypto patches to form, easily fifty years or more. You will recognize the cryptobiotic soils by looking for a blackish-colored covering over the sand, which looks like a little village. It is hard to describe, but you will recognize it when you see it. These microorganisms form filaments that bind together the fragile sandy soil, providing safe haven for plant life. One step on it by you or your dog will destroy it. On

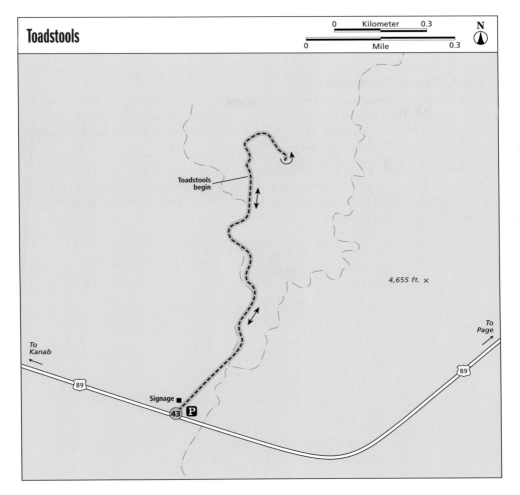

this fun hike you'll be surrounded by colonies of cryptobiotic crust, and it will be tempting to walk through it, especially for children, but please keep your small ones in check.

There are a number of trails winding around these beautiful sandstone features. As you move toward the white cliffs, be sure to take a look back toward the Paria River Canyon for another perspective. Explore at will, but please keep to the existing trails before returning the way you came.

## MILES AND DIRECTIONS

**0.0** The trail begins to the north of the parking area indicated by a sign.

**0.6** Arrive at the hoodoos, wander and enjoy, then return the way you came.

**1.5** Arrive back at the trailhead.

## NEARBY HIKES
Buckskin Gulch, the Wave in Arizona

## CREATURE COMFORTS
**Best Friends Animal Sanctuary**, 5001 Angel Canyon Rd., Kanab, UT 84741; (435) 644-2001; www.bestfriends.org. Best Friends Animal Sanctuary is an animal welfare agency located north of Kanab. They offer pet-friendly lodging options and encourage volunteers to socialize with the animals living there.

**Peekaboo Canyon Wood Fired Kitchen**, 233 W. Center St., Kanab, UT 84741; (435) 689-1959; www.peekabookitchen.com. Peekaboo offers vegetarian and vegan options including wood-fired pizza, salads, and more. They have a great pup-friendly patio and frequently feature live music.

# 44 PARIA RIVER

## WHY GO?

The Paria River hike is down the famous Paria Canyon alongside the winding Paria River. The mileage is up to you: from a morning wander after visiting other dog-friendly sites in the area to a dawn-to-dusk excursion, to a planned overnight adventure outfitted with permits. This area is as flexible as you and your dogs need it to be. Although there is a lot of water on this hike, bring snacks for you and your dog if you are planning a long hike. Also pack extra layers because deep canyon water can get cold.

### THE RUNDOWN

**County:** Kane
**Start:** From White House Campground
**Distance:** 14.0 miles +/- out and back
**Hiking time:** Flexible 1–8 hours
**Difficulty:** Difficult due to river crossings, sand hiking, and possible length
**Trailhead elevation:** 4,311 feet
**Highest point:** 4,311 feet
**Best season:** Fall
**Trail surface:** River bottom, sand, some slickrock
**Other trail users:** Backpackers, horses
**Canine compatibility:** Voice control; leash up when appropriate
**Land status:** Bureau of Land Management: Grand Staircase National Monument/Vermillion Cliffs National Monument
**Fees and permits:** Small per-person and per-dog day-use fee
**Trail contact:** Paria Contact Station, 2040 Long Valley Rd., Kanab, UT 84741; (435) 644-1200

**Nearest town:** Kanab
**Trail tips:** The Paria River is one of the world's famous slot canyons and the Buckskin Gulch connector has made its way to many of the "world's best hikes" lists, making it a worthy adventure. This hike can be done as an out-and-back or a shuttle and is typically done as an overnight. This area is extremely dangerous during a flash flood. Check the weather at the ranger station before entering the Paria River area. Be prepared for water crossings and an adventure. Depending on how far you are planning to travel down the canyon, bring snacks for you and your dog. Also pack extra layers because deep canyon water can get cold.
**Nat Geo TOPO! Map (USGS):** 7.5-minute *West Clark Bench, Bridger Point*
**Nat Geo Trails Illustrated Map:** *859: Paria, Kanab Vermillion Cliffs National Monument Escalante National Monument*

### FINDING THE TRAILHEAD

From Kanab, drive east on US 89 toward Page, Arizona, for 44 miles. After you pass Paria Outpost and Outfitters, turn right (south) onto White House Trailhead Road at the Paria Ranger Station. As you pass the turnoff for the ranger station, stay left, heading east for 2 miles to White House Campground and Trailhead. Parking is available near the vault toilet, with the fee station just to the south. The trail begins to the west of the parking area.
**Trailhead GPS:** N37 04.819' / W111 53.456'

## THE HIKE

Paria Canyon and its tributary Buckskin Gulch are two geological celebrities among the many that reside in this area, including the Wave, North and South Coyote Buttes, and the Toadstools. The word "Paria" has been adopted from the Paiute language, meaning muddy or salty water. The river collects sediment from the sandstone cliffs upstream and carries it down from the headwaters near Bryce Canyon, giving the water its opaqueness.

This area for a long time was considered one of the more remote corners of the United States, making the hike down the Paria River toward the narrows an adventure into the deep, dark places few have ever seen.

From the White House Trailhead, head to the west of the parking area following a small trail that will drop you into the Paria River Drainage, an open wash with the river running through it. Over and over, you and your pup will cross the river as you shuffle from one wall to the other. It is possible to avoid a couple crossings by following obvious trails along the banks, but for the most part, you will have to cross when the river demands it of you.

Use caution, especially with smaller dogs, when crossing. While the river isn't particularly deep, there are parts that may require you to assist your pup across. There is also a likelihood of experiencing mild quicksand along the water's edge. Walk where rocks are visible in the sand for more stable footing.

As you follow the wash, approximately 0.3 mile from the trailhead, look to the east of the river and you'll see the ruins of an old homesteader's cabin. As you continue your dog will love galloping through the shallow parts of the river. If you are planning on traveling a great distance, monitor your pups closely and leash your dogs if they are expending too much energy too soon.

Martin avoiding the chilly river.

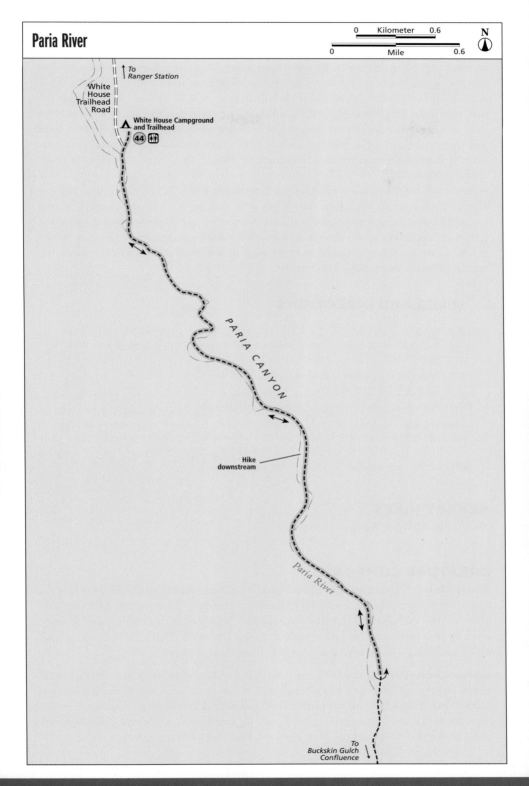

Paria River

0   Kilometer   0.6
0   Mile   0.6

**N**

*To Ranger Station*

White House Trailhead Road

White House Campground and Trailhead

44

PARIA CANYON

Hike downstream

Paria River

*To Buckskin Gulch Confluence*

As you continue you'll occasionally come across a number of hidden panels of petroglyphs on the west side of the canyon. After approximately 4 miles you'll approach the narrows. At this point the walls will become very close together, something hard to imagine as you began your walk up the wide river bottom at the beginning of the wash. As you continue south, approaching the confluence with Buckskin Gulch at approximately 6 miles, you'll find Slide Arch, and the canyon begins to narrow. Continue on until you reach the confluence at mile 7.1, surrounded by sheer sandstone walls. After you have traveled as far as you would like, simply turn around and travel back to your vehicle. A permit is required for this adventure. More information is available at www.blm.gov/node/7623.

Areas like the Paria are very prone to flash floods and it is imperative that you use caution. Typically these regions have large watershed areas above the canyons as well as significant upstream tributaries that feed the washes and rivers flowing through the canyons. This makes it very dangerous with even a small amount of precipitation. When it rains in Bryce, miles north you may see signs of it in the Paria Canyon, so please use caution when entering these canyons.

## MILES AND DIRECTIONS

**0.0** From White House Campground. The trail begins at a sign for the Paria River to the south of the restrooms and just to the right of the first campsite. Walk downstream.

**0.1** Pass signs for White House and Paria River. The trail is in the wash bed. Continue downstream as long as you'd like.

**4.0** You will be hiking through the narrows of the Paria River.

**7.0** Arrive at the confluence of the Paria River with Buckskin Gulch. Whenever you are finished exploring the canyon, turn around and walk back upstream to the White House Campground/Trailhead and your vehicle.

**14.0** Arrive back at your vehicle.

## NEARBY HIKES

Toadstools, the Wave, Wiregrass Canyon

## CREATURE COMFORTS

**White House Campground**, White House Trailhead Road, Kanab, UT 84741; (435) 644-4600; www.recreation.gov. White House is a primitive campground with five tent sites near the Paria River. The area is spectacular, but there are no reservations or amenities so plan to arrive early and bring everything you need. There are vault toilets and picnic tables at each site as well as a fire pit. A small fee applies.

**Kanab Creek Bakery**, 238 W. Center St., Kanab, UT 84741; (435) 644-5689. Kanab Creek Bakery is a great spot to grab breakfast or lunch on your way to the Kanab-area hikes. Their pastries are all made in-house, and they do their best to source regional ingredients that are in season. They serve quiche, sandwiches, salads, and global-inspired goodies like shakshuka and breakfast burritos. And their coffee is great too!

# 45 LICK WASH

## WHY GO?

Lick Wash is a spectacular narrow canyon through Navajo sandstone skirted with majestic ponderosa pine. If you are seeking a quiet, photogenic hike, this is a perfect option. There is no water available on this trail, so you will need to carry water for you and your dog.

### THE RUNDOWN

**County:** Kane
**Start:** From Lick Wash Trailhead
**Distance:** 5.6 miles out and back
**Hiking time:** About 6 hours
**Difficulty:** Easy. This is a longer hike but has few obstacles and little elevation gain.
**Trailhead elevation:** 6,230 feet
**Lowest point:** 5,901 feet
**Best seasons:** Fall, spring, winter (weather permitting)
**Trail surface:** Gravel and sand
**Other trail users:** Hikers
**Canine compatibility:** Voice control
**Land status:** Bureau of Land Management
**Fees and permits:** None
**Trail contact:** BLM Kanab Visitor Center, 45 E. US 89, Kanab, UT

84741; (435) 644-1300; www.blm.gov/visit/kanab-visitor-center
**Nearest town:** Kanab
**Trail tips:** This often overlooked hike is such a gem, well worth the drive to the trailhead. No water is available at the trailhead, so bring plenty! In the side canyons of Lick Wash, you can view arches and faint petroglyphs and experience mini–slot canyons. Keep your eyes peeled. Take lots of water. Do not attempt this hike in the heat—hot sand will burn paws.
**Nat Geo TOPO! Map (USGS):** 7.5-minute *Deer Spring Point*
**Nat Geo Trails Illustrated Map:** *714: Grand Staircase*

## FINDING THE TRAILHEAD

From Kanab, drive east toward Page, Arizona, on US 89 for 9.5 miles and turn left (north) onto Johnson Canyon Road. Travel 16.2 miles, passing Hog Canyon. Turn right (north) onto Skutumpah Road (BLM 500), a maintained dirt road. After 14.8 miles and just past a sign that says "Flood Area," the parking lot will be on your right. The trail is obvious and heads southeast toward the canyon opening. Because of its clay base, Skutumpah Road can be slippery and impassible if wet.
**Trailhead GPS:** N37 21.877' / W112 11.311'

## THE HIKE

The name "Skutumpah" is an interesting one: a hybrid of the Ute and Paiute languages, it means both "the place where squirrels live" and "the creek where rabbitbrush grows." Rabbitbrush, or rubber rabbitbrush, is a common plant in southern Utah with silver stems topped with bright-yellow flowers. This is one of the first plants to rebound after a fire, their roots providing stability to the fragile desert landscape. Rabbitbrush provides winter forage for mule deer and shelter for many songbirds. Baskets can be made from its limbs.

Lick Wash is steeped in cattle history. You may be treated to the sight of a free-ranging long-horned cow and calf as you travel up Skutumpah Road. Because of the salty soil, cows licked the dirt as they were herded through Lick Wash to Park Wash, hence the

**Heading into the wash.**

name "Lick Country" as noted by Cal Johnson in *Utah's Canyon Country Place Names* by Steve Allen.

The walk through Lick Wash is a gentle one through the sandstone canyon lined with towering ponderosas. The cross-bedding in this canyon is noteworthy throughout the early part of the walk. In ancient times prevailing winds shaped the dunes, back and forth sculpting the sand into distinct layers. These layers are now frozen in time and line the lower canyon.

The walk begins from the parking area through the sage toward an opening in the cliff. After 10 minutes or so, the scenery changes as you slip gently into the canyon. Upon entering, it is a wonderful walk to the east with little chance of losing your way. Just follow the wash up the canyon. You will encounter a huge boulder and ponderosa pines in varied angles, some even creating huge bridges overhead. All these are easily bypassed. Keep an eye out for faint petroglyphs as you walk through the narrower parts of the canyon. You may enjoy exploring the side canyons while traveling toward the confluence of Park Wash. You will know you have reached Park Wash as you come upon a large confluence of canyons. Lick Wash opens up to a large pasture. History and geology intertwine beautifully as you reach the end of Lick Wash. Return the way you came. Water is an issue, so be prepared. Exposure can be brutal on the sage flats in the desert.

Ponderosa pines (*Pinus ponderosa*), also called western yellow pines, stand as one of the great faces of the western United States. These giant trees can be found in high and low elevations, sand, clay, salt, alkaline, and everything in between. Their extensive root systems are the most impressive of any pine. The taproots are deep, and the roots and rootlets are extensive and almost as wide as the crowns of these trees. Due to these root systems, ponderosas are usually spaced fairly far apart. Their seeds spread by luck and full-cheeked chipmunks stocking up their winter fare. Barring death by beetle or the axe, these trees can live to be 500 years old. To most people, ponderosas are almost identical to the Jeffrey pine. Their puzzle-piece bark and faint smell of vanilla or butterscotch is a delightful addition to their beauty. Young ponderosas have dark edges to their back, and as the tree ages, the bark gets more yellow and tan. Look for these old trees as you walk Lick Wash. They are special, having survived flood, fire, and drought. They are a rare treat in the harsh desert climate. These trees have written within their majestic trunks the record of the years, as ring by ring they tell the story of yearly weather patterns. When you and your dog have walked far enough, head back the way you came.

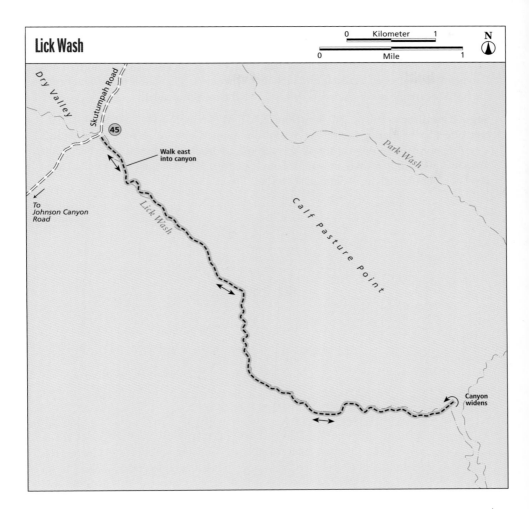

## MILES AND DIRECTIONS

**0.0** Start at the parking area for Lick Wash on Skutumpah Road.

**0.2** Pass the sign and trail register for Lick Wash.

**1.8** Look to your left: Twisted Pine Arch will be visible on the cliffs to the north.

**2.8** Arrive at Park Wash, a good place to turn around. Or you can continue exploring.

**5.6** Arrive back at your vehicle.

## NEARBY HIKES

Willis Creek Narrows, Wire Pass, Buckskin Gulch

## CREATURE COMFORTS

**Parry Lodge**, 89 E. Center St., Kanab, UT 84741; (888) 289-1722; www.parrylodge .com. Parry Lodge is a landmark in Kanab with vintage digs and pet-friendly rooms. Extended-stay suites are available and include kitchenettes. The staff is very friendly and the breakfast, while not included, is delicious. Highly recommended!

**Sego Restaurant**, 190 N. 300 West, Kanab, UT 84741; (435) 644-5680. Sego Restaurant offers an unexpected selection of globally inspired options in a beautiful setting. Their menu includes options for all diets. Some favorites include the pork-belly-and-watermelon salad, artichoke-and-mushroom appetizer, and Malaysian BBQ wings. Sego also has a pup-friendly patio and great service. This is a must-go!

## SKULL CRACK

**Start:** Causey Reservoir
**Trailhead elevation:** 6,063 feet
**Distance:** 4.9 miles out and back
**Hiking time:** About 2 hours
**Difficulty:** Easy
**Best season:** Summer
**Fees and permits:** None

**Trail contact:** Ogden Ranger District, 507 27th St., Ogden, UT 84401; (801) 625-5112
**Canine compatibility:** Voice control
**Land status:** Forest Service
**Nearest town:** Huntsville

## BASIN RECREATION TRAIL SYSTEM: PARK CITY, UTAH

**Favorites:** Glenwild, Ecker Hill, Armstrong
**Start:** Various trails around Park City
**Trailhead elevation:** Approx. 7,000 feet
**Distance:** Varies
**Difficulty:** Easy to strenuous
**Best season:** Year-round

**Fees and permits:** None
**Trail contact:** Basin Recreation, 5715 Trailside Dr., Park City, UT 84098; (435) 649-1564; www .basinrecreation.org
**Canine compatibility:** On leash
**Land status:** Public
**Nearest town:** Park City

## BUTTERFIELD PEAKS/MIDDLE CANYON

**Start:** Middle Canyon
**Trailhead elevation:** 8,368 feet
**Trailhead GPS:** N40 27.976' / W112 12.317'
**Distance:** Approximately 3 miles out and back
**Hiking time:** About 3 hours
**Difficulty:** Moderate
**Best seasons:** Early summer, fall
**Fees and permits:** None
**Trail contact:** None
**Canine compatibility:** Voice control
**Trail surface:** Mixed
**Land status:** Private with public access
**Nearest town:** Herriman

Martin at the top of Butterfield Canyon.

## LEATHAM HOLLOW: LOGAN CANYON/CACHE COUNTY

**Start:** Leatham Hollow Trailhead
**Trailhead elevation:** 5,148 feet
**Distance:** 4.4 miles out and back
**Hiking time:** About 2.5 hours
**Difficulty:** Moderate
**Best seasons:** Early summer, fall
**Fees and permits:** None

**Trail contact:** Logan Ranger District, 1500 E. US 89, Logan, UT 84321; (435) 755-3620
**Canine compatibility:** On leash
**Trail surface:** Mixed
**Land status:** National Forest
**Nearest town:** Logan

## HISTORIC CANAL TRAIL: ST. GEORGE

**Start:** Historic Canal at Hurricane River Rim
**Distance:** 4–6 miles
**Hiking time:** 2–4 hours
**Difficulty:** Moderate
**Trailhead elevation:** 3,604 feet
**Best season:** Fall
**Trail surface:** Rocks, dirt trail
**Other Trail Users:** Hikers
**Canine compatibility:** Voice control
**Land status:** Bureau of Land Management
**Fees and permits:** None
**Trail contact:** BLM St. George, 345 E. Riverside Dr., St. George, UT 84780; (435) 688-3200; www.blm.gov/office/st-george-field-office
**Nearest town:** Springdale/St. George
**Trail tips:** This hike has a cliff section with a chain to hold on to.
**Trailhead GPS:** N37 11.782' / W113 14.104'

Running in the mountains.

# DAY HIKE AND BACKPACKING CHECKLISTS

## DAY TRIP CHECKLIST

Your supplies will need to be altered depending on location, time of year, and dog's needs.

- ❏ Water for long hikes without water. Bring a water-purification system in case you need to refill your bottle.
- ❏ Extra food and snacks (know/ask if anyone in your group is diabetic or has other medical needs)
- ❏ Extra clothing: layers, socks, and gloves (wool keeps you warm even if it gets wet)
- ❏ Poncho/rain gear
- ❏ Wide-brim hat
- ❏ Sunglasses
- ❏ Sunscreen (Reef Safe, especially if swimming). Protect our wild waters!
- ❏ Map/compass/GPS
- ❏ First-aid kit, including a blister kit

**Wren keeping our gear safe.**

- ❒ Survival kit, including fire-starting kit, hand warmers, headlamp with extra batteries, feminine hygiene products with bag to carry them out with you
- ❒ A knife, preferably with a tang
- ❒ Bug repellent, preferably without DEET, especially if you plan on swimming
- ❒ Toilet paper and a baggie to bring it back with you. (Pack out any trash. Make a positive impact. Leave no trace.)
- ❒ Extra plastic bags
- ❒ Biodegradable hand soap
- ❒ Hiking/trekking poles
- ❒ Hiking journal

## DOG CHECKLIST

- ❒ ID tags on collar and/or harness
- ❒ Leash (nonretractable)
- ❒ Dog water. Always refill the water bottle or dromedary carrying your dog's water at streams and lakes in case your dog needs water in between.
- ❒ Dog treats: kipper snacks, kibbles, cooked sweet potato
- ❒ Bowl
- ❒ Biodegradable doggie poop bags
- ❒ First-aid supplies
- ❒ Hunter's orange dog vest if hiking during rifle/hunting season

## BACKPACKING CHECKLIST

- ❒ A well-fitting pack with a waterproof liner. Take the time to break it in!
- ❒ Shelter: tent, tarp, or whatever you are comfortable using that will cover both you and your dog
- ❒ Sleeping bag and pad
- ❒ Small sleeping pad for your dog (extra layer for them to get off the ground especially if it is cold or if they have stiff joints)
- ❒ Clothing: wool base layer (long johns), thick wool socks for sleeping, wool hat, balaclava, wool sweater, down coat . . . whatever you need to be warm and dry!
- ❒ Shoes for water crossings, if applicable
- ❒ Toiletries
- ❒ Food: lightweight, nutritious food—oatmeal, rice, pasta, quinoa, crackers, bread, butter, salami, pepperoni, cheese, sardines, hard-boiled eggs, smoked salmon or trout, hummus, olives, sun-dried tomatoes, dried foods, nuts
- ❒ Stove and fuel, consider a Billy stove (non-gas stove)
- ❒ Waterproof matches and dependable lighter

- ❏ Cooking pot
- ❏ Cooking spices (make your food taste good!)
- ❏ Cooking and eating utensils
- ❏ Parachute cord (about 20–30 feet) and bear bag

## DOG BACKPACKING

- ❏ Food: three meals a day
- ❏ Small Maglite powerful light to get a close look at paws, ears (for ticks or fox tails)
- ❏ Life vest, if applicable

# TRAIL EMERGENCIES AND FIRST AID

Lots of hiking in Utah is remote backcountry. Having knowledge about first aid in the backcountry is one of the most important things you can do to stay safe. Getting CPR training and becoming a Wilderness First Responder will help in any backcountry scenario. A wilderness first responder is trained to evaluate an injured person in the backcountry, determining what the next course of action should be.

For your dog, it is imperative that you have a list of veterinarians that have emergency care or after-hour availabilities in the areas where you will be hiking.

Carrying a first-aid kit is essential on any hike. The most cost-efficient way to put together a proper first-aid kit is to purchase a premade kit and then alter it. Keep it as small and light as you can for packing purposes. Remember, each kit will need to be tailored to your and your dog's individual needs. Also remember to replenish your kit after using items from it.

Wren showing off her paw bandage.

## BASIC DOG FIRST AID

Diagnosing and treating your dog should for the most part be left to a qualified veterinarian. Hiking injuries that are left untreated could ultimately lead to more suffering for your dog. If your dog's behavior changes, including how they walk, their eating patterns, drinking, bowel movements, vomiting, and obvious discomfort, contact your vet ASAP.

Below is a list of the most common minor hiking injuries and ideas about how to take care of them on the trail or in the backcountry.

**Abrasions, including paw care:** Keeping your dog's paws in good shape is part of the vigilance needed as a dog owner while exploring the backcountry. If your dog begins to limp, take the time to thoroughly check your dog's paws and between the pads for stickers, abrasions, or burrs. Cockleburs can also get caught in the armpit area of your dog, so be sure to check them over from time to time to catch any objects stuck in your dog's coat that can cause them discomfort or abrasions. Your dog will often show you by licking an area that has been injured. Wrap the paw with vet wrap if the pad shows signs of abrasion; if the limp does not improve try something else. Do the best you can to keep the abrasion clean and free of debris. If it seems to be getting worse, make sure you take your dog to the vet to get it properly cleaned.

**Hyperthermia:** High temperatures in the summer months around Utah can be dangerous for your dog, potentially causing their body temperature to rise too high. This occurs when a dog's self-cooling mechanisms cannot keep up with the rising internal temperature. Dogs can get too hot quickly, and it is important to know what your dog can and cannot tolerate when it comes to the heat. Overheating can cause organ failure and death. Excessive panting, being lethargic, laying down over and over are all signs that your dog is in a precarious situation. The best medicine for heat exhaustion and stroke is prevention. Do not hike with your dog during the hot parts of the day, or pick a trail that has easily accessible water. Make sure you have lots of water available for your dog, and stop frequently and allow your dog to hydrate.

**Hypothermia:** Cold tolerance is also a very breed-specific issue. Elderly, short-haired, and fine-boned dogs, such as whippets, may need special care when confronted with chilly or cold temperatures. Shivering is the most obvious sign. If your dog is wet and shivering, encourage movement, as exercise will warm up your dog quickly. Wrap them in a blanket, get them dry as soon as possible, and use your body heat and conduction to help them get warm.

**Dog bites:** If your dog gets into a brawl with another dog, it is important to immediately check over your dog. Look for blood, puncture wounds, broken skin, or any other injuries. Irrigate any wounds with clean water to remove any foreign objects. Keep an eye on the spots of injury if they get worse or begin to turn red. Your dog may have an infection and will need veterinary care.

**Sore muscles:** Just like when you hike too much, your dog can experience muscle fatigue and pain. Allow your dog to rest and apply cool compresses to tight muscle areas to reduce inflammation. Elderly and stiff or sore dogs could benefit from a massage after a day of exertion.

## FIRST-AID KIT

### WOUND CARE

- Gauze pads: two 2" x 2", two 4" x 4" (for cleaning wounds, absorbing blood)
- Non-adherent pads: two 2" x 2", two 4" x 4" (for covering wounds)
- Combine ABD pad: 5" x 9" (for absorbing blood)
- Perforated vinyl tape 1" x 15' (for wrapping and adhering gauze to wounds)
- Bacitracin ointment: 1 oz. (to prevent infection of small wounds)
- Iodine wipes: four pieces (for cleaning wounds)
- Alcohol wipes: four pieces (for cleaning wounds)
- Knuckle fabric bandages: five pieces (wound protection)
- Fingertip fabric bandages: five pieces (wound protection)
- Elastic strip bandages: five pieces 1" x 3" ten pieces (wound protection)
- Irrigation syringe

## MEDICATIONS

- Ibuprofen 200 mg: twenty pills (for pain relief, fever reduction, anti-inflammatory)
- Acetaminophen 325 mg: ten pills (pain relief)
- Calcium carbonate 420 mg: four tablets (antacid)
- Antihistamine (Benadryl) 25 mg: ten pills (allergy relief)
- Glucose tablets (to raise blood sugar, boost energy) 5-10 tablets
- Bismuth subsalicylate (Pepto-Bismol) 262 mg: ten tablets (relieves upset stomach, anti-diarrheal)
- Cold medication: twelve pills (cold and flu symptom relief)
- Drowsy cold medication: four pills (sleep aid and cold and flu symptom relief)
- Hydrocortisone cream: 1 oz. (itch and sting relief)
- Eye drops
- Any medication that you or your hiking group requires

## MISCELLANEOUS

- Tweezers: flat nose and pointed (for wound cleaning and splinter extraction)
- Scissors
- Safety pins 1": six
- Moleskin 3" x 4": two
- Vinyl gloves: two
- Duct tape or equivalent adhesive tape

## DOG-SPECIFIC ITEMS

- Any medication your dog is taking
- Extra vet-wrap/Coflex for creating a makeshift bootie
- Booties (in case of emergency)
- Veterinarian information
- Muzzle option if your dog will bite someone when receiving first aid
- Extra poop bags to be used creatively, from makeshift water bowls to waterproof temporary bandage cover

## WILDLIFE CONFLICTS

Wild animals that have become habituated to humans and their trash are a danger to themselves and others. It is important to keep wild animals, such as bears, wild. Do your part and practice positive impact and leave no trace. Do not give an animal the opportunity to become dangerous.

Utah is home to large predators, such as bears and mountain lions. Because Utah is still wild and animals still have the space they need, there are fewer dangerous encounters with these animals. You and your dog are far more likely to encounter the following animals in Utah:

**Rattlesnakes:** During the summer, especially in the Wasatch Range, rattlesnakes will emerge in the morning to sun themselves on rocks before it gets too hot. The best policy with snakes is to leave them alone, and don't touch! In Utah you are most likely to encounter a rattlesnake on rocky talus slopes. Rattlesnake aversion training is a good idea when hiking in Utah.

**Moose:** A cow moose with a calf can be very protective and dangerous, charging when threatened. Pay attention when traveling through moose country, which in Utah is mountain forests and wetlands. Moose are often found near streams and lakes, particularly those surrounded by willows.

**Skunks and porcupines:** These creatures can inflict a great deal of damage on dogs and anyone around them. A dog getting skunked is a horrible situation, and it is a good idea to have de-skunking shampoo available in case your pup ends up getting sprayed. Porcupines are also an incredibly painful run-in for a dog. It is vital to spend a lot of time on recall with your dog if you choose to have them off-leash, so you can protect them from their chase instincts. You will find skunks and porcupines throughout Utah in wooded areas and grasslands. Occasionally, you can spot one of these creatures in urban areas.

**Coyotes:** Coyotes can be found throughout Utah. They are adapted to a wide range of habitats, including urban and rural areas that border Utah's mountains and deserts. Coyotes will often call out and draw your dog away from you to attack it. Coyotes, especially in stressed areas, are dangerous for your dog. Small dogs are especially vulnerable.

**Wren getting teased by a squirrel.**

# SOURCES FOR POOCH GEAR, USEFUL WEBSITES, AND BOOKS

## WEBSITES:

- Airbnb.com: offers listings for vacation rental properties
- Bestfriends.org: Kanab-area animal welfare nonprofit. Volunteer, donate, or stay at their cabins.
- Natgeomaps.com: online source to purchase trail maps
- Recreation.gov: reservations for camping on public lands
- REI.com: source for gear, maps, and local knowledge. REI has two locations near Salt Lake City.
- Reserveamerica.com: campground reservations
- Ruffwear.com: offers pup hiking gear

## BOOKS:

- *Animals Make Us Human: Creating the Best Life for Animals* by Temple Grandin
- *Being a Dog: Following the Dog Into a World of Smell* by Alexandra Horowitz
- *Braving the Wilderness* by Brené Brown
- *Dog Songs* by Mary Oliver
- *The Genius of Dogs: How Dogs Are Smarter Than You Think* by Brian Hare
- *Inside of a Dog: What Dogs See, Smell, and Know* by Alexandra Horowitz

# LOCAL INTEREST TRAIL FINDER

## UTAH CLASSICS

- Bonneville Shoreline Trail: Thousand Oaks Section
- Bowman Fork to Alexander Basin Trailhead
- Corona Arch
- Dog Lake
- Eagle Crags
- Fehr Lake Trail
- Grandeur Peak
- Grandstaff Canyon to Morning Glory Natural Bridge
- Paria River
- Stewart Falls
- Warner Lake
- Water Canyon
- White Pine Lake
- Wild Horse Canyon

## OVERNIGHTERS

- Battle Creek Loop
- Bay Bill and Merwin Canyons
- Crystal Lake Loop
- Little Grand Canyon
- Lofty Lake Loop
- Lone Peak Trail to the Second Hamongog
- White Pine Lake–Logan Canyon
- Willow Creek

## PUPPY FRIENDLY

- Bloods Lake
- Bonneville Shoreline Trail: Thousand Oaks Section

- Corona Arch
- Dog Lake
- Eagle Crags
- Miners Trail
- Neffs Canyon
- Onion Creek Narrows
- Pipeline
- Red Reef at Red Cliffs Recreation Area
- Run-a-Muk
- Toadstools
- Water Canyon
- Yant Flat

## RUGGED AND REMOTE

- Bay Bill and Merwin Canyons
- Chute Canyon
- Deseret Peak
- Eagle Crags
- Lick Wash
- Little Grand Canyon
- Lone Peak to the Second Hamongog
- Mountain View via Miners Basin Trail
- Paria River
- Warner Lake to Dry Creek
- Water Canyon
- Wild Horse Canyon
- Yant Flat

# HIKE INDEX